MW00467351

BISON
BOOKS

Jesse James
WAS MY NEIGHBOR

By

HOMER CROY

Introduction to the Bison Books edition by
Richard E. Meyer

University of Nebraska Press
Lincoln

∞ The paper in this book meets the minimum requirements of American National Standard for Information Sciences—Permanence of Paper for Printed Library Materials, ANSI Z39.48-1984.

First Bison Books printing: 1997
Most recent printing indicated by the last digit below:
10 9 8 7 6 5 4 3 2 1

Library of Congress Catloging-in-Publication Data
Croy, Homer, 1883–1965.
Jesse James was my neighbor / by Homer Croy; introduction to the Bison Books edition by Richard E. Meyer.
p. cm.
Originally published: New York: Duell, Sloan, and Pearce, c1949.
ISBN 0-8032-6380-5 (pbk.: alk. paper)
1. James, Jesse, 1847–1883. 2. Outlaws—West (U.S.)—Biography.
3. West (U.S.)—Biography. I. Title.
F594.J27C76 1997
978'.02'092—dc21
[B]
97-163 CIP

Reprinted from the original 1949 edition by Duell, Sloan and Pearce, New York.

To

Elmer L. Pigg

Jefferson City, Missouri, who has been a lifelong student of the James story, and who has been a great help in wrestling with the elusive matters set forth in this book. Besides, he's a fine person.

INTRODUCTION TO THE BISON BOOKS EDITION

Richard E. Meyer

> Frank and Jesse James,
> They knowed how to rob them trains;
> Always took it from the rich and gave it to the poor.
> They might've had a bad name,
> But they both had a heart of gold.
>
> Hank Williams Jr., "A Whole Lot of Hank" (1983)

The song lyrics quoted above are remarkably similar in both style and sentiment to the numerous popular folk ballads celebrating the life and deeds of Jesse James that began to appear shortly after the outlaw's death in 1882. But this is not a song about Jesse James: rather, the real subject is its composer, Hank Williams Jr., one of the primary gurus of the "outlaw country" movement of the 1970s and early 1980s. Reacting against what they perceived to be the restrictive, ultra-conservative constraints of the Nashville music establishment, these proponents of progressive country music—who, in addition to Williams, included Waylon Jennings, Kris Kristofferson, Jerry Jeff Walker, and Willie Nelson—self-consciously viewed themselves as artistic "outlaws." In his song, Hank claims "I'm an outlaw from the South," and "I've got outlaw in my bones." The metaphoric comparison to America's historical outlaws is a consistent and recurrent theme in the songs he and the others composed and sang.

From the time of our earliest literature and folklore—and reflecting similar trends in cultures older than our own—rebellious figures who challenge and often transcend established authority have emerged to strike a sympathetic chord in the hearts of average Americans. And sometimes, when these figures are actual, historical individuals whose character, deeds, and surrounding circumstances combine in such a way so as to fit the age-old patterns of legend-making peculiar to oral tradition, they become folk heroes. At this point a curious phenomenon, at once both frustrating and utterly fascinating, begins: as history and myth, fact and fancy, collide, mix, and eventually meld, a new kind of reality emerges. It consists of the popular beliefs and attitudes that cluster about folk heroes and determine their lasting cultural impact.

Perhaps no period in American history has created so many folk rebels as the decades stretching from the end of the Civil War to the turn of the century. Shaped by the violence that tore a country in two and the chaotic social conditions that were its legacy, there emerges the classic figure of the American outlaw operating along the fringes of a still-expanding geographic frontier. Opportunistic and bold, blessed with an entrepreneurial aptitude for larceny, these historical individuals combined their natural abilities with a string of good luck lasting long enough to allow the formulaic elements of the outlaw folk hero's ethos to coalesce about them: champion of the people, surrogate "righter of wrongs," confounder of conventional opponents, and, ultimately, betrayed martyr. And, amongst them all one name, more recognizable to most Americans than the majority of their past presidents, stands supreme: Jesse James.

The historical record concerning the life of Jesse Woodson James is actually more complete than one generally finds with American outlaws. The bare outlines are clear, almost predictable. Born the son of a Baptist minister in 1847, Jesse's boyhood in Clay County, Missouri, moved inexorably into a young adulthood steeped in border-state Civil War violence and the traumas of post-war reconstruction. Riding with such Southern guerilla notables as William Quantrill and "Bloody Bill" Anderson, he served a meaningful apprenticeship in their incredibly savage brand of irregular warfare. Following the war, he led a gang of bank and train robbers that included, among others, his older brother Frank and various members of the Younger clan on a crime spree spanning some twelve years and seven states. Robert Ford, a sometime gang member destined to be forever stigmatized as a Judas figure in the Jesse James legend cycles, shot Mr. Howard (one of Jesse's aliases) in the back while the semi-retired outlaw was arranging a wall picture at a house in St. Joseph, Missouri, on the morning of 3 April 1882.

Such are the prosaic facts. But it is not too difficult to see why a formulaic transformation of reality took place at this moment in American history. Sympathizers of the lost Confederate cause, rankling under both the ignominy of defeat and the forced accommodation to Northern economic and social institutions, found in the actions of Jesse James a strong measure of vicarious satisfaction. Jesse robbed banks and trains after all, hated symbols of the forces ordinary folk saw as responsible for their protracted misery. As Homer Croy, author of the book you are about to read, notes: "[T]imes were hard. Banks were unregulated; they ground the people down, and the people hated them, and blamed them for the times" (37). And as for the railroads, Croy tells us: "When a train killed a farmer's cow, he had to wait years to be paid. Sometimes sparks from the engine set farmers' haystacks on fire. The farmer would write a handful of letters, and not even get a reply" (54). Better than another letter, perhaps, would be the image captured in one of the standard Jesse James ballads of the time:

> With the agent on his knees, he delivered up the keys
> To them outlaws, Frank and Jesse James.

The persistence of the Jesse James mythos, handed down by the poor nineteenth-century farmers of Clay County, Missouri, may owe much to our continuing infatuation with the simpler, more individualistic values of a lost frontier. Perhaps we cry out for figures who, like Jesse James, don't passively wait for circumstances to come to them but rather go out and forcefully shape events to their own needs. At an even deeper, more subconscious level, it may be that we citizens of a nation born of rebellion identify positively with those who flaunt authority and who seek dramatic means by which to assert their independence.

Whatever the reasons, the Jesse James phenomenon has continued to fascinate for more than a century. Witness the vast amount of printed material focused on Jesse James. At best estimate, well over two hundred books alone, ranging from dime novels to purported attempts at serious history, have been published since the 1880s, dealing exclusively or substantially with the premier American outlaw. Most of these are long out of print, and in the vast majority of instances this might be considered a very good thing as few among them contain anything of value to the general reader. There are, however, a few notable exceptions to this rather depressing assessment, one of them being this remarkable book by Homer Croy first published in 1949, *Jesse James Was My Neighbor.*

Those familiar with Homer Croy's earlier works (between 1914 and the late 1940s he produced scores of novels, screenplays, and various types of nonfiction works, frequently humorous) might have been somewhat surprised at his decision in later life to focus on biography. During these years, in addition to this book, he produced readable and worthwhile biographical studies of Will Rogers, film director D. W. Griffith, Mary Todd Lincoln, Frank James, frontier marshal Chris Madsen, and "hanging judge" Isaac C. Parker. Tall, gangling, mild-mannered, and known throughout his life for his keen sense of humor (in his New York years he liked to refer to himself as "Two-Gun Croy, the law north of 125th Street"), the author never forgot his formative years as a poor farm boy in northwestern Missouri, and when he died at age eighty-two his obituary in the *New York Times* on 25 May 1965 recalled him as "a gentleman from Missouri" who always had "a twinkle in his calm eye."

Of Croy's historical/biographical works, many of them about frontier subjects, *Jesse James Was My Neighbor* remains perhaps the most significant. Certainly it is unique in style, technique, and indeed purpose, among nonfictional works devoted to Jesse James, and thus deserves serious attention. The book has always been highly regarded by those whose opinions count in such matters. Ramon F. Adams, whose *Six-Guns and Saddle Leather* authoritatively (and sometimes mercilessly) critiques and annotates almost 2500 books and pamphlets dealing with Western American outlaws and gunmen, calls it "a most refreshing book on Jesse James." William A. Settle Jr., author of the only truly definitive biography, *Jesse James Was His Name,* accurately pinpoints both its essential nature and principal value when he labels it "an entertaining and refreshing telling of the tales in which Croy was steeped."

Croy himself stresses in his introduction the role of oral storytelling in keeping alive the memories of the James boys in the area of Missouri where he grew up, and one soon realizes that the "neighbor" of the book's title refers more to the constant presence of these memories than to the actual living person, who did after all die the year before the author was born. The entire book, in fact, is the result of Croy's deliberate and careful searching out of these memories: though some of his sources are printed, the greater number of them are living people, many of them in their eighties and even nineties at the time he interviewed them. To me, one of the most remarkable features of Croy's achievement in this work is that, without formal training or experience in these areas, he somehow managed to employ with considerable skill the fieldwork techniques of the professional oral historian and folklorist in producing a work of historical biography quite different in texture and emphasis from the standard models of his time.

Though the author states unequivocally that "I am not putting in this book any legends or folk tales" (12), there is little doubt that more than a few have found their way between its covers. Chapter 9, "Jesse and the Widow," is an Ozarks version of a centuries-old anecdote concerning Robin Hood and is, moreover, a tale found in the oral traditions surrounding several other American outlaws, including Sam Bass and Pretty Boy Floyd. Equally suspect is the fabled chance meeting between Jesse James and Billy the Kid detailed in chapter 14: absolutely no reliable historical documentation exists to support such an incident, and the whole concept seems suspiciously grounded in the type of tantalizing "what if" fantasies which in more recent times have produced such entertainments as computerized "superbouts" and Steve Allen's highly successful "Meeting of the Minds" television series. Whether it is simply Croy's naiveté that allows these dubious narratives to enter the work or whether (more likely) the author, tongue in cheek, at times surrenders to the temptation to engage in the traditional Ozark practice of telling a "windy" or two, is something we may never know. In any case, these distinctions are superseded in importance by a far more significant point: *all* the material in this book, spurious or not, contributes to what most certainly is Croy's primary intent, which is not so much to tell the "true" history of Jesse James as to present an accurate and detailed picture of the way people *feel* about the outlaw hero.

Perhaps, when all is said and done, this has always been what I have liked best about Homer Croy and his treatment of Jesse James. He has no axe to grind here: missing is that self-righteous "debunking" zeal that taints so many works on western history in general and western outlaws in particular. Rather, the author is content to present to us, often in the words of others, the composite portrait of an individual whose mythic role in the American consciousness may ultimately be of far more importance than the once living, breathing man who bore the name of Jesse Woodson James. I can think of no other work on the subject that comes close to matching this accomplishment, and I am genuinely pleased to see it once more in print and readily available to readers of many backgrounds and interests.

This introduction began with lyrics from a contemporary song. I would like to end it with the last stanza of one of my own songs, written some years ago in an attempt to understand the importance of western heroes to Americans like myself. If you look closely and don't blink, you should find an old friend there.

So here's to the legends of the great Wild West—
Here's to Billy and Wyatt, and all of the rest;
Here's to good old Sam Bass, and of course Jesse James,
And the whole Texas Rangers, whatever their names;
Here's to John Wesley Hardin, and to Doc Holliday,
And the famous gun battle at a place called O.K.;
Here's to Judge Isaac Parker, and Calamity Jane,
And to all of the outlaws ever held up a train —
Yes here's to the daydreams that we tried to fulfill;
We needed some heroes, and they sure fit the bill;
Yes we needed some heroes, and I guess we do still.

AUTHOR'S NOTE

In order to make this a flowing narrative I have avoided putting footnotes and numbered references in the main text, and have instead moved all this material into the section entitled *Sources*. Here the reader may find information, chapter by chapter, on the origin of all stories, anecdotes, and facts the authority for which is not included in the text.

Acknowledgment of the many and varied sources from which I have obtained my material on Jesse and his times is made at each appropriate place in the course of the book.

——H. C.

CONTENTS

CONTENTS

PRINCIPALS IN THE DRAMA

Name	*Born*	*Died*
Robert S. James	July 17, 1818	Aug. 18, 1850
Zerelda Cole James (Samuels)	Jan. 29, 1825	Feb. 10, 1911
Alexander Franklin James	Jan. 10, 1843	Feb. 18, 1915
Robert R. James	July 19, 1845	Aug. 21, 1845
Jesse Woodson James	Sept. 5, 1847	April 3, 1882
Susie James Parmer	Nov. 25, 1849	March 3, 1889
Reuben Samuels	Jan. 12, 1829	March 1, 1908
Sallie Samuels Nicholson	Dec. 26, 1858	Sept. 15, 1915

PRINCIPALS IN THE DRAMA

Name	*Born*	*Died*
John T. Samuels	May 25, 1861	March 15, 1932
Fannie Quantrill Samuels Hall	Oct. 18, 1863	May 30, 1922
Archie Payton Samuels	July 26, 1866	Jan. 26, 1875
Zerelda Mimms James	[?], 1845	Nov. 30, 1900
Ann Ralston James	Jan. 25, 1853	July 6, 1944
Jesse Edwards James	Aug. 31, 1875	
Mary James Barr	July 17, 1879	Oct. 11, 1935
Robert Franklin James	Feb. 6, 1878	

As copied from the James family Bible now in the possession of Frank's son Bob James. It will be noted there were eight children, one dying when a month old.

He was hunted and he was human.

—*From the writings of John N. Edwards, the most famous newspaperman in Missouri at the time of Jesse James.*

Jesse James
WAS MY NEIGHBOR

INTRODUCTION

Jesse James was betrayed the year before I was born, but his memory was all around me. We talked of 'Jesse'—and that's what we called him—as if he still lived. We never said the 'James gang'; it was the 'James Boys,' or merely 'Jesse and Frank.' Or sometimes 'the Boys.' As a lad, I went around screeching at the top of my voice, "It was a dirty little coward that shot Mr. Howard and laid poor Jesse in his grave." And I meant it; it had seemed a ghastly deed.

Frank James, a few jumps away from my home in Maryville, Missouri, lived until 1915. His widow until 1944. Later I want to tell their love story. But it will have to fit in its place.

The stories that floated around us! Sometimes, at night, I could imagine the Boys were still riding. But of course they weren't, for Jesse was in his martyr grave and Frank was a horse starter at country fairs and with a circus.

Now as to some of the stories I grew up with. They happened in the county, one about five miles from our farm. I tell you it made us shiver—delightedly, of course. But late at night when we had to go out and pump up a drink of water just before going to bed . . . well, the shivers were pretty real, then.

I'll tell the 'five-miles-away' one first. To freshen my memories, I went back, when I started this book, and checked up on my childhood. Most of my memories, I found, were correct. But how could a boy forget the big, the exciting, the thrilling deeds of Frank and Jesse?

The Carmichael farm! How many times I had ridden past it and stared like a grasshopper. Old Mr. Archibald Carmichael was living on it, then. But when I went back, he was gone. I had his son, John Carmichael, tell me the story. It was, surprisingly, just about as I had remembered it from his father.

We sat on the back porch and visited. He mentioned first what a good farmer my father was (very pleasing to me), then got down to the story.

"I was just a little sprout, but I don't have no trouble remembering it," said John Carmichael. "About dusk two men rode up, their horses showing evidence of having been pressed. We didn't know it, then, but they were Frank and Jesse. Even if we had known it, they'd been mighty welcome to food and shelter. They said they were officers of the law, chasing horsethieves. That was perfectly reasonable, for the county was overrun with horsethieves. They asked if my mother could set them a bite. I went out with them while they were rubbing their animals down. I was too young myself to appreciate it, but my father said they were extremely fine specimens of horseflesh.

"We were always glad to have visitors, and, after supper, sat around and visited with the travelers. They were as pleasant men as you'd want to house. They asked about prices hereabouts, how the roads were and where the streams were fordable. My father gave out the information as best he could. This was the year 1871. Roads have changed considerable. You could bear across the country, then, any way you saw fit. Finally bedtime came upon us. My mother was assigning them to beds when the tall one cast a look at the short one and said he thought he'd patrol the yard and let his fellow officer get in what sleep he could; he said the horsethieves might pass and they'd know which way to pursue them the next morning. So we retired to bed, except the tall one I just mentioned. Some time in the middle of the night, the tall one came to the window and tapped and the two exchanged places. The next morning my mother fixed them a substantial breakfast. After consuming it, the short one asked my father if he cared if he engaged in some pistol practice. Said some of the horsethieves they were pursuing were good shots and that it didn't pay to exchange shots with them unless you were in practice. My father said he could understand that.

"Well, I went out with the stranger to a spot behind our smokehouse and stood beside him while he got ready. There was a shellbark hickory about ninety yards off. Every time he fired, the bark flew. Lots of men with a rifle couldn't given him odds. Finally he put his pistol up, saying, 'It don't pay for an officer of the law to get rusty on his pistol work.' Then he went to the house and offered to pay my mother for their lodgment, but she wouldn't accept anything, so agreeable and entertaining had they been. Finally they rode off, us standing there watching and hating to see them go.

"It wasn't till my father went to Maryville, about two weeks later, that we found our visitors had been Frank and Jesse. We had considerable to talk about that night when Pa returned from the city. But we were glad to shelter them. They didn't ever cause farmers any trouble. Mostly they robbed banks and railroads and express companies that had plenty of money. On the whole we were real pleased we could provide for them for the night. Always when I see or hear about good shooting, I think of Jesse out behind the smokehouse, makin' the shellbark fly."

And that is the story as John Carmichael told it to me in August, 1948, substantially as I had remembered it.

Anecdotes featuring Jesse's persuasive way with shooting machinery are numerous and good, when you can be sure they're true. Here's one told to me by Buck Darrell, who lives at 3207 South Seventeenth Street, St. Joseph, Missouri. When I talked with Buck Darrell he was eighty-nine. In the 1870's he had been a traveling gunsmith, going from town to town repairing rifles. He arrived one evening at Pattonsburg, Missouri, and was sitting in the hotel lobby, smoking and reading, when a .22-caliber pistol he was carrying dropped out of his pocket and fell on the floor.

A man seated nearby looked up with interest, then said, "You can't do much damage with that article, can you?"

"I've got one that will make up for it," said the gunsmith, and from a shoulder holster drew out a .45.

The stranger gazed with even more interest. "Do you fancy yourself as a marksman?" he asked.

Buck Darrell, who knew all about guns, said, "I guess I can hold up my end."

The whiskered stranger studied him a moment. "Would you like to do a little shooting?"

"I wouldn't mind."

"Let's take a walk," said the stranger.

When they got outside the town, the stranger took out a long-bladed, sharp-looking hunting knife and held it in his hand a moment. Then he cut a mark in a tree, and the two began to fire at it. Buck Darrell won.

The stranger gazed at Buck with more interest than ever. "How are you on moving targets?"

"I guess I can hold up my end," said Buck.

"Did you ever see this?" asked the stranger. He proceeded to whittle out a stick about as long as his finger, which he drove into a tree. When he finished this, he cut a piece of string about the same length, pried a bullet out of a cartridge, cut a notch in the bullet, and drove one end of the string into the bullet.

He then tied the free end of the string to the peg in the tree, started the bullet swinging back and forth like a pendulum, and thrust the end of his hunting knife into the tree just at the point where the bullet crossed. The handle of the knife was pointed down, the tip of the blade up and the cutting edge out.

Then the stranger said: "The idea is to hit the bullet as it passes over the edge of the knife. If you do it right, you will cut, or shave, both bullets at one shot. We'll shoot from five paces."

Buck took his position and shot four or five times unsuccessfully.

The stranger stepped up, and on the third try hit the swinging bullet.

Then, with great satisfaction, Jesse James pocketed his gun and the two walked back to town together.

Of course, this was extremely good marksmanship, but at that time all men were marksmen. Some of their skill had come down from the trappers, Indian fighters, and the pioneers. Most of the men in the section had been in the Civil War and were accustomed to guns. Shooting matches were held frequently; in addition, there were turkey shoots at which the prize was a gobbler. A good shot was proud of his ability and he had a right to be, for nearly all men wanted to be marksmen. The Jameses were exceedingly good marksmen; they had always handled rifles and six-shooters and they kept in practice, which, everything considered, was a good idea.

Another childhood story. Just west of us was Quitman, Missouri, where Tom Bond lived. How we hated him! He was one of the Federal soldiers who had swept down on the James farm during the Civil War, and had been one of the men who had helped torture Dr. Reuben Samuels, Jesse's stepfather. It had been a dreadful scene. His stepfather had rope burns on his neck till he died. Jesse was fifteen; he had witnessed the cruel act, and went sobbing to his mother and said, "I'm going to kill every one of them." He didn't, but hate was always in him.

So one day he and Frank stopped in this town looking for Tom Bond. They walked up and down the street looking for him. They waited about two hours, then started on again, and then—plop-plop—in the middle of the road they met Tom Bond driving in a buggy with his wife. After they passed, one of them said, "I believe that's Bond."

Bond heard and knew who they were. He handed the lines to his wife and ran into the timber. Jesse and Frank sat on their horses debating whether to chase him or not; finally they rode on. They came back one other time, but Tom Bond was warned by old William Allbright, who knew the Boys by sight, and escaped. But it was too much for Tom Bond. He might not be so lucky the next time. He left Nodaway County. Only his close kin knew where he had gone.

Another farm we used to drive past—with me staring like a hoot-owl—was the Richard Stafford farm, not so far from the Croy farm. A very exciting, yes, a very thrilling thing had happened there.

Washday on a farm! Do you remember the kettle of boiling water out in the yard, and the stove in the kitchen going great guns? And the way your mother used to take a damp cloth and run it along the non-rust metal clothesline to get off the rust? Some way or other it always rusted.

Anyway, on this Blue Monday, shortly before noon, Mrs. Stafford had just finished her washing and was ready to hang it out. She was cross; any woman would be, after doing a farm washing. It was then that two strangers cantered in from the main road and asked if they could feed and water their horses. This was nothing unusual, for men on horseback felt free to ask such a favor. And usually a farmer was glad to have them; company.

Mrs. Stafford didn't want anybody messing up things today. Not on top of a farm washing. But she told them they could water and feed.

In a short time they came up from the barn. "Where's your husband?"

She told them he had gone to town, which, then, was an all-day trip.

"Would it be askin' too much to ask you to cook up a meal for us?"

On washday! It certainly was; and Mrs. Stafford said so, directly and to the point.

"We'd appreciate it," said one, "and we wouldn't try to drive a bargain about the price."

"No," she said firmly, "I've got my washing to hang out."

The men looked at the heaping baskets of clothes, then at each other.

"Ma'am, I reckon we could do that," said one of them. "You could spend the time cooking."

"There wouldn't be no quarrel about the price," urged the other.

"Well," said Mrs. Stafford, more agreeably, "all right, I'll do it. I'll run down a chicken."

She started to the chicken yard. One of the men left the clothes and asked her to show him which chicken she wanted. She pointed one out.

"There won't be any running-down," he said. Drawing a pistol out of his pocket, he followed the fowl for a moment, then shot its head off.

"You'll have to help pluck it," said Mrs. Stafford.

The man mumbled something about getting more than he'd bargained for, but when she immersed the chicken in scalding water he began to pull off the feathers. The other man—having finished his job—came and watched the process, seeming to enjoy it hugely. "Get all the pinfeathers. You know you want to do a good job for the lady."

The other gave him a sour look, but plucked on.

"Get the little ones there on the wing. It pays to do good work."

At last the job was finished and the two men stretched out on the grass in the yard and rested.

When dinner was ready the two came in, and they ate heartily, according to Mrs. Stafford, who waited on the table.

When the meal was over, one of the men handed her a five-dollar bill—a tremendous sum.

"When your husband gets home, you can tell him you had the pleasure of having Frank and Jesse James for dinner."

Smiling, the two men rode away.

Another I used to gaze on in popeyed wonder was 'Red Bob' Wilson. Why, it was almost as good as seeing Jesse! And lest my mind had done me tricks, I went to see him again in my hometown. He is now Robert E. Lee Wilson. But to me he's still Red Bob. And there, at 915 East First Street, you can find him.

He was a newsboy in St. Joseph, Missouri, on That Day. He chose the day to go catfishing in the Missouri River. When he came home that evening his mother said, "It's a pretty time for you to go skylarkin' around. This is the biggest day there ever was to sell papers. Jesse James was killed today!"

Red Bob was a bit flabbergasted, but he wasn't licked. He rushed to the office of the *St. Joseph News* and got a cartload of papers. Jesse was then at the undertaker's and a line of people was waiting to see him. Red Bob went up and down the line selling his papers.

"It was the best day I ever had," he said reminiscently.

Then Red Bob went in and saw *him* himself.

"I wish I could say he had been one of my customers, but I can't. I had never seen him before."

Red Bob was the first person I ever knew who had seen Jesse 'strapped to the board.' I could shut my eyes and almost see Jesse, myself.

In questioning old friends and sons of the oldtimers as to what they knew about the Boys, I came upon a new story, one I had never known before. It has to do with Don Alexander, now the dignified president of the Maryville School Board.

One summer, between school terms, he had a job working in the house where Jesse gave up his life. Jesse fell upon the floor and died without speaking. His blood ran out on the floor. It was Don Alexander's duty to sell shavings from the boards to the morbidly curious—the grisly boards with Jesse's lifeblood upon them. Fifteen cents admission was charged, with another fifteen cents for a bloodsoaked shaving. But tourists were many and sales problems were many. The owner of the house solved them neatly. Each morning he had Don smear the boards with chicken blood. Today, in America, there must be a hatful of shavings, all smeared with the lifeblood of ill-fated chickens.

Another hometown story new to me till I began scouting around for this book comes from Mrs. Stella Rankin, 1021 East Jenkins Street, Maryville, Missouri. Stella Rankin I have known a long time, but not the story. I believe the story is true, for I am not putting in this book any legends or folk tales. Only the truth as nearly as I can determine it. Jesse James has been a hobby with me for a good many years—long, long before I ever dreamed of putting him to paper. During this time I have sieved out a great deal of chaff. I believe what is left is wheat.

Stella Rankin's grandmother was Mrs. John Nanson. She lived in what was called the 'Congrave-Jackson' house near Fayette, Missouri. One day Mrs. Nanson was canning peaches with the aid of 'Easter,' the family's 'Mammy.' Suddenly three men rode up. Mrs. Nanson recognized them, for they were neighbors and she had seen them before. They were Jesse and Frank and Cole Younger. They were restless and uneasy and showed signs of having ridden fast. They asked Mrs. Nanson if she would have Easter cook dinner in an hour. Easter agreed to try.

The men conferred, then asked Mrs. Nanson if she could suggest a place for them to hide their horses. In the rear was an old cave which some years before had been used as an icehouse. Around it had grown up a thicket of brush. Mrs. Nanson suggested they could use this; the men led their horses to the abandoned icehouse and put them in it, then came to the house. Mammy Easter was busily flinging about. Soon the meal was ready.

But just as the meal was about on the table there was again the sound of horses outside—this time it was Federal troops. The soldiers were between Frank and Jesse and Cole and their horses.

Mrs. Nanson told the three to go upstairs, where she would hide them between featherbeds. She put Frank and Jesse in one bed, but Cole was so big he couldn't go in with them and had to have a separate bed. In they went, each between featherbeds; soon they were as cooked as the peaches downstairs.

The Federal soldiers came in and asked whom the meal was for. Mrs. Nanson said it was for her father and two neighbors. The Federals were delighted and sat down to a fine, leisurely meal. They complimented her upon her ability—and ate some more. Meanwhile Jesse, Frank, and Cole Younger cooked some more.

The Nanson family had a dog, 'Jo Shelby,' named in honor of the great Confederate general, Jo Shelby. Inadvertently Mammy Easter called him by name.

Instantly one of the soldiers got out of his chair. "Anything with that name ought to die." Ordering the dog outside, he drew his pistol.

Mammy Easter begged for his life, saying she had cooked their dinner and they ought at least to do this for her, so the man relented, sitting down again.

At last the soldiers got up and left. Jesse, Frank, and Cole came downstairs again, dripping like hay hands. They looked at what was left of the sumptuous meal. Mammy Easter gathered up the remains, but they were afraid to be served downstairs. So they sat upstairs, where they could see the road, and nibbled at the leftovers.

Frank James looked up from a chicken neck and said, "If

that man had shot Jo Shelby, I would have leaned out the window and shot him." Then he went back to the chicken neck. The others gnawed on in embittered silence.

This was not all. On August 29, 1903, Frank James and Cole Younger came to our town with a circus and had dinner with Mrs. Rankin in the very house where I was hearing this story. It made the picture doubly vivid.

Oh, the tales I collected, about Frank as well as Jesse. Uel W. Lamkin of California, Missouri, told me the one about Frank James and the young interne. Later, Mr. Lamkin became president of the Northwest Missouri Teachers College in Maryville, but when he heard this story he was a boy in California, where it happened.

John Patrick Burke had grown up in California, become a medical student, been seized by wanderlust, and had gone to Texas where he became an interne. One day Frank James had been brought to him, a victim of typhoid fever. At that time Dr. Burke had not known who the tall, thin, rather hawk-nosed man he nursed safely through the illness was. But Frank was immensely grateful, and when he was ready to go he had identified himself and said, "If there is ever anything I can do for you, you let me know and its performance will be a pleasure."

Later young Dr. Burke returned to his old hometown and set up in practice, but he found it hard to get started. One day, as he was going to his office, he was surprised to see several horsemen moving slowly through the street, then doubly surprised to see that one was Frank James. The Moniteau County National Bank was on the corner, and immediately Dr. Burke put two and two together.

He did not hesitate, but went up to Frank, called him by name, and asked him if he were going to rob the bank. Frank appeared a bit embarrassed, then admitted that was his intention. Whereupon Dr. Burke said that people knew he had met Frank James in Texas, and would think he had served as a spy and had tipped Frank off about the bank, with the result that he would never be able to build up his practice.

Frank considered a moment. "There's something to what you say, Doc. When does the next train leave?"

Frank would not let his men rob the bank, for that would harm a friend. But the train was different.

Another story is Elmer Frazier's. Elmer is now dead, but I have heard him tell it, myself quaking pleasantly meanwhile. Marshall E. Ford of Maryville refreshed my boyhood memory of it. One day Elmer was sitting in Mike Hilgert's saloon watching the men at their pleasures. Mike's saloon had two pool tables. At one of these was playing a character called 'Omaha Charlie.' He was a tough egg; no one wanted to play with him because he was so quarrelsome and insulting. Hardly ever did he get into a game but words were shouted and fists flourished. Later, indeed, they had to take him out and hang him to a railroad trestle. He had killed a man; many men engaged in the hanging went about it with great enthusiasm, so mean was Omaha Charlie.

On this day Elmer saw a rather handsome young stranger with a brown beard come in and seat himself. Omaha Charlie, unable to get anybody to play with him, approached the stranger. In no time they were playing and in no time a quarrel arose. The stranger was soft of voice and pleasant of manner. During the game, Omaha Charlie accused him of cheating. Not only that but came toward him with upraised cue. Instantly the stranger took on a deadly calm and his blue eyes became icy-cold.

"Stop where you are. You are threatening the wrong man."

And so meaningly did the stranger say it that Omaha Charlie stopped, knowing that the stranger meant every word. Not only did Omaha Charlie stop, but he put up his pool cue and left the place. Later he said, "I could see hell in that man's eyes."

The stranger stayed a few minutes, then left.

It was not long before Elmer Frazier went, with a crowd of men from our town, to St. Joseph to see Jesse James at the undertaker's, and there, on the slab, was the mysterious stranger whose deadly coldness had made Omaha Charlie tread water.

No one ever knew why Jesse James was in our town that day, except that he had come 'to look things over.' His usual method was to go in a bank and ask to have a bill changed; while this was being done, he would cast his eyes about him, especially at the time lock, a subject that interested him profoundly. No one at either of our banks remembered him, or, at least, paid any attention to him. This happened just a short time before he was killed, when he was planning, with Bob Ford, another bank robbery. They settled upon Platte City, a town a short distance away. Our people always thought if he hadn't been frightened away by the pool game and attention drawn to him, Jesse would have robbed one of our banks. Sometimes I almost wished he had.

I

THE BOYHOOD OF JESSE JAMES

ON THE old James farm near Kearney, Missouri, are the sworn papers of the 'tobacco bride.' She was Zerelda E. Cole, the mother of Frank and Jesse James. She was only sixteen, a minor, and Robert James, who wanted to take her in marriage, didn't have enough worldly goods to indicate he could support her. So he had to put up a bond of fifty pounds of tobacco in order, as the documents say, 'to intermarry' Zerelda E. Cole. But he wasn't considered a good risk, so he had to get a co-guarantor, and there, on a sworn copy of the official papers, is the latter's name—J. J. Milliken. The girl had a guardian named James M. Lindsay who demanded the last pound of tobacco.

She was attending a Roman Catholic convent in Lexington, Kentucky. (In those days convents were sometimes the only schools available.) She fell in love with Robert James, who was going to Georgetown College, Georgetown, Kentucky. It was a Baptist school and is still in existence.

He was studying to be a preacher; he was twenty-three and a senior. It was the old story; they 'couldn't wait' so they were married while he was still in school. The time was December 28, 1841, and the place was the bride's uncle's (Judge Cole) on the 'Stomping Ground Road' about four miles out of Lexington.

The bride left the convent and came over to live with her husband. Some way or other he managed to keep his mind on his studies and managed to graduate. Now what was he to do?

His mother had gone to Missouri, so the young minister and his bride trekked after her. His mother had located in Clay County, not far from Kansas City, and thence went Mr. and Mrs. Robert James, wondering what the world had in store for them. It had a great deal indeed. That young bride, as the years went by, saw unfold before her one of the most amazing dramas ever to be played in America. She was picked up by a force far greater than herself and carried along to a tragic and moving end.

The young minister got hold of some land and started both to farm and to preach, which, in that day, was not at all uncommon. A son came along on January 10, 1843; they named him, rather impressively, Alexander Franklin James. He was soon to become 'Frank,' and hereafter, in this book, he will be only that.

The first house was about a quarter of a mile from the one where the father and mother soon moved. This latter house still stands and is known as the James home. Heartbreak and tragedy—and humor—became part of it. How many anxious nights have dragged by in that old log house! In its early days there were loopholes in the top story. They are now gone. The house has been changed some since Frank was taken there as a lad. But not much. For the most part it stands just as it did when the young couple moved into it.

There, in what they called the 'new house,' Jesse James was born. He was named after two uncles: Jesse Cole (his mother's brother) and Drury Woodson James (his father's brother). And now the date: September 5, 1847.

Young Robert James organized two neighborhood congregations into churches. One was the Providence Church, the other was New Hope. He preached at them both and they both stand today. Not only this, but he was a 'traveling preacher'; he went to other churches in the county where he held 'revivals' and 'protracted meetings.' His wife—who had gone to the convent—seems to have supported him wholeheartedly. She was, all her life, a religious woman. And so was her son Jesse religious; sometimes, before he went on a 'raid,' Jesse read the Bible. Frank James was not of this turn of mind. He liked politics and—strangely enough—Shakespeare. Frank's education was scanty; he added to it by reading and studying Shakespeare. Jesse thought it was boring. Jesse was the man of action; Frank the student. This must not be thought of in terms of today, when Shakespeare study is wide and deep, but in terms of that day. Sometimes, when the Boys were hiding out, Frank would sit and read Shakespeare. This disgusted the other members of the gang. They said he would never get any place as a bandit. Once, in later years in Baltimore, Frank went to see a Shakespeare play, and as a result was almost captured.

A daughter was born—Susie, two years younger than Jesse. Then a boy who lived only a month. (That is all there ever were of the James children.) So there was the little log cabin and there were the three children; and there was the young minister engaged in farming and plowing, and the world ahead seemed to lie as straight as a furrow.

But preaching wasn't all for Robert James. He was interested in education, too. P. Caspar Harvey is with William Jewell College at Liberty, Missouri. He breathes and exudes the belief that William Jewell College is the greatest in the land. In his office is a printed copy of the college's charter. The charter was granted by a vote of the legislature of Missouri and was signed by the governor on February 27, 1849. There, almost at the top, is the name 'Robert S. James.' The men listed were prominent citizens, and it would seem that Robert S. James was considered a man of some importance in the state.

Now there came an unexpected turning in the furrow. In the very town where he had helped establish William Jewell College, covered wagons were then being outfitted for faraway California. The Gold Rush was in the air; it was everywhere. Go west, get rich. And so Robert James joined up and started on the long journey. It proved to be a long journey, indeed, for he never came back. He died and was buried near Marysville, California. Once, years later, Frank went there to see if he could find his father's grave, but failed. And so passes the young preacher-educator-farmer. He never dreamed the story his two sons would give the world.

With three children on her hands, the young widow looked about her and married a neighbor named Benjamin Simms, a farmer, on September 30, 1852. She was married in Kearney and the man who performed the ceremony was the Reverend Franklin Graves. But the marriage didn't turn out well. Simms was sixteen years older. The chief reason, however, seems to have been the way he treated Frank and Jesse. She said, later, that he was cruel to them and once whipped Frank. In those early days, divorce was not a matter lightly to be entered into, but she was preparing to go ahead when Benjamin Simms died.

It was not long until she took a third chance, this time with a fellow-Kentuckian named Dr. Reuben Samuel. He had come to Missouri from near Samuels Station, Kentucky, where his family was a proud one. He was a doctor-farmer, as was often the case in the early days in this southern fringe of the Middle West. Search of the marriage records bureau of Clay County shows that Reuben Samuel and Zerelda Simms were married September 26, 1855, by Ellis Williams, justice of the peace. (For some reason or other, the marriage was not recorded till December 17th of that year.)

(A word as to the spelling of the name. It was really 'Samuel' and was spelled that way on the marriage license and it is spelled that way on the tombstone in the little cemetery at Kearney. But the neighbors called him 'Samuels' and the newspapers referred to the family as the Samuels family, so, in this book, I am using the spelling most frequently found; from now on Zerelda will be Mrs. Samuels, as she was indeed to everybody in that section, and later, when she became the central figure of a national drama, to everybody in America.)

Dr. Samuels, it developed, liked the boys, and when trouble came defended them—once almost with his life. As a result she liked him and they got along, on the whole, rather well, this despite a trait of Mrs. Samuels' character which threaded importantly through her life: her temper. It was hot and fiery; she talked first and thought afterward. This quick temper she passed along to Jesse. Frank, on the other hand, was like his father: calm, judicious, slow to go off. Frank was more 'brainy' than Jesse, though Jesse had excellent brains for his specialty—banditry. Indeed, Jesse was a strange character; he loved fun and had a sunny, equable disposition until his mother's temper went off; then he was a madman; he was a killer.

Jesse and Frank were typical farmboys of that period. They went to the Pleasant Grove School; it still stands, and other boys—who must be very much like them—go there now. Out in front is a 'teeter-totter' and an old automobile tire used as a swing. In the old days there was a woodshed. But that's gone. Kerosene now. At home the boys had to chore; in summer they plowed corn and farmed. Always there were horses; and there were guns. In due course Sallie and John Samuels came along. Sundays the family got in the hack and drove to Kearney—about three miles—and went to the Baptist church, the father's influence thus lingering.

The first character trait of Jesse's that became evident was his interest in religion. It seems to have been more than the interest that sometimes strikes boys at a certain age, for, according to local tradition, he went to church regularly and insisted that other members of the family go when they would much rather have passed the Sabbath morning at their own pleasures. Once he startled the good brethren and sisters by standing up and praying aloud for his brother Frank. But it seems to have done little good, for Frank went to his reward a doubter. Jesse himself seems never to have questioned the Divine Scheme.

There were other interests. George Mereness lives in Liberty. His stepmother was Jesse's first sweetheart. Her name was Martha King and she lived at Prathersville, a short hop from the James farm. Jesse was so shy that he would not court her outright; didn't have the courage, Mr. Mereness said. So Jesse went about the matter in his own way. He would ride down the road to her house, and when he came opposite he would give a peculiar whistle. Then he would leave some lead in an old woodpecker hole in a fence post, and ride on again. In a day or two he would come back, reach into the woodpecker hole, and there, wrapped in paper, would be bullets. Bullets were especially valuable then, being mostly home-molded. A few days later Jesse would ride by again. But it didn't do him any good; he lost her to a young man who probably didn't whistle at all but rode right in and told her she was wonderful, without any foolishness about woodpecker holes.

But the thing which worked upon Jesse's life as a boy and played perhaps the largest part in making him what he became, was not something personal out of his home life but something broader and wider and out of the history of America as it was then. Students of the period say that there was more bitterness during the Border Warfare between Kansas and Missouri than in any other phase of the warfare between the states. It arose over whether Kansas should come into the Union free or slave. Apples of bitterness grew on that tree. Neighbor was set against neighbor, family against family, brother fought brother. The warfare began about the time of the Kansas-Nebraska Act in 1854, and continued up to and through most of the Civil War. The people of Missouri, who in Jesse's section were largely Southern sympathizers, marched over the border and killed all the Kansans they could. The Kansans marched right back.

The people of Missouri were called 'Bushwhackers,' a title very appropriate, for they whacked with their rifles from ambushes in timber and covert. The Kansans were called 'Jayhawkers,' after the Jayhawker bird. There never was such a bird on land or sea, but the name got started and it's still going. Sometimes the armed bands were called 'Redlegs,' this from the red-morocco leggings they wore in the early days. These bands, on each side, were really guerrillas; they were not attached to the regular uniformed forces, but operated separately; they were their own bosses and rode and robbed and slaughtered as they pleased. The leaders of the Kansas men were General James H. Lane and General Jennison. The military leaders of the Missourians were William C. Quantrill,

William F. Anderson, and George Todd. Anderson was called 'Bloody Bill,' which was almost praise, considering what a scoundrel he was. But, compared to Quantrill, Anderson was a Sunday-school teacher with cookies in his pocket. This will give an idea of Quantrill: In 1863 he rode into Lawrence, Kansas, with his bloody legionnaires (Frank James was one of them) and ordered every male shot to death and their houses burned. When the day was done, so were one hundred and eighty-two men. Bloody Bill Anderson attacked a railroad train at Centralia, Missouri, found twenty-three Union troops aboard, captured them, lined them up alongside the railroad track, and shot them to death. Not pleasant reading, but that was the way things were in the Border War.

The warfare was carried into the homes, not just of the town people, but of the farmers as well. Suddenly one side would swoop down on a farmer and demand to know if he had anyone there from the other side. If he had, they shot him. If he hadn't, they wanted to know where their enemies might be. It was bad business. It is impossible to overstate the bitterness of this warfare between two sister states. It was as black a mark as has been made on American history—this ghastly matter of riding across an imaginary line and killing people just because they lived on the other side.

The very heart and center of this bloody business of the 1850's was two counties in Missouri—Jackson (where Kansas City is), and Clay. And it was in the latter that the Jameses lived. Mrs. James, being from Kentucky, was an ardent Southerner. She had that fiery temper; she had ideas about who was right and she spoke them. Union sympathizers were scoundrels; Southerners were God's people. (Curiously enough, the James family had no slaves. They acquired two colored people later, who worked at the house and on the farm, but this was after the slaves had been freed.) She had many neighbors who were Northerners; she told them where they could go. But they did not want to go there, highly as she recommended it. It all made her talk louder; neighbors warned her to be careful, but with her nature she could not be cautious-tongued. Dr. Samuels was thoroughly Southern, too, but he didn't take it out in the road and show it.

Every day Frank and Jesse listened to this; the result was inevitable. They played 'Hang Old Jim Lane' and they named stumps 'John Brown' and lammed stones at them. In this atmosphere they grew up.

When Fort Sumter was fired on, Frank joined up as fast as he could manage it; he was eighteen. He enlisted under General Sterling Price in the Missouri State Guards, a Confederate force in a state that had come into the war on the side of the Union. In almost no time at all he got a taste of fighting, at Wilson's Creek near Springfield, Missouri, less than a month after the Battle of Bull Run. It was the fiercest battle ever fought in Missouri, and Frank James's side won.

Frank came back to the James farm elated with victory. There is no record of what his mother said, but it could have been only one thing. Frank talked so long and loud he was seized by the Unionists. There wasn't a place in Kearney to contain him, so he was taken to Liberty (where his father had climbed in the covered wagon to go after California's gold) and was clapped into jail. That was pretty difficult to take. He had just helped win a victory at Wilson's Creek and now he was on the inside looking out.

His mother came to his rescue. She went to the commander of the Union forces in the county and asked him to release Frank. He agreed to do this if Frank would sign an oath of allegiance and if the Stars and Stripes were flown in the yard of their house. But three days after Frank signed the oath, this officer was moved to another command, and so the flag did not fly. The new commander tried to capture Frank, but Frank 'went into the bush.'

Frank felt he couldn't go back with General Price, so he made a decision that changed both his life and Jesse's: he joined Quantrill's guerrillas.

Jesse remained at home, farming. And then, one day, something dreadful happened.

II

THE BORDER WARFARE MAKES ITS MARK

ONE day in June, 1863, a squad of Union soldiers rode up to the log cabin that was to see so many scenes of violence and tragedy. Dr. Samuels was busy in the rear; he came around the corner—and his heart must have beat faster when he saw the ominous horsemen.

"What do you want?" he asked.

"We want you," one of the men said. "You and your wife both. You've been talking too much. And your son has joined Quantrill. Not only that but you put up his men when they came through!"

Dr. Samuels tried to defend himself, but what the men had said was true, and Dr. Samuels did not do a good job of it.

"Where's your wife?"

"In the back yard making soap," answered the dignified doctor.

The men looked at each other significantly; a plan had been prepared and they began to carry it out. One of the men went back to his saddle and returned with a rope. Two others seized the doctor and bound his hands behind his back, the rope was tied around his neck, and they marched him to a coffee-bean tree and threw the end over the limb. The doctor—gasping and struggling—was lifted off his feet. Then the rope was tied and the men calmly marched out to the barn.

The moment they turned the corner of the house, Mrs. Samuels rushed up and untied the rope; the doctor fell to the ground, an inert mass. She worked desperately, loosening the cord from around his burned neck. His eyes opened. He was alive! She helped him into the house. Now he was safe. Or was he? . . .

The men thought young Jesse had hidden in the barn, but he wasn't there. They found him in the field plowing—this blue-eyed lad of fifteen and a half.

"Here's that Quantrill-man's brother," one said.

"We'll learn him, too," said another.

They proceeded at once with what they had in mind. Two of the men seized him and the third began to beat him with a rope. A dreadful scene—grown men lashing a boy—but that was the way it was, for feelings in this border state were deep, especially in this county which was at the dead center of the conflict.

And now, having accomplished their purpose, the men went back to the house. Dr. Samuels was no longer hanging in the yard, but that was all right; his wife had probably carried the body in. So the men got on their horses and rode away.

After a time young Jesse came in. It took only a glance from his mother to know something had happened. She got his shirt off—and there were the welts and blood. And so she took care of both of them, her son and her husband.

Then it was that Jesse made a decision that changed his life, and the lives of many others. He was too young to enroll as a regular Confederate but there was something else.

"Mother, I'm going to join Quantrill."

What could she say, with her husband half-dead and her

son's back lashed and swollen? What a choice she had to make! But she hated the bushwhacking Federals; and Frank had done well as a soldier and had gone to ride with Quantrill.

Jesse was never one to say something he did not mean. All through his life he had that trait, like marrow in a bone. The next day he got in touch with some men who were with Quantrill, but who were temporarily at home. They had bad news for him. He was too young. Quantrill wanted only the toughest and most daring. And so he returned.

The neighborhood was small; news got around. About a week later the Union men returned and again tied their horses to the hitchrack. They would really teach him a lesson.

"Where's that boy of yours?"

"He's not here," said Mrs. Samuels.

The men would not believe it and went to the barn, then to the field. By a lucky stroke Jesse and his stepfather were away. But it was not wholly lucky, for they ordered Mrs. Samuels to come with them—the so-called 'military arrest.' She was taken in a wagon to Kearney and then sent in a roundabout way to St. Joseph. That night, when Jesse and his stepfather returned, she was not there.

Mrs. Samuels was kept in prison about two weeks. What a scene that must have been, when she returned to the little log cabin! But they had to be ever-watchful, for conditions were growing very dangerous. More and more often Federal troops rode up to cabins and demanded answers to their questions.

Jesse found that what the men had said was true—being not yet seventeen he was too young for Quantrill, who had the bloodiest and most dangerous group of men in America; but there were ways around this. So Jesse joined one of the side-commands under the direction of Quantrill: Bloody Bill Anderson's. (Jesse served under both Todd and Anderson, and later, in Texas, under George Shepherd. But in this book he will be referred to hereafter simply as serving 'under Quantrill.')

The first week that Jesse was in the band something happened that is important to record. He had been brought up with guns; he knew all their tricks. But not quite all, for as he was cleaning his pistol it went off and so did the tip of the third finger on his left hand. The boy shook his hand and said, "That's the dod-dingus pistol I ever saw."

The hardened old murderers laughed uproariously. If one of them had shot off the end of *his* finger, he would have cursed till hell would not have it. But Jesse—with religion so deep in him—never swore. The men began to call him 'Dingus,' and Dingus he was as long as he rode with them.

In September of 1864 Anderson's massacre at Centralia took place. On the afternoon of the same day, September 27th, pursuing Union forces under command of Major A. V. E. Johnson were ambushed, and between 175 and 264 soldiers (the estimates vary), together with their leader, were killed.

Jesse James, it is believed, was the one who shot Major Johnson. This, so far as is known, was the first man Jesse ever killed. The date was twenty-two days after his seventeenth birthday. The boy was getting a good start.

Sometimes Frank and Jesse were under the same command, sometimes not. Jesse ranged as far south as Texas. But wherever he went the war was going against him. He had been lucky; his only wound was the 'dingus.' He was seeing and he was fighting a war of hatred, though, and that gave other wounds.

In August, 1864, Anderson brought his men to Rocheport, Missouri, to capture the steamboat *War Eagle*, which was owned by Northerners. He hid his men behind a tobacco warehouse near the levee, close to where the boat would land.

The men waited silently as the boat came heading in. During the wait one of them became so nervous that he accidentally discharged his pistol. The pilot of the boat, realizing something was wrong, pulled the bell and signaled the engineer to reverse the engines. The boat began to back into the current.

Anderson, maddened at seeing the rich cargo escaping, ordered his men to open fire. The pilot, to escape with his life, left the wheelhouse and let the boat drift. Noting the boat's helpless state, Anderson commanded four of his men to row out and finish the capture.

The men procured a rowboat and soon came up to the steamer. Just as the first man stood up to go over the gunwales, the pilot blew his right arm off with a shotgun. The rowboat, with the injured man, came back to shore.

Anderson was infuriated and ordered his men to open fire on the steamer and to kill every man, woman, and child.

A young fellow named Lyons, who had joined Anderson only the day before, was shocked at this brutality, and, stepping up to the leader, said, "Captain Anderson, here are my pistols. I cannot make war against women and children."

Anderson glared at him, almost bursting with rage. Then with his pistol he knocked him down and began to kick him. Some women, who had come down to the levee to see the boat land, ran up to Anderson and begged him to stop. Anderson began to argue with them, and while he was doing this the young man got to his feet and managed to run away.

After the trouble with the women was over, Anderson turned to Jesse James and said, "Capture that man. I'm going to kill him as an example to others."

Jesse started after Lyons. But he, too, had been shocked by Anderson's brutality and did not press his pursuit and let the young man escape.

The war went on.

Came Easter Sunday at Appomattox. The Confederate soldiers surrendered honorably, but there was the matter of the guerrillas. The bands and contingents were required to come in separately. One of the surrender points was Lexington, Missouri, not far from the old home; and to it Jesse started. The war was over. He could go back to farming.

What happened this morning became important in his life. There has been much confusion about it, but it has been possible to get, from original sources, what seems to be the truth. The person I am indebted to is A. L. Maxwell, Route 2, Lexington, Missouri. His father was a cavalryman in Frost's Division. Mr. Maxwell lives on the land where the event occurred. It was his brother-in-law who obtained the facts concerning it from Barnett Lankford before Lankford's death in the late 'eighties.

The time was April 23, 1865. Jesse was riding with a small group of guerrillas coming to surrender at the Burns schoolhouse. In this group was Jesse Hamlett, a friend. Suddenly they saw a band of five horsemen coming from the direction of Salt Pond Road. These men charged the Southerners, firing on them. Hamlett's horse was killed under him and Jesse James was shot three times—twice in the right breast and once in the leg. But in spite of his wounds, Jesse got his friend up behind him and the two rode away as fast as they could.

It is not known what happened to Hamlett thereafter, but Jesse was so seriously wounded that he had to dismount and crawl off the roadside into the brush. The Union soldiers caught the horse and began to search for him. There was an old abandoned coal mine near, and into this Jesse crawled. When night came on he went to a house which proved to be the home of Barnett Lankford. The latter was a Southern sympathizer and willingly took Jesse in, and there he remained two days. At the end of that time he was able to stay on a horse, painful as this was, so he started toward the Hill place two miles southeast of Mt. Hope, where his wounds were treated by Dr. A. B. Hereford. Lankford's horse was sent back to him by a recently returned veteran of Price's Army, who came with Jesse to the Hill farm.

On the farm was a semi-abandoned log house, in which he hid. When he was again able to travel, he went to his mother's. Jesse had gone through the war without having been wounded, but on the day he was to surrender he was almost killed. The mother received the son who had gone to avenge his stepfather's hanging, her imprisonment, and his own beating, and who had returned with two ghastly chest wounds and a lesser wound in the leg. He was now seventeen and a half.

Jesse went to bed and Dr. Samuels did what he could for him. But instead of getting better, the wound got worse. A tube had to be kept in it. Dr. Samuels thought he was going to die, but his mother did not give up hope, mothers being what they are. Week after week went by, and he was still in bed.

The neighborhood remained filled with bitterness. Jesse belonged to the conquered, and the Northerners made it uncomfortable for him and for his family. Dr. and Mrs. Samuels decided a change would do the boy good, so he was placed in a wagon and taken to the very town where he had gone to surrender, and there carried on a stretcher to a steamboat going up the Missouri River.

Why the family chose the town of Rulo, Nebraska, to move to is not known. It may have been having a boom and its future may have seemed all smiles. But in any event it must have seemed a place of cheer to Jesse and his mother and stepfather. He was carried ashore, a house was secured, and Dr. Samuels started practicing medicine. They lived under their own names, for there was no thought of concealment.

Jesse did not get better; day after day he lay in bed, his faithful mother waiting on him. There was no Border Warfare feeling here, no sectional bitterness. But they were not his people. Not Southerners at all.

Finally Jesse said, "Mother, I don't want to die up here in the North. Please take me back."

Dr. Samuels closed out his practice, Jesse was carried to the boat, and the trip home, in August, 1865, was begun. On the way something happened that changed his life.

The family decided to stop and see Dr. Samuels' sister, who was living in Harlem, now part of North Kansas City. So they got off there and Jesse was carried to a rooming house run by his aunt, Mrs. John Mimms. And there Jesse met his cousin Zerelda Mimms, named for his mother. She began to wait on him; and when she came into the room his eyes were upon her eagerly. He began to call her 'Zee.' (His mother was known among the kinfolks as 'Aunt Zerel.')

One day a band marched past the house. Zee went in to open the window so he could hear better, but he was already up and sitting in a chair beside the bed. She pulled his chair over to the window and the two, side by side, watched the band march by.

The mother began to see 'there was something doing,' and sought to discourage it. A sick boy; the girl, his cousin. It would not do.

He began to get better, and his mother put him in a wagon and started back to the old James farm. As the wagon jolted along, Jesse said, "Mother, I want to marry Zee."

"Hush! Don't talk about it. You're too young and you are sick."

Back in the old home place, which Jesse loved all his life, he improved even more. Frank had been farming it, but they were postwar sufferers. Their horses had been stolen. Prices were at starvation levels; it took hard scratching to make a living.

Meanwhile, Jesse had good days and bad days. Sometimes he would be up and around; then his wound would open and he would have to go back to bed. As he got better he began to go to the Baptist church in Kearney; not only that, but he sang in the choir. (It is not known if he did any more praying for Frank.) In the neighborhood there was a boy named Leonidas Leavell, who was the same age as Jesse. Every Sunday the two went to church together; usually Jesse came home with him and had Sunday dinner at the Leavell house.

One Sunday Jesse sat through a long sermon, sang with the congregation, and, when the young people gathered in front of the church, seemed as lively as any there. On arriving at the Leavell home, the two boys watered, stabled, and fed their horses, then went to the house to wait for dinner. Others had come and it was a gay party. But Jesse seemed to become uneasy. Excusing himself, he went behind a large lilac bush, took off his shirt, and unwound the bandage from his chest. Putting his hands around the wound, Jesse squeezed out about a half-pint of pus, replaced the bandage, got into his shirt, then came back and calmly began to mingle with the other guests. In the afternoon he mounted his horse and rode leisurely home.

In later years the Leavell boy became Judge Leavell. He often said that what Jesse did that day was a superb example of grit.

The Civil War was over, but lawlessness wasn't; men, in these Border counties, had been fighting for eleven years—from 1854 to 1865—and they didn't easily put bloodshed aside. Everywhere they went armed; the taking of a life wasn't a very serious matter. Armed bands constantly were on the roads; sometimes they were horsethieves, sometimes cattle-stealers; a few highwaymen. At night the inns and hotels housed hard-looking crews.

Meantime the country was 'settling up.' People were pushing in from the East; covered wagons, with land-seeking families in them, were clucking along the roads. Men were looking for new land, new opportunities. On the last day of 1862, Abraham Lincoln had signed a bill creating homesteads for settlers. But the war was on then, and little could be done about it; now the war was over and people were taking advantage of the so-called 'free land'—and it was almost that, for only $14 had to be paid down to file on a quarter-section. So everywhere people were beginning to stake out new homes. The first homestead in the United States was at Beatrice, Nebraska, not far from where the James family lived.

The keynote was lawlessness. There was little respect for the law. Now and then a man was lynched for stealing a horse; people took it calmly. After the terrors of Border Warfare, a man dangling on a limb didn't mean much.

One of the disturbing factors of the period and the place was the 'loyalty oath' which the government made the residents of this section take. No one was permitted to practice law, teach, or preach unless he had first taken what was called the 'Ironclad Oath.' Ministers, or preachers, who had even given a meal or a night's lodging to a Confederate could be thrown in jail. In Liberty there was so much resentment against the North that the Confederate flag continued to fly over the courthouse; indeed, it was not pulled down until almost 1870.

The feeling of hatred was never stronger. Francis P. Blair, who saved Missouri to the Union, was running for Congress. His life was openly threatened. In 1866 he was to make a speech at Louisiana, Mo. When he was ready to speak, he walked to a table on the platform, took out two pistols, put them on the table, then said: "I understand that I am to be killed here today. I have just come from four years of killing and am familiar with that kind of business. Let the man who tries to kill me take good aim." Then he launched into his speech; there were no interruptions. Once, however, in St. Louis, a man in the audience suddenly rose up, and from a distance of twenty feet fired at Blair, missing. Immediately the man was seized. Blair said, "Let him shoot. If I am wrong I ought to be shot," then went ahead with his speech.

This was the sort of thing that colored Missouri life in that day, especially in the county where the James family lived. On top of it, times were hard. Banks were unregulated; they ground the people down, and the people hated them, and blamed them for the times. The men who had ridden with Quantrill and his lieutenants didn't mind the idea of something happening to the smug bankers. These men needed money, and they began to think about how to get it.

The geography of the country was admirably suited to outlawry. There were few fences; not many bridges. Armed men on horseback could cut across the country in almost any direction they wished; they were not nozzled down at bridges where officers could pounce on them. An outlaw could ride a few miles and completely disappear; if he rode fifty, it was as if he were in a new country. People knew nothing about him and very kindly asked no questions.

The result was almost inevitable. On February 13, 1866, ten men rode up to the bank in Liberty, Missouri, and the first bank robbery in America took place. So closely upon the end of the Civil War did it follow that when the ex-guerrillas rode down the street, they gave the famous, terrifying rebel yell. On the way to William Jewell College at the time was a youth named George Wymore. The robbers yelled at him to get inside, but the boy was so taken by surprise that he could only stand and stare. It cost him his life, for he was shot down.

The robbers went inside, and then made its appearance an article that was to become famous—the grain sack. The men swept up the money from the counter, and into the grain bag it went: $62,000. A posse was raised which got nowhere impressively. After a time it came back, saying it had 'pressed them hard.' And that was the end of that.

From the point of view of the robbers, the holdup was a tremendous success. No one was ever jailed, no one ever suffered . . . except a young college boy.

Frank James was in the robbery. After the affair cooled down he came home, and he must have told Jesse about what had happened and must have shown Jesse the money. And Jesse—who had been thinking about being a farmer, about joining the church—must have looked at it and had other thoughts. It must not have seemed so terribly wrong to rob a bank. Hadn't he seen far worse at Centralia? Hadn't he seen more than a hundred men die in cold blood in one day? And hadn't he killed one of them, himself?

He was eighteen and a half years old.

III

JESSE JAMES BEGINS TO RIDE

THERE was talk that the Jameses, somehow, had been mixed up in the Liberty robbery. They were rough and tough and carried guns wherever they went. But so did the other young men in the neighborhood. And Jesse was going regularly to church and was singing whenever he had the slightest opportunity. Frank was definitely suspected, but nothing was done about it. Proof was conspicuously lacking; everywhere Frank and Jesse had friends. The two did not know it at the time, but these friends were to become tremendously important assets, for they were to hide Frank and Jesse when the law was on their heels. In a short time the robbery blew over.

Jesse had begun to get better; he carried scars now, not open wounds. He had become his old self. He joked and he was full of fun. And he was in love. But there were greater forces working upon him—the aftermath of the war, the poverty of his family, . . . and the easy way Frank had made some money.

The James family was poor; they did not have enough horses—work stock—to take care of the crops. But what they did have was riding stock, light, fast horses for getting about on the roads. And now, for the first time in his life, Jesse got upon a horse and rode away to rob. He headed for Lexington, the town where he had stopped the bullets. The date was October 30, 1866 . . . about eight months after the easy pickings at Liberty.

Five mounted men rode into Lexington at the noon hour. This did not arouse any special attention, for they did not come together, but one by one and from different directions. Mounted men were constantly arriving in small towns, for the railroads were few and far between; horseback was the way men traveled.

'Noon hour,' in this Southern town, meant something; the place just about closed down. There was only one man in the bank, the cashier. He had already had his dinner and was about two-thirds asleep.

The five strangers tied their horses to the hitchracks and casually sauntered across the street. One of the men detached himself from the others and went in the bank. He put down a $50 United States bond, at this time bonds being used as money.

"Can you change this?"

"I reckon I can," said the cashier agreeably. That was the way to make a friend for the bank.

He opened the cash drawer and began to get the money. As he did so, two other men sauntered in, but once inside they became extremely businesslike. The cashier looked up to find himself gazing down the barrels of three pistols. Instantly he became less sleepy.

"Who are you?" he demanded.

"Bank examiners," came the answer. (That could have been only one man.)

One of the others produced a grain sack . . . just like the one that had done so well at Liberty.

"Put everything you've got in there," said the examiner.

The cashier put it in.

The three men began to back toward the door, their pistols pointed at the still-befuddled cashier.

"If you poke your head out inside of ten minutes, we'll shoot it off."

Confused as he was, the cashier knew he did not want his head shot off, so he said he would not poke it out. He would have use for it as the years went by, he thought. This can be considered a good example of clear thinking.

In a few minutes it was all over and the bank examiners were galloping down the street. The cashier did come out finally. The bewildered citizens did not know what to do; it was an hour before some of them could get on horses and start after the five unceremonious strangers. And they didn't go any too fast. They followed the trail for two days—not any too ardently—then returned and said they guessed the robbers had got away.

The citizens had a mass meeting and said something should be done. After the way of such meetings, nothing was.

In a short time the cashier was back in his old place, going home early to dinner, but exceedingly cautious about cashing $50 United States bonds for out-of-town people.

When the contents of the grain sack were counted they amounted to $2000. Not a big haul, but better than working by the day.

And thus Jesse at nineteen got his first taste of pistol money. If he had had the strength of character not to go on that expedition, he would probably never have been a bandit. And I would not have had a book.

As there had been rumors that Frank had been in the Liberty affair, so now there were rumors that both of the boys had been callers on the Lexington bank. But nothing was done about it. Many others were suspected, too. (The gang in the early raids was made up of men whose names do not yet become a part of the record—a changing group which included men from Clay or the adjoining county of Ray, or friends of the James Boys. Mostly they were ex-guerrillas.) Jesse and Frank worked in the field . . . but not as industriously as they once had. Now and then the neighbors spoke of the 'James Boys.' They were a bit wild—especially the younger one, but that wasn't surprising, considering the hell he had gone through on the Border. He would soon straighten out.

Not far from the James farm was Savannah, Missouri, a prosperous pioneer town, with money in the bank. At exactly noon—as had happened at Lexington—five men rode into town. The date: March 2, 1867.

Four of the men sauntered into the bank, leaving one on the street to hold the horses. The banker sized things up, leaped to the safe, and slammed the door. That took a good deal of nerve, but he had it. Then—still on the initiative—he seized a pistol from under the cash counter and began to fire. It was extremely heroic, but it was extremely bad judgment. In a moment he was shot down.

His son rushed out and shrieked, "Robbers! The bank is being robbed!" The man who had been left to guard the horses began to shoot at him, but the horses plunged and he missed.

The four men in the bank came boiling out, mounted their horses, and the five went racing ignobly down the street. The men did not get a cent.

A posse was formed and galloped grimly after them. Two days later they came slowly back. The robbers had escaped in thin air. One reason they could escape so easily were the back roads and dim trails. The men dispersed and rode off in different directions; the posse would be looking for a band. But no one had seen a band.

Again there was talk about the James Boys, but there was no proof and nothing was done about it. Two men were arrested, but both were freed.

The Savannah raid had a sobering influence on Jesse; there were two sides to this raiding business, it appeared. He returned to farming and to attendance at church. He was feeling strong and sturdy now, except for the fainting spells on hot days which were to be the lifelong after-effect of his wounds. He attended some neighborhood parties, and was remarked to be the most spirited boy there.

In most matters Jesse was honest; this sounds paradoxical but appears to be true. On April 7, 1867, Charles McKinney, a farmer living in Clay County, discovered that his dappled mare was not in the barn. He went from neighbor to neighbor, making inquiries, thinking she might have strayed, but became convinced she had been stolen. He went to the printing office and had a handbill set up offering a reward of $50 for information which would lead to the return of his mare.

Two weeks later Jesse James stopped in at Lee's Summit, Missouri, to stay overnight on his way home to see his mother. As he was putting his horse in the livery stable, he saw an animal answering the description of the stolen mare. Horses were important at that time, and they were especially important to Jesse James, his line of work being what it was. He went to the livery stable owner—a man named Poteet—and told him he thought that the horse had been stolen. Poteet agreed not to let the horse leave the stable.

A day or two later Jesse went to the owner of the horse and reported what he had seen. The owner went to the stable, identified the mare, and claimed her. Jesse James could have collected the reward money, but he was evidently interested only in seeing the right thing done, for he did not claim the money.

But the older men in the gang felt that at Savannah they had been defeated only by bad luck, and that if they tried again they could do better. Jesse allowed himself to be talked into agreeing, and in this the fatal weakness in his character again showed up. If he had had the strength to reject their persuasion he might have gone no further with outlawing.

The older men decided on Richmond, Missouri, a town about fifteen miles from Jesse's home. They also decided to do the job in the big way that had been so successful at Liberty. A little over two months after the Savannah fiasco, fourteen men rode down Richmond's main street, shooting right and left and giving the blood-chilling rebel yell. It worked; it scared the living daylights out of the people. The robbers dashed into the bank with the grain sack, and when they came out they were $4000 to the good.

But everything did not proceed entirely right, for at this point the citizens went into action and began taking potshots at the mounted bandits. The outlaws answered and killed three men, there on the streets in Richmond. Then they rode away as fast as they could. A posse was formed and went clattering after them, but as usual accomplished nothing.

The robbery must have made Jesse think some more. Three men killed on the streets. The country outraged. More and more suspicion directed at the James Boys. But still nothing had been proved. No officer had come with a warrant. And there was their family position. It was so good and the family was so respected in the neighborhood that no one made any foolish moves.

In the meantime, another side of Jesse's life was becoming important. He had been corresponding with Zee Mimms; now came exceedingly good news. She was coming to Clay Seminary in Liberty, only about a dozen miles from the James farm. Clay Seminary was the fashionable school of the section and drew students from all over Missouri and the Southwest. Girls were not admitted to William Jewell, but it was nice to have 'em in town, the boys said.

Jesse was still shy in the presence of girls, even with his cousin. But he would get to see her, that was the point. Zee was blonde, had blue eyes like himself, and was taller than the average girl—but that was all right; his mother was tall, too.

He wrote and made arrangements to call on her. When he got to town, he saw the boys walking on one side of the streets and the girls on the other, for they were not allowed to mingle. He had had to stop school when he was fifteen, but he felt vastly superior to the boys he saw sauntering around. He had ridden under Quantrill, he had been wounded, and he had helped rob at least two banks. And he was a far better rider than any of the dudes parading the streets.

But Zee had disturbing news. She told him that the Seminary had rules and regulations, and that the only place she could see him was in the 'social parlor' of the school. He didn't know what a social parlor was but he knew it sounded ominous.

When he got to the parlor that evening he came upon a dreadful scene. Instead of being alone with Zee, as he had expected, he was ushered into a stiff and formal room where there were two other couples—girls from Clay Seminary and 'young gentlemen' from William Jewell. And that was not all. Over them—a kind of grim general—was a woman he had never even heard of before: the college chaperone. He was not one of the students. He looked suspicious; certainly he didn't have the polished manners of the college boys. When she introduced him around he mumbled and stammered and made an unfavorable impression. Zee tried to help him, but she was new to the school and not any too much at ease herself.

Jesse, gazing at the polished shoes of the college boys, became conscious of his farm boots and shifted them awkwardly. When he had seen the boys on the street he had looked down on them, but now he was in a new world; they knew this world and he didn't. He pulled at his fingers, trying desperately to think of something to say.

There was a long pause during which he sat tonguetied, staring at the grim-lipped woman. Each moment he became more selfconscious. He must speak.

"I hope you are enjoying good health, ma'am," he said solemnly.

"I am, thank you," replied the humorless creature.

A little snicker rippled through the sophisticated college students. He knew he had said the wrong thing; he would cover it up.

"I hoped you'd be able to report that." He swallowed painfully. "There aint any satisfaction like being able to enjoy good health in your old age."

A guffaw burst out.

"I didn't mean you especially," he said hastily, becoming more and more embarrassed. "I meant people in general."

Painful as this was it was finally over. The students began to chat about the world he knew nothing of—debates, studies, teachers, classroom jokes.

He became more conscious than ever of his exclusion. He must speak. Again he addressed the chaperone:

"It's good weather we're having now. If it holds out it'll be all we can ask."

Then, for something to do, he drew his watch out of his pocket and looked at it. All eyes fastened on him.

"I—I just thought I'd see what time it was," he mumbled and shoved the watch back into his pocket.

The dreadful evening wore on. If he could only escape! But he would have to think of some good reason.

He stood up. "I'm worried about my horse," he said, trying to assume a look of concern. "I rode hard today and he showed it 'long toward the end. If you'll excuse me, I'll go and see him and call it an evening."

Getting up, he hastened out as if the poor animal might die any moment.

The heartbreaking evening was over. He stayed with a boy friend, and the next morning rode back to the James farm.

The first formal call on Zee had been a failure, but he continued to see her from time to time. While she had doubtless heard some of the rumors about the James Boys, she probably didn't believe them; they were her cousins and Aunt Zerel was an exceedingly fine woman. And she had helped nurse Jesse back to health. He had his health now—and he had good looks, too, with his blue eyes and jaunty turned-up nose.

IV

THE DUAL NATURE OF JESSE JAMES

THERE is a story told about Jesse James by General Jo Shelby, the famous Confederate leader. Jesse was going to Lafayette County to buy horses for his stepfather; on the way he stopped at Jo Shelby's, but Shelby was away. Jesse said he would like to feed his horse and rest awhile, himself. Mrs. Shelby was pleased to have him there and made him feel at home.

She had a colored houseboy named Joe Miller. She sent him to a small town named Aullville, and while he was in town he got into a fight with a white boy of his own age, which was about fifteen. The white boy was named Catron. As the two fought, a crowd collected, most of them taking sides with the white boy.

Joe Miller started home.

The white boy then ran to his own home, got a gun, mounted a horse, and started to follow the colored boy. He began to gain, and as he came closer Joe ran and got behind the gatepost at the Shelby home. Catron fired his shotgun, but none of the shot struck the colored boy. Before he could reload, Joe rushed at him, pulled him from the horse, and began to belabor him. Just then Joe looked up and saw a mob coming down the road from town. Knowing what would happen to him, he rushed in and implored Mrs. Shelby to protect him.

Jesse James said, "I'd be pleased to take care of that for you, ma'am."

He made a quick survey. The mob, to get to the house, would have to cross the Davis Creek bridge nearby. So he hurried out and got to the bridge first. There he drew his two pistols, and when the mob came up he said, "This is as far as you go. Turn around and go back."

The mob debated, studying the man with the cold-blue eyes, with the two pistols in his hand. Finally they thought better of it, and went back down the road in the direction whence they had come.

This story illustrates the dual quality of Jesse James's nature. He was as quick to defend life as to take it; something had intervened here that was stronger than his natural feelings as a Southerner under the Reconstruction. But on another occasion he was to shoot a defenceless man without consideration and without qualm.

As he approached his twentieth birthday, the time when the course of his life would begin to take a permanent direction one way or another, the two natures in Jesse were struggling against each other. He had been taught honesty by his mother and stepfather; no more honest a person ever lived than his mother, and his stepfather was scrupulously upright. He had ridden and shared life with some of the lowest, thievingest, most blasphemous rascals and cutthroats in the War Between the States. But he did not swear, he did not thieve, he had not (so far as is known) had any adventures with women, he did not even smoke. The name 'Dingus' still clung to him, with all that it connoted of gentlemanly manners under stress. On top of all this was his interest in religion, inherited from his father and furthered by his mother.

Jesse had a deep and abiding affection for his mother. In July, 1864, Jesse and two other guerrillas were near Fayette, in Howard County, Missouri, when they heard that a Union soldier named Allen Bysfield had come home on a furlough. A Union soldier! They surrounded the house, then demanded the door be opened. It was, but the young Union soldier had got word and had escaped.

The men surmised that he must have rowed across the river; going down to the Missouri, they succeeded in finding a rowboat and managed to get across into Cooper County. There was an old shanty near the landing; they went to it—and there was the Union boy.

They decided to shoot him, then and there.

The boy began to beg for his life, but they paid hardly any attention; then he said he had come back to see his mother. Jesse knew this but now, with the boy saying it, it made an impression. Jesse looked at the piteously begging boy with renewed interest, then began to ask questions. Finally he turned to the others and said: "He's come back to see his old mother. Any man ought to be willing to go through hell to see his mother, and that's what this boy has done. Let him live. He deserves it."

There was a short conference between the three. What Jesse said carried weight and in a few minutes the three walked out, leaving the young Union soldier, who could hardly believe his good fortune. The three men rowed back across the river and disappeared.

Frank was never the complicated character Jesse was. When he was asked to go on an 'expedition,' he went and that was all there was to it. He would never have dreamed of getting up in church and praying out loud for Jesse. If Jesse wanted to go to

Heaven, he would have to do it on his own. No help from brother.

The days of moods and meditations continued for Jesse. God wanted him. Perhaps; but so did his bold friends. He was an expert shot, he was a fine horseman, and he was fearless. He was an addition to any band. And, young as he was, he was beginning to show qualities of leadership. It seemed easier to make a living robbing a bank now and then than it did farming. There is a good deal of evidence—too detailed to go into here—to indicate that Jesse was violently pulled between the requirements of a religious life and the demands of banditry. He became moody; his mother complained that he would no longer 'talk' to her. She had lost his confidence. Once she told her husband, "I don't understand him any more."

Not far away was another powerful influence. The Youngers. Big, portly Cole Younger also had a great interest in religion (sometimes the others called him 'Bishop'), but he didn't allow it to confuse the issue; the issue with Cole was banditry. He had been in the Richmond raid, although he always said he hadn't been. But then, he was the most sanctimonious liar in three counties.

Cole Younger had ridden with Quantrill in Kentucky and thought he knew all about it. He began to talk up Kentucky as a land overflowing with gold and banknotes, and finally convinced the others this was true. In his whole bandit career Cole never did anything above and beyond the intelligence of a sheep dog. Sometimes, it would seem, the dog had it on him a little.

He said that Russellville, Kentucky, was just waiting to be plucked, so he was sent down to scout it. He used the method that had, almost unconsciously, been adopted by the gang. He went to the window and said, "Can you change this $100 note for me?"

The cashier looked Cole over and smelled something.

"I'm a cattle buyer from Louisville," said Cole.

He looked about as much like a cattle buyer as he did like a musk-ox.

"No," said the cashier, "I'm afraid I can't."

The cattle buyer returned his $100 note to his pocket and left.

A week later, on March 20, 1868, Cole led the gang back; among the six was Jesse James.

By a streak of good luck, the gang galloped out of town with $14,000 in the faithful grain sack, and without killing a single man. They didn't even give the inevitable posse a chance not to get too close to them.

But the Russellville bankers were not satisfied with half-hearted pursuit and a hue and cry that quickly died down. They wired to Louisville and engaged a detective to get on the trail—D. T. Bligh. He began to work with an assistant, William Gallagher, and they soon discovered that Jesse James was suspected but that nothing had been done about it. Bligh and his man decided to do something. And now, for the first time, Jesse had detectives to deal with.

Jesse was accustomed to outdistancing posses. He didn't know about the kind that came in the silence of the night and listened at keyholes. But some way or other he found out that they were on his trail, and he realized that he had to do something and do it fast. He had plenty of money, so he did a surprising thing. He went to New York, saw the sights, got on a boat and went to Panama. He crossed the Isthmus, got on a steamship, landed in San Francisco, then, his trail well confused, he headed for Paso Robles, California, the place where he had intended to go all the time.

Paso Robles was thirty miles north of San Luis Obispo, and the reason Jesse went there was his uncle, Drury Woodson James, the one whom he was named after. 'Mr. D. W.,' as he was called, had been one of the founders of the present incorporated city of Paso Robles, at that time called El Paso de Robles. In 1860, with John D. Thompson, he had bought 10,000 acres of government land on La Panza Rancho and stocked it with 2500 head of cattle. D. W. realized the value of the mineral springs. He and Thompson built a wooden hotel and cottages, and the place soon became famous for its hot sulphur springs and mud baths. On September 15, 1866, D. W. James had married, and now, to visit his uncle and pay his respects to his new aunt, came Jesse James.

Jesse was driven twice a week to take the baths, and soon looked less like a hunted man. He then began to ride the range with the cowboys; sometimes he would be gone with them for days. The men noticed that he had a couple of peculiar traits, but at the time they did not think what might be behind them. When the men rode in a group, Jesse always rode on the outside. At night, when the men rolled up in their blankets, Jesse always went off and slept by himself.

One of the cowboys was a boy younger than Jesse, named Charles Morehouse. Jesse took a fancy to him. The young boy had an inferior lariat, made out of horsehair interwoven with grass fiber. The best lariats were made of rawhide. Jesse had one of these.

One day Jesse said to the boy, "Is that your best lariat?"

"Yes."

"Here's mine. You keep it. I won't need it any more."

The next day he disappeared.

Some time during 1868 Jesse and Frank were back on the James farm. They thought things had blown over. There is indication that they wanted to settle down, for they began to farm again. Jesse began once more to attend church regularly, singing in the choir, and was 'converted' and baptized in the Kearney Baptist Church. (By a strange irony the church was located on the spot which later became a graveyard, the place where Jesse lies buried today.) His mother, according to local legend, is reported to have said, "This is the happiest day of my life."

The year that followed must have been a happy one for Jesse as well. He was twenty-one, a husky young man an inch under six feet, friendly and more approachable than his brother Frank. He had the solace of religion, and he was still courting his cousin. In addition, the times were settling down. The bitterness of the Border Warfare days was partially subsiding. Now and then the rebel yell was heard, but for the most part Clay County was more peaceful than it had been in fifteen years.

However, a new phase in local feelings had come along: the dislike of *both* banks and railroads. The banks squeezed the farmer till he bled. When a train killed a farmer's cow, he had to wait years to be paid. Sometimes sparks from the engine set farmers' haystacks on fire. The farmer would write a handful of letters, and not even get a reply. The feelings the railroads aroused were soon to be reflected in the career of Jesse James, a career which—despite the calm and promise of a change for the better—was soon to be resumed.

Just a little over a year after Jesse had returned from California seemingly finished with 'road work' and persuaded to life on the farm, he mounted his horse and, together with Frank and Cole Younger, rode off toward Gallatin, Missouri, about forty miles from the James farm. They appeared in the town on December 7, 1869. Cole and Jesse went in, leaving Frank outside to hold the horses. Cole used his old dodge—could the cashier change a $100 bill? The cashier said he could and started to count out the change. As he was doing so, Cole drew his pistol and said, "Don't make a move or I kill you."

Out came the grain sack and Jesse began to toss in all the money he could see, which, goodness knows, wasn't much—$700.

Two or three persons had started to enter the bank, but Frank warned them off. Suddenly the people realized what was happening and scurried away after their guns. Frank yelled to Cole and Jesse to hurry.

A characteristic of Jesse's was his loyalty to friends. Now, as he was filling the sack, his attention was suddenly caught. Where had he seen that cashier before? Stepping over to Cole, he talked in a low undertone, both of them looking intently at the cashier. And then suddenly Jesse shot him. The cashier fell dead in as cold and cruel a murder as Jesse ever committed.

By this time Frank was popping away right and left. The other two rushed out, but in attempting to mount Jesse was thrown. He was in a pickle. He had no horse and the citizens were beginning to come up with their hardware. The tricky situation was solved by Frank, who pulled Jesse up behind him and out of town they galloped, Jesse clinging to the sack.

Luck was with them. In fact, luck was with Jesse all his life, until the last. The two met a man on a horse. In no time at all Jesse had a horse and an honest farmer had none.

As they approached the next town they met another man and made him pilot them safely around it. Something was on Jesse's mind; finally he said: "We were just up to the Gallatin bank. I killed a man there. I think it was S. P. Cox. He killed Bill Anderson and I always said I'd get that man if I could."

The Anderson he referred to was Bloody Bill. But Jesse hadn't killed S. P. Cox; he had killed Captain John W. Sheets, a local man.

A posse rode out to no avail. But something else happened. The riderless horse was caught and was identified as belonging to Jesse James. The local talk about the 'tough James Boys' boiled up again with a vengeance, and became more than just talk, for the Gallatin men went to Captain Thomason, the sheriff of Clay County, gave their proof, and asked the sheriff to 'bring 'em in.'

The sheriff knew Jesse's and Frank's courage and their ability to take care of themselves, and didn't hanker after the job. But he had to do it. So he swore in three deputies and rode over to get the Boys. They turned in from the main highway and advanced toward the house. Frank and Jesse saw them coming, but instead of trying to get out the back side of the farm, they rode out to meet them. This was more than the deputies were counting on.

"You boys've got to go to town with us," called Captain Thomason.

"We don't want to go to town with you," said Jesse with complete logic.

The four deputies glanced at one another, then one said, "You boys think it over."

"We've thought it over," said the Boys.

"I'll count ten," announced the sheriff.

"You can count all you want to, but it won't do you any good. We don't figger to change our minds."

Frank glanced at his brother. Jesse's pistol flashed out, and, taking careful aim, he shot the horse the sheriff was on. The animal reeled to the ground, Thomason managing to keep from being entangled with it.

Whirling, Frank and Jesse dashed away. The deputies fired a few shots, hitting nothing but the wind.

The humiliating part came when the sheriff had to go to the house and get Mrs. James's permission to borrow a horse. She gave him her permission and something he hadn't asked for—a piece of her mind. She was very liberal with this; it steamed a little around the edges.

The deputies started back to Liberty, pretty well ashamed of themselves. They had gone out to bring in the James Boys. All they were bringing in was one of their horses. And *he* would have to go back.

There is a footnote to this story which illustrates Jesse's sense of fair play. He was honest except when he went out to rob (there was no paradox in that to him). Captain Thomason's term as sheriff of Clay County expired, and his son Oscar was elected. In 1872, after Oscar too had served out his term, he started to Texas with a friend to buy cattle. They traveled by covered wagon, with a fringe of horses to take care of the cattle on the way back.

As they were jogging along in northern Texas, they saw two men on horseback coming toward them. After they had passed, Oscar Thomason exclaimed, "Why, that's Jesse and Frank James!"

They looked back and saw that the two men seemed to be puzzled and quite a bit disturbed, for they had halted and were conferring. One of the men got off his horse and went behind a tree with his rifle at ready; the other rode slowly back displaying a white handkerchief. When he came up he called, "Are you looking for us?"

The man who called was Jesse James.

"No, we're not," Oscar shouted in return. "I'm not sheriff now. We're on our way through Texas to buy cattle."

"Oh!" exclaimed Jesse, relieved.

He came closer and waved Frank out from behind the tree; all four caucused a while.

Then Oscar Thomason invited them to have dinner. A fire was started beside the road and a meal cooked, the men still talking in a friendly way. At the end of the meal, Jesse said, "I've had it on my conscience about shooting that horse from under your pa that day, Oscar. How much did he value that animal at?"

"Well, I would say he was worth fifty dollars."

"I would say about the same thing," replied Jesse. "I'd like to square that off here and now." Pulling out his purse he counted fifty dollars.

The men continued to visit, then Jesse and Frank rode off in one direction, and Oscar and his friend in the other. Jesse had squared his conscience.

There was so much feeling from the Gallatin raid and the murder of Sheets that the Boys had to clear out—this for the second time. And although they didn't know it, D. T. Bligh and his man were still on the trail.

It is not established where they went; the early writers said they went to Kentucky to their mother's folks and that would seem to be as good a guess as any.

The deacons, who had welcomed him in less than a year before, called a hasty meeting and read Jesse out of the church. They didn't want that kind of member, even if he could sing in the choir.

And now Jesse was twenty-two years and four months old. He had seen a great deal of life. He was to see more.

V

THE BOYS IN IOWA, KANSAS, AND KENTUCKY

JESSE was now definitely 'on the dodge,' as his mother phrased it. He returned to the James farm; all his life he was returning, and all his life he was having to scurry away. There was no reward on his head, but he was wanted. And yet, so strange a person was he, he was getting quite a bit of fun out of living. He was courting Zee Mimms, he was living better than the average young man of his day. He wore good clothes and kept himself neat and clean. He never looked like a suspicious character. He did like to play pool, but did not drink or gamble—that is, outside of a friendly poker game.

But always he had to be on the alert; never a moment could he relax. This was so ingrained and so deep in him that it became second nature. His very existence depended on it.

On a hot, lazy afternoon one August, Jesse and a friend were riding along near the Little Blue River, not so far from Kansas City. They came to a lovely stretch of water, with trees extending invitingly over it. Jesse looked at his friend and his friend looked at him. It was more than human nature could stand. Getting down, they tied their horses and soon Jesse and his friend were having a wonderful time.

Suddenly they saw a man ride up and begin to dismount. The rude intruder carried a shotgun. Marching in between the two nature-lovers and their clothes, he leveled his gun at them and bellowed, "Throw up your hands!"

The nature-lovers threw up their hands.

"Now," said the intruder, "you two come out. I know who you are."

Jesse and his friend looked around desperately. A few minutes before, the place had seemed so lovely and enticing. But now the dancing shadows were cold and chilly.

Their clothing and revolvers were on the bank behind the gentleman with the shotgun. Jesse advanced toward him with his hands where the man had commanded him to put them. Jesse's companion walked slowly behind, still in the water. Suddenly he gave a shriek and dived into the water. Startled by the noise, the man holding the gun turned to see what was wrong.

Instantly Jesse grabbed the weapon and the two rolled on the bank and in the weeds in the biggest wrestling match that had been seen on the Little Blue River since the Indians had discovered that lovely body of water. Jesse's friend came plopping and they soon had the man crying uncle.

But to their astonishment he wasn't looking for them at all; he was a county constable searching for horsethieves!

Jesse blinked. Well, that was different.

"Look here," he said sternly, when he'd got his senses together, "you about scared the life out of us, so we're going to teach you a lesson before you do that to other innocent people."

And so saying the indignant Jesse dipped the man's gun in the water, took the ammunition, and rode away with his friend, injured expressions on their faces.

This was the first time Jesse was ever 'captured' and it lasted only a few moments. It is also the last time there is any record of Jesse ever going in for a dip, however inviting the water or languid the afternoon.

How did Jesse live during this period? This historian has no easy answer—nor had the sheriff and detectives. But the main outlines are known. The Boys never rode together in a large band—alone, or by two's and three's. They rarely hid in the woods, unless hard-pressed. They never carried blankets or bedrolls, or anything else that might slow them up when they wanted to be quickly on their way. Anyhow, they were nearly always under shelter. Sometimes they would be registered at country hotels just like any normal cattle buyers, and paying their bills. Sometimes it would be in a church or a schoolhouse (never in farmers' barns, for the latter breed have a habit of getting abroad early, and also have been known to talk). But the great protection was friends and relatives. Clay and Ray Counties were full of family, and all over Missouri and Kentucky were the ex-guerrillas with whom Jesse had ridden. Many of them were farmboys like himself, and he was in their midst. They didn't like the banks the James Boys and the Youngers were doing business with. If Jesse wanted to visit any of his old friends for a while, why he was welcome.

I had heard that James Womack, a farmer living near Fulton, Missouri, had an 'interesting Jesse James story,' so I wrote him and this is the story.

The Womack family is a well-known family living in the most famous county in Missouri—Calloway County, sometimes called 'the Kingdom of Calloway.' It claims to be the last county to surrender after the War Between the States. A great many Confederate soldiers came from there, and quite a sprinkling of guerrillas.

James Womack was a boy when the incident occurred, but writes that he remembers it clearly. One day a mounted man rode up and said a neighbor had recommended this as a place that would be willing to take in a stranger. James Womack's father said he would be pleased.

The man announced his name as John Franklin. He was given a room, and was considered 'good company.' About a mile from the house was the Unity Baptist Church. One day the stranger said, "How would you like to have a singing school?"

The children and the neighbors were delighted, and one was organized. It developed that the stranger had a good voice and that he especially liked to sing hymns. The singing school ran for two months in the summer.

The neighbors became exceedingly curious about their strange singing teacher, and sometimes, at night, crept up and peeked through the window. But the stranger's ears were extremely sensitive to suspicious sounds. One night he suddenly got up, stepped quickly out of the house, and shot.

In a moment he came back, smiling. "A rabbit was stomping around outside," he said.

No more rabbits were heard.

At the end of his stay he revealed who he was. "I am really Jesse James from Clay County," he said.

Then he rode away; the family missed him very much.

"And so," writes James Womack, "I suppose I am one of the few people living who can say he had Jesse James as a singing-school teacher."

Now the story moves along to June 3, 1871, and to the town of Corydon, Iowa, about two jumps above the Missouri-Iowa line. The place was agog with excitement—not because seven strangers had ridden in on horseback, but because an outdoor political meeting was being held on the edge of the town. The subject up for debate was the location of a schoolhouse, and neighbor was ready to shoot neighbor, as so often happens in a small town.

The reason Jesse had fixed on Corydon was that he knew the taxes had just been collected and the banks were bursting. Going in to one establishment, he hauled out the usual $100 bill and required some change. But the teller explained that the bank's treasurer was at the meeting, and only he had the combination to the safe; so no change. But the teller aimed to be accommodating. He informed the stranger that a new bank had opened just that day, across the town square, and that in view of the fact that it had one-half of its capital on deposit, it might quite likely be able to take care of the $100 bill.

Jesse went out and consulted with his men. Never was there a harder decision. Then over to the new bank he walked, and laid down the bill. The cashier went to the safe to get the money; when he returned he was gazing down into the machinery of a six-shooter. He was promptly taken into the back room and tied up. Jesse and his much-encouraged gang started to fill the sack, but as they were going about their business in walked a Negro preacher to make a deposit. The men received his contribution gratefully, and invited him to join the cashier.

Shortly the inspection was over. The gang mounted their horses and started down the streets of Corydon in a state of pleasurable accomplishment. Soon they reached the spot where the meeting was being held. They rode up as close to the speaker's platform as they could, and then one of them—it was Jesse, of course—called out, "Excuse me for interrupting, but may I ask a question?"

The speaker gazed at him sourly. "Well, what is it?" he asked, none too pleasantly.

"Did you know there's something wrong at the bank?"

The speaker thought Jesse had said there was something wrong with banking, and for a moment the two had to shout back and forth.

"I mean in your new bank," said Jesse, and rode away.

It had seemed a curious interruption, and nothing was thought of it right away. Then somebody from the audience figured it might be a good idea to look anyhow. It turned out to be an exceedingly good idea, for, threshing around in the back room, they found the cashier and the minister.

Interest in the speaking immediately fell off. The farmers unhitched their work mares, straddled them, and went clipping down the road after riders who had the finest and fastest horseflesh in the State of Missouri. The usual happened. They came drooping back after a while, without even having caught sight of the callers from out of state. The next time they had a political speaking in the town, 'tis said a great many of the men sat facing the bank.

A good day's work. Seven men had taken in $40,000.

Robert A. Pinkerton himself took charge of running down the Boys. He followed them to Cameron Junction, Missouri, where he gave up the pursuit, saying he found that the men had so many friends who were ready to protect and 'falsify' for them that it was useless to trail the gang any farther.

Jesse and Frank were questioned, but proved by neighbors and friends that they had been at home during the robbery, hard at work as all honest citizens should be. In the course of their career the Boys were many times kept from arrest by this kind of testimony; sometimes it arose out of fear, but mostly it arose from friendship or from a sharing of the Boys' attitude toward banks and railroads. (The incident when Jesse and Frank stayed overnight and Jesse practiced pistol-shooting with young John Carmichael is supposed to have taken place after the Corydon affair, for the Carmichael farm lay on their path back to Clay County.)

The Boys disappeared again. Jesse was now twenty-three years and six months old.

The strange combination of God and deviltry forever persisted. As an example of how much his religion meant to Jesse, I take a story given in *The Chronicles of Oklahoma* by William J. B. Lloyd, who was a preacher among the Choctaw Indians near Old Bennington, Indian Territory. Mr. Lloyd was also the first postmaster of Bennington when the post office was established, August 7, 1873. But at the time the incident happened he served only as a minister. The event took place, according to him, either late in 1872 or early in 1873.

At this time an Indian named Wilson N. Jones was the 'principal chief' of the Choctaw Nation. The government was paying money to the Choctaws; Wilson N. Jones was the one who took care of it for them. At that time in the Indian Territory there were very few banks, and, as a result, handling money was a problem.

One day Mrs. Lloyd rode over to the house where Chief Jones lived and talked to him about a preaching service for her husband. When she was ready to leave, the chief said: "I have just received a shipment of gold and I am nervous about it, there are so many outlaws around. I want you to take it home and keep it until I call for it. No one will ever expect a preacher to have money."

"How much is it?" asked Mrs. Lloyd.

"Ten thousand dollars in gold."

Mrs. Lloyd was rather flabbergasted by such a large sum,

but Chief Jones urged her to take it, and at last she reluctantly did. After discussing the matter with her husband, they decided the best place to put the bag was at the foot of the spare feather-bed. This was done. Now and then company arrived; then the bag would be taken out and hidden elsewhere.

Suddenly one day, when she was alone, Mrs. Lloyd was alarmed by the arrival of five hardlooking men. Without beating around the bush they asked that their dinner be cooked. Pressed by them, she finally agreed to cook a chicken dinner. One said, "Show us your fowls."

She led them to the chicken yard and pointed out two fowls. A shooting contest developed between two of the men as to which would be the first to shoot off a chicken's head. The arrival of strangers had made the chickens nervous, and now they began to run excitedly about the yard. The men began firing away, each trying to win.

The Lloyds had a son John who was just a small boy. Amidst the shooting and confusion he ran to his mother and said, "Mother, what are we going to do about the bag of gold?"

Jesse James, who was standing near, watching the sport, immediately plucked up his ears. "What bag of gold?" he demanded.

"It was just childish talk," said Mrs. Lloyd, trying to appear innocent.

Jesse came nearer and said in a hard voice, "I want to know about that bag of gold."

Fearing for her life, Mrs. Lloyd admitted she had some gold her husband was keeping for the Indians. Immediately the others came up and began to listen. Then the men withdrew a little distance, where an earnest discussion went on amongst them.

Finally Jesse walked back and said, "We are not going to disturb your gold because your husband is a preacher and we don't want to rob a preacher."

There was no further reference to the matter. The men ate their chicken dinner, paid for it, mounted their horses, and rode away.

There are many examples of this same attitude. In 1874 the Reverend George Bayer was living in a small town in the foothills of the Ozarks. One day, as he was preparing his sermon, he heard a horse coming along the highway. He saw it was a stranger; then he saw the man dismount and tie his horse to the pole hitchrack. But this was not unusual, for people unknown to him often stopped in for advice, or sometimes to have funerals preached.

Instead of knocking, the stranger strode abruptly in and asked, "Are you that German preacher?"

"I am the Lutheran minister," said Mr. Bayer.

The man began to ask him about the members of his church. Finally he said, "Do any of them keep money in their homes?"

The preacher said they were mostly immigrants and had little or no money.

The man listened carefully, asked a few questions, then walked over and unceremoniously pulled out the drawer of the writing desk. In it was a cigarbox and in this some coins.

"Is this all the money you've got?" he asked.

"Yes."

"How much salary do you get?"

"Two hundred dollars a year."

"I need money, but I guess I don't need it badly enough to take it from a poor preacher. Maybe you would like to know who I am? Well, I'm Jesse James and not as bad as some people think."

Going outside, he discharged his pistol. In a few minutes two other men came up on horseback. Jesse sat on his horse, evidently explaining something to them, for they kept looking at the house. Then all three rode away.

Forty thousand dollars is a great deal of money, even when divided among seven, but money slips away, and Jesse's general principle was to live comfortably when he had it until what he had was about gone; then he would start to stew around how to get more. Frank, on the other hand, was more provident. It didn't slip through his fingers as it did Jesse's. Frank wasn't the harum-scarum Jesse was; nor was he as much fun.

So now things move along to April 29, 1872, a little less than a year after the public-speaking in Corydon. The place is Columbia, Kentucky. Five men canter down the street; three enter the bank. But the affair doesn't go well. When they come out the cashier is dead and all there is in the grain sack is $1500.

The posse comes back and tells how it almost got them, once.

This robbery did have one serious effect. It made the detectives redouble their efforts. But as yet no arrests were made.

More and more the James Boys were being talked about; their fame was spreading. Yet neither had been arrested and the only one who had ever been inside a jail was Frank and that was during guerrilla days. Was Jesse to go to jail?

Jesse was soon desperate for money again. And at this juncture, most providentially, Kansas City held a fair. Why, this was just at his back door! Suddenly, on the afternoon of September 26, 1872 (six months after the Columbia call), three masked men swooped down on one of the gates of the fairground and seized the cashbox.

The money was in bills, quite a bit in silver. Arrangements had been made with the First National Bank for the bank to stay open after hours and the money taken to it; the bandits had a different idea. The box was dropped into the faithful sack and the three rode happily away. The amount taken has never been definitely established, but it is believed to have been about $8000.

But this time no posse. The matter was turned over to the police, which promptly ended it.

And now Frank and Jesse had to make themselves scarce, a matter in which they were perfectionists. They proved by friends, neighbors, and ex-guerrillas that they had been far away when those low characters had taken the tin box at the fairground.

Ste. Genevieve is a Mississippi River town in 'Swampeast' Missouri. It had been settled by the French; many of them had recently come and still spoke with an accent. The town was known as 'quaint.'

On May 26, 1873, five strangers rode into town. Three of them went into the bank to transact some business. The cashier looked up, pleased to see so many new customers, smiled, and said, "*Bonjour, Messieurs.* What is it we can do for you today?"

"You can hand over your money—and damned quick," said one of the *messieurs*, who had no claim at all to culture.

"But that will not do!" said the cashier.

"Damn you—the money!" exclaimed the rude man.

This social interchange ended at once, and at least half-pleasantly, for when the men came out there was $3600 in the grain sack, and not a disturbing shot had been fired.

The men mounted their horses and galloped happily out of town. But all of a sudden a horse stumbled and fell. Its rider was the one carrying the heavy sack. He clung to it faithfully, though he was a bit shaken up. When he went to remount, he placed the bag on the horse in front of the saddle and started to hoist himself up. The horse, already frightened and now made more nervous by the sack, suddenly gave a leap, freed itself, and bounded riderless away—with the grain sack.

The men said things that have no place here. There were the fruits of all their hard work rapidly bobbing down the road; and there, firmly planted on the ground, was one of their own men, wholly and completely horseless. It was a trying moment.

Just then, by mere chance, a Frenchman came riding up. One of the men pointed desperately at the runaway and said, "Catch that horse! Go after him! We've got to have him!" He meant every word of it.

"*Oui, Messieurs*. But how much is it you choose to pay?"

At that the men stared hard indeed. "You get that horse, damn you!" said one of them, recovering his wits and drawing a gun.

"*Vraiment!*" replied the Frenchman, and galloped off hard after the gaily trotting animal. By a piece of good luck he secured it and brought it back to the men waiting in the road.

"*Voilà!*" said the Frenchman, beaming with tremendous satisfaction at his good deed. "And now, *Messieurs*, how much is it you wish to pay?"

"You get to hell out of here," replied the *étranger* with the gun.

"*Mais non!*" cried the Frenchman indignantly. "*Jamais!*"

It ended suddenly. One of the men slapped the horse and the Frenchman went bounding down the road, shrieking things that, fortunately, the men didn't understand.

A posse was organized, but it didn't do any better in French than the others had in English.

VI

THE JAMES BOYS LOOK TO THE RAILROAD

JESSE JAMES was now so heavily involved in banditry that there was no turning back. Every robbery added new perils and pulled him in deeper. He and Frank were notorious. 'The James Boys!' The words were on everyone's tongue. It was growing more difficult for him to get back to the farm to see his mother. Nevertheless, Jesse and Frank—especially Jesse—began to enjoy the reputation that was coming to them. (All his life, Jesse liked to talk about it.) And they considered new ways of enlarging it.

Jesse was becoming more and more the leader. He was the most daring, he would take chances the others wouldn't. And with leadership came problems to solve. It wasn't all easy pickings. For one thing, there was the matter of organizing his men. This was a problem not because it was difficult to get men, but because most of them were no good. He was discovering that it was extremely difficult to get a group of men who could take all the punishment that was necessary and not be at each other's throats. Rain and storm and snow—they had to meet all these. Men who could be depended on in a pinch were a problem. And loyalty too; that was extremely important. In the early part of his career Jesse was very trusting.

But toward the end he trusted hardly anyone. He had learned by bitter experience.

Jesse's gang was not static at all; it was constantly changing. From the time he started until he was no more, he had a total of twenty-eight men in his band. One of them he had to kill.

About this time, something began to make an impression on the now-accepted leader of the James-Younger enterprise: this was the increasing number of train robberies.

Hasty historians have said that the 'James-Youngers,' as they came to be called, committed the first train robbery, but this hardly bears inspection. The first train robbery in the United States occurred the same year as the first bank robbery, which *was* the handiwork of the James-Youngers. The first train robbery was at Seymour, Indiana, and the date was October 6, 1866; the first bank robbery had been in February of that year. The train robbers were the Reno brothers and they did right well by themselves, getting $13,000. (Strangely enough, the second train robbery happened in the very same town, a little less than a year later, the exact date being September 28, 1867; the performers were not the Reno brothers but two men living in that section. The take was $7000. The catch was that both were hanged.)

The Reno brothers did have this in common with the James brothers: they were farmboys and they had been in the Civil War, the Renos in the Union Army. But their careers did not remain parallel very long, for soon John Reno, the leader, was making binder-twine in the penitentiary and his three brothers were dead from rope strangulation. Not properly and sedately hanged by a sheriff but lynched by ill-natured mobs. Their career had lasted only two years. It just goes to show the difference between Missourians and Indianians. The latter never did get the knack.

In all, there had been about twenty train robberies in the United States before the James Boys cocked an eye at it. And when they did, the fate of the Renos didn't worry them even a little bit. One robber never seems to think that because another robber has had his fires slaked that he himself will perish, too. No, he tells himself. He is smarter. He won't make the mistakes the other did. So he hoists up his pants and wades in. Pretty soon his pants are full of lead and his mother weighted down with grief.

By some means the James-Youngers discovered that gold was being shipped out of the West and was coming through Omaha on the Chicago, Rock Island & Pacific Railway; so they decided to inspect this gold. It was less than two months after the Ste. Genevieve robbery. Two of the men—believed to have been Cole Younger and Frank James—were sent to Omaha to take a short course in gold operations. Jesse, in the meantime, led his stalwarts north into Iowa. They came to the quiet little town of Adair, which had never had anything more exciting than a hair-pulling, and went outside of town a short distance to inspect a railroad track which they thought might be in bad condition.

Breaking into a handcar shed they took a spike-bar and hammer, pried off the fishplate, and pulled out the spikes. Then they tied a rope to the rail in such a manner that the rail could be pulled out of alignment. When everything was set, they hid behind the embankment on a curve where the train always slowed down.

The train came along, the rope was pulled. The men had thought the train would merely stop; instead, the engine balanced for an agonizing moment, then toppled over on its side, instantly killing the engineer. Men, women, and children were tossed about in a dreadful scene. But with the tragedy there was also comic relief.

In the day coaches were thirty Chinese who were being brought to this country to be educated. Their passage money had been put up by a church organization which wanted to take them out of heathen China and show them how Christians lived. Some of the Chinese could talk a little English; all wore their queues and long black skirts.

Suddenly the Chinese were thrown violently about in the day coach. They screamed at the top of their voices, not realizing this was part of the American educational system. Then they came tumbling out of the coach. But by this time the bandits had taken command, and to frighten the Chinese they began to fire in the air. It worked perfectly. The Chinese went screaming back into the coach. As if this wasn't enough, one of the bandits, who had entered one end of the coach, now began to pop his pistol. The Chinese screamed louder than ever, not realizing they were receiving an advanced course.

Meantime other things were happening. The gang entered the express car and forced the guard to open the safe, but all they found was $3000. Frank James and Cole Younger hadn't done such a good job after all, for they had made a mistake; the next night—just twenty-four hours later—$75,000 went over that very spot. It was enough to embitter them in their new work.

The troubles of the Chinese were only beginning. Angry because of the small amount of money in the express car, the bandits started down the aisles of the cars with the familiar grain sack, ordering the passengers to toss in their money and valuables. In a few minutes they reached the coach where the Chinese were, and commanded them to throw in. The Chinese didn't understand this part of the curriculum, either, and only stared at the grain bag. One of the bandits made signs of emptying his pockets, but the Chinese didn't have pockets—only sleeves—and so they merely continued to stare at the collection bag and the strange antics of the Americans. In disgust the bandits left, saying things the Chinese had not learned in the church schools. Getting on their horses, they rode away into the night.

Since it was obvious that it would be hours before the train could be righted, it was decided to walk the passengers to the nearest town, which was Anita, Iowa. After a great deal of shouting and badgering, the passengers were started down the track, following the brakeman with a lantern. As the weird procession got underway, one of the Chinese was heard to say (or so it is reported), "Amelica one hellee countree."

An emergency telegraph set had been rigged up and cut in on the regular line. Word was dispatched for a wrecking train; and word was spread of the robbery.

Meantime the robbers were on their way back to Missouri. The train crew tried to arouse the farmers and get them to pursue the bandits. The farmers said they hadn't lost any money and that the railroad men could chase them themselves, being as the farmers bore no particular love for the iron horsemen. The railroad then dispatched word to all agents along the way to organize posses. This was backed up by special trains leaving Council Bluffs with men armed to the teeth; they stopped along the way and picked up rented horses that the local agents had arranged for. Then the railroad men went bouncing and jolting along in what they thought was hot pursuit of the robbers.

The State of Iowa leaped to action and offered the princely reward of $600. The railroad got busy and offered $5000.

After a time the pursuers came dragging back, and it developed that not one had seen a bandit. Some of the farmers mumbled behind their hands that the railroad men hadn't wanted to. As for the James Boys and their companions, they were back in Missouri. Not a single arrest was ever made.

While it is not true that the James-Younger gang were the first American train robbers, they were the first to wreck a train to further a robbery. The date was July 21, 1873. Jesse was twenty-five and eight months.

The outlaws didn't know it, but they had now begun to deal with an entirely different group. The banks had done great quantities of nothing; the railroads really meant business. They had been aroused by the previous robberies; now an engineer had been killed. So they not only put up reward money but they also engaged the Pinkerton Detective Agency to kill or capture. And the agency meant to do exactly that.

But the Boys were pretty experienced, and they had had marvelously good luck. Not one of the band had been killed in action. True, three of them had been hanged afterward by fire-snorting citizens, but none had died while engaged in the raids. The Boys were feeling their oats; they must have felt them pretty well, for it was not long before they participated in two robberies inside of two weeks. One was at Hot Springs, Arkansas; the other at Gad's Hill, Missouri. Both went well. The former was a stagecoach robbery, a comedown for men who had been doing bank and train work. The date was January 15, 1874. The grain sack took in about $800, which probably soured the Boys on stagecoaches. The real money was in banks or trains. The Gad's Hill robbery occurred on the last day of that month—January 31, 1874. Better luck this time—$12,000; and no one killed, no one caught.

Posses, of course. For appearances.

THE JAMES BOYS LOOK TO THE RAILROAD

Now with Jesse James, at the age of twenty-six, becoming a national synonym for banditry, it seems wise to point out the difference between an outlaw and a 'bad man.' They were two vastly different creatures. Jesse James was never a bad man in the sense that the term is usually used.

At this time the western outlaw was just coming in—the men who, later, made Dodge City, Abilene, and other cow-towns famous, the men who 'operated' in Tombstone, Arizona, and in Texas and New Mexico. These men were killers; they swaggered up and down the streets, rolled into saloons, shot the lights out, and created unpleasant scenes at card tables. They killed to impress others and to achieve fame in the saddle set. They were not robbers, in the sense of holding up banks, trains, or stagecoaches; sometimes they grabbed the money on a faro table and departed into the night without any clear indication of where they were going.

Jesse James was not this kind at all. He never shot a light out in his life, never took a drink at a bar as he watched in the mirror some other man with a view of disposing of him, never rode down a street shooting right and left for the fun of it. He was in the business of train and bank robbery. And he made a success of it as no other man in America has ever done.

VII

JESSE IS MARRIED

IT IS astonishing that Jesse could keep on courting his cousin with sheriffs and detectives hot upon his trail. One thing that helped him was that she was in Liberty part of the time; and the rest of the time she was in Kansas City, not too far away. Her mother had died and she had gone to live with her sister, Mrs. Charles McBride, in Kansas City.

Jesse was twenty-six and a half; he had courted her nine years. She knew he was being sought, knew he was part of the 'James gang' which was attracting so much attention.

One day she came to the James farm and there Jesse arrived to see her. All day they were together and the early evening, too. But about nine o'clock Jesse became suspicious, and, creeping out, found five Pinkerton detectives stealthily approaching. He and Zee had only a moment to slip away. She went to a corner of the yard and hid there; near the house were some flower bushes and into these he crawled. From them he could peep into the house.

The detectives unceremoniously threw open the door and entered, demanding of Mrs. Samuels where her son was. She told them she did not know; they searched the house, and finally, convinced by her earnest manner, departed. Jesse said later that he could have killed at least two of the men, but there would have been crossfire and Zee might have been wounded.

Zee's mother had tried to dissuade her from the marriage, and so had her uncle, the Reverend William James. But they got nowhere, for Zee loved Jesse, and had ever since the time she helped nurse him back to health. Against all opposition, the day was set.

At this time marriage licenses were not necessary. The preacher could take care of everything. (If somebody had told Jesse that he would have to have his blood sampled in order to get married, he'd have shot him on the spot.) The local tradition is that he wanted to be married in the Baptist church in Kearney, but the church had read him out, and he still resented it. At this juncture another sister stuck up for Zee. If Zee loved Jesse and was willing to pay the price, then she should get married. This sister was Mrs. W. Boling Browder, who lived on a farm near Kearney; so it was decided to have the wedding there. The day fixed was April 24, 1874. Uncle William was fetched from Kansas City.

Jesse rode in out of nowhere, and the moment Uncle William saw him he began to upbraid him for his deeds of violence, and to say that Jesse could not properly take care of a bride and that she should not marry anybody on whose head was a reward of $10,000.

Zee defended Jesse loyally, saying that many of the deeds that Jesse was accused of were not true. To support this, Jesse took from his pocket newspaper clippings attributing desperate deeds to the James gang on the same days in different states. Finally, after urgent solicitation, Uncle William agreed to perform the ceremony, and in the presence of Zee's sister and her husband, at about nine o'clock at night, the two were finally married. I like to think of that scene—Jesse, with the two pistols he always wore, and beside him Zee Mimms, looking up at him so trustingly.

They could stay only two hours, so closely was he watched; then they rode off together into the night. It is not known where they spent their honeymoon. Was it at his mother's? Or was it at her sister's in Kansas City? Or was it at some roadside inn? Anyway, before long they turned up in Sherman, Texas, at the home of Jesse's sister, Susie James Parmer.

Meantime other things were happening.

They had been after the James-Youngers since the Columbia, Kentucky, robbery. When the railroads got involved, the word went out that the gang must be exterminated. The word was mainly carried by the Pinkertons.

Pinkerton's National Detective Agency was an organization dreaded by all lawbreakers. It had been founded in Chicago by a Scotsman, Allan Pinkerton. During the Civil War it had been a spy system for the Union armies. It had uncovered a plot to assassinate President-elect Abraham Lincoln. It had broken up many gangs of counterfeiters and express-company robbers. It seems to have been feared by all lawbreakers except the James Boys, who even taunted the Pinkertons because they could not find them. Headquarters of the agency was in Chicago, but, to be close to the Boys, a branch was opened in Kansas City, thirty miles from the James farm.

The first detective-bandit blood was drawn near Osceola, Missouri. Captain J. W. Allen and another Pinkerton man had reason to believe that part of the gang was hiding near there. Engaging a former local sheriff, Edwin B. Daniels, to show them the roads, the detectives rode here and there, posing not very successfully as cattle buyers. But on one of the roads they met two members of the Younger family. The Youngers began to question them about their cattle-buying. The city detectives knew as much about cooking whale blubber as they did about cattle-buying, so in no time at all Allen was dead. Also the ex-sheriff who had so foolishly undertaken to 'show them around.' The other detective put spurs to his horse and ran away. One of the Youngers fired, and, even with this bouncing target, put a bullet through his hat. The hat fell off. The detective let it stay where it fell, as he had other hats at home.

But John Younger had been killed. That was the first blood. The score: two detective-sheriffs; one Younger. The date: March 16, 1874.

Neither of the Jameses was there. The members of the gang split up immediately after a 'ride,' and didn't get together again until they had business to attend to. But the Jameses did know that they were being pressed and that, more and more, detectives were becoming a problem. The easy days of riding and reaping were over.

Now came the next move in the game. A rough-looking man who gave his name as Jack Ladd got a job as hired hand directly across the road from the James farm. The house still stands, much now as it was then. It is almost opposite the gate that leads up to the James home. You can stand on its porch and see the James home. The name of the farmer who owned it then was Daniel Askew.

Ladd worked in the fields where he could see the Jameses. Sometimes he went over to the well and pumped himself up a drink of water. He even went to the Baptist church.

Ladd was a Pinkerton detective, reporting to the Kansas

City office. But so well did he manage things that he was not suspected. There is evidence that he even went to Jesse James's wedding. But apparently it was felt that not enough results were coming out of his peeping and spying, so the Pinkertons sent another man to hurry things along.

This man pursued a plan that was incredibly stupid. He seems to have thought of the Jameses as one cut above mentally retarded jackasses. He didn't know the boys were far from stupid and were protected by the finest armor in the world—friends.

At any rate, brisk, businesslike John W. Witcher arrived in Liberty to take care of the Boys in short order. Going to the bank, he made a deposit of Pinkerton money, then asked to see the president. "I've come here to capture the James Boys," he announced smugly.

"Well," said the bank president, "you'd better think twice. They're surrounded by friends and they're dead shots. In addition, they're as smart as you can find them."

The Chicago detective smiled.

Then he went across the square to an ex-sheriff and asked him to cooperate.

The ex-sheriff advised care, but the Chicago go-getter said, "Oh, I've worked out plans! Don't worry. I'll soon have your boys where they belong."

Then Mr. Witcher went to a hotel, rented a room, and stayed overnight. The next morning he bought some new farm clothes, went back to his hotel, and put them on. Then he asked the hotel man to check his bundle of clothes.

There was an afternoon train to Kearney, and, with a pistol in his pocket, the confident detective got on that train. When the train reached Kearney, he descended and started to march down the road to the James farm, a distance of about three miles.

Suddenly a man stepped out of the elderberry bushes.

"Hello," said Jesse.

"Hello," Witcher returned confidently.

Jesse surveyed him carefully. "You seem to be a stranger in the neighborhood."

"Yes, I am," said the man genially. "In fact I've just got here."

"Have you? said Jesse, with companionable interest. "Then maybe I can help you. I've lived here for some time."

"Maybe you can. I'm looking for work."

"What kind of work?"

"Farm work. I work as a hired man and I want somebody to employ me."

Just then two other men stepped out of the alders.

"He's a hired man looking for work," explained Jesse significantly.

"Where's your grip?" asked one of them.

"I haven't got one," said Witcher, a bit awkwardly. "I was going to wait till I got settled down."

"Search him," said one of the men. A revolver was discovered.

"Where have you been working?" the men asked.

"At Beatrice, Nebraska."

"Who for?"

The detective gave a name.

"Did you work there long?"

"About five months."

"Let's see your hands."

The detective extended them. They were as soft as a baby's.

That was the end of the hired man with the soft hands. He was shot and killed.

But not there. In order to divert suspicion the detective was taken across the Missouri River at the Blue Mills ferry late at night, and the deed done in another county. The body was left by the side of the road. When the coroner rolled up the right shirt sleeve he found the initials 'J.W.W.' tattooed on the forearm.

It has always been believed locally that Witcher had the audacity to be going to the James farm to apply for work. He got about halfway.

In spite of the gathering clouds the James-Youngers engaged that year in two more robberies. The first came on May 12, 1874, at San Antonio, Texas. This was a comedown, for it was a stagecoach. But the returns were good—$3000. It just showed that humble means must not be overlooked. A posse was organized to chase the robbers slowly.

This time Jesse James had a watertight alibi. He said he was in Kansas City at his brother-in-law's. And he probably was, for he had been married only eighteen days and no man in his right mind would want to give up a honeymoon to rob a stagecoach.

December 13, 1874, at Muncie, Kansas; that was the second. About $2000 was taken. The farmers got up a posse, and that was as far as they got.

All in all, 1874 was a tremendously active year for Jesse James. A thumbnail summary:

January 15—Hot Springs, Arkansas.
January 31—Gad's Hill, Missouri.
March 10—Detective Witcher killed.

March 16—Two Pinkertons killed near Osceola, Missouri.
April 24—Jesse marries.
May 12—San Antonio stagecoach robbery.
December 13—Train robbery at Muncie.

Of course Jesse did not participate in all of these affairs, but they all affected him. It can safely be stated that he alone participated in the honeymoon.

VIII

THE BOMB EXPLOSION

THERE is no record of what Detective Jack Ladd thought when Detective Witcher was killed, but it must not have been very pleasant, for he was doing the same thing that Witcher had set out to do. But he was playing his part far better; not telling the neighbors his plans, not checking his city clothes with a hotel keeper. He was just a dumb farmhand.

Every day he looked across the road to the James farm and talked to members of the family. The household was rather large; in addition to the mother and stepfather there were Fanny, John, and Archie Samuels, Charlotte, an old colored woman, and Ambrose, a small Negro boy. And Frank and Jesse . . . when they were there.

One day in January, 1875, Jack Ladd got word that the boys were coming back to see their mother. On their heads was a reward of $10,000 in an offer that practically amounted to 'dead or alive,' although it wasn't phrased that way. Big news. Just what he had been waiting for.

He got the word to the Kansas City office. (It would be interesting but it has not been possible to find out how he communicated with his headquarters.) Plans had been made, and now they began to go forward. Nine Pinkerton men got on the train in Kansas City and rode to Kearney, on their way to the farm which knew nothing of these grim preparations. They rode past Kearney to the point nearest the farm, a distance of about three miles. Since the agency was working with the railroads, the conductor stopped the train at the place requested. Then the nine men started walking in the silence of the night toward the log cabin. Jack Ladd crept out of the Askew farmhouse and joined them; now they were ten.

Timber came down to the house (later it was cleared and became a cornfield; it's now pasture).

The ten silent men arrived at the stable and one of them opened his bull's-eye lantern. Two of the horses showed signs of having been recently ridden. Just what Jack Ladd had reported! Except that it was wholly and completely wrong. Fanny and John Samuels had been to a party at one of the neighbor's; they had stayed late and, afraid of being scolded, had ridden fast.

Jesse and Frank were not at home.

The ten detectives approached the house.

Creeping up as silently as shadows on the peacefully sleeping household, they threw a black-powder bomb through the window. I have held half of the brass shell in my hands; it is about the size of half a football. The bomb had a fuse, but there was danger that the fuse might be extinguished, so the detectives had thoughtfully wrapped the bomb in gunnysacking saturated with kerosene. And there it lay, smoking and stinking. The family awoke in consternation.

In the room was a fireplace. Groping through the dim light, Mrs. Samuels got the fire shovel and began edging the devilish mass toward the fireplace. Too late. It went off with a terrible explosion, taking with it her hand.

The scene became vivid to me when I interviewed E. Price Hall, who saw part of it with his own eyes. At the time we talked together he was eighty-seven years old. Once, for six years, he had been a deputy sheriff. He had an oldfashioned silver watch, with a heavy chain, in his vest pocket. His vest was open and the chain and the watch held the two sides of the vest together. He was living in Liberty. We sat on the front porch in rocking-chairs and rocked and talked and watched the cars go by. Now and then a neighbor passed and called out, "Hello, Price!"

At the time of the explosion he was a boy; his father's farm and the James farm adjoined. The Halls were awakened by the commotion and screaming, and young Price hurried to the James house. The father did not go.

"When I arrived the stench was still in the house," said Mr. Hall. "Mrs. Samuels' hand was still clinging to her arm by a shred of skin. Dr. Samuels had heated water and was preparing to cut the pieces of skin. Little Archie Samuels was lying on a cot, groaning. A fragment from the bomb had been driven into his side, and his lifeblood was running out in spite of all his father could do. Dr. Samuels was trying to wait on both at once. Archie continued to groan and his voice got weaker. At dawn he died. When he was going out, his mother came and stood by his cot, sobbing—not for her arm but for her boy. It was the most dreadful scene I ever saw.

"Shortly after dawn I went out to explore the yard. There had been a light snow and there were the tracks of the men. I followed the tracks a short way and found where the men had sat down on a log. I found a pistol one of them had lost. On the handle was stamped the letters 'P.G.G.' This stood for 'Pinkerton's Government Guard.' Allan Pinkerton had organized the United States Secret Service and he had official government standing.

"We followed the tracks to the railroad and saw where the men had stood waiting for the train. They had enough authority to stop the train. Then they got on."

I asked E. Price Hall if he still had the pistol. He said he had kept it several years, then it had disappeared; he does not know what became of it.

The detectives did not go quite free. Ambrose, the Negro boy, seized the family shotgun, rushed out, and fired at the gray figures. There was a groan, then the sound of a body falling. The man was carried off by the others, but he died on the train as it was pulling into Brookfield, Missouri. The body was taken to Chicago for burial. The man turned out to be Jack Ladd, which made things as they should be.

There are two sides to any story. I insert here the point of view of the Pinkerton Agency regarding the alleged bombing. It was given to me in an interview with Ralph Dudley, general manager of the agency, at the New York offices:

> The facts, as we understand them, are based on the circumstances as reported by Allan Pinkerton and from utterances of Dr. Samuels and Frank James to relatives and neighbors. Our men, and other law enforcement officers, approached the James homestead. They found it was a citadel, with the windows shuttered and barred. They called to those inside to open up and be questioned, but those inside refused to do this. One of our men then pried open a window.

The interior was dark except for a fireplace which gave off insufficient illumination to locate and identify those concealing themselves therein.

Our men had with them a device for illuminating a darkened place. It was something akin in nature to the firepots which later came to be used on the highways. It was shaped roughly like a globe, with a long neck; in this neck was a wick. The device itself was of light metal but on the bottom were strips of iron; this was so that if the firepot rocked over on its side, the weight at the bottom would make it return to an upright position. The contents were probably kerosene and turpentine, although this is not exactly known. At the time, Allan Pinkerton referred to the illumination that the device gave off as 'Grecian fire.'

The device was tossed in to illuminate the interior. The family then displayed activity. Dr. Samuels took a firestick and began to push the device toward the fireplace, finally getting it in. The device—coming in contact with the hot embers—created gases. These expanded. The result was an explosion. One of the heavy straps struck Mrs. Samuels in the arm; another struck Archie Samuels in the head. Archie died from his wound and later the lower portion of Mrs. Samuels' arm was amputated in consequence of complications which set in.

If the fireplace had not been in use and if hot embers had not been in it, there would have been no explosion. These entire occurrences must be viewed in the light of the extremely vicious character of Jesse and Frank James, their established murderers' reac-

> tion to attempts to restrain them. The methods employed by this posse were necessary under the circumstances. The unfortunate and tragic results would have been avoided had Dr. Samuels and the mother of Jesse and Frank James responded to the call of the posse and revealed that these outlaws were not in the house.

The shock of what had happened to their mother, and the death of their half-brother, embittered Jesse and Frank James. They were now more definitely aligned against the law than ever. Especially detectives. They became merciless toward detectives. Their wives acted as listening posts for the Boys, and when communicating with them by letter would pass along all the information they could about the detectives.

Now came the problem of Daniel Askew. Did he know? Did he suspect? Those must have been tense days for him.

A little less than three months after the explosion, on April 12, 1875, he took a bucket from the shelf in the kitchen and went down to the spring to dip a pail of drinking water. He got the water and was carrying it back when there was a rustling behind the woodpile. Three shots rang out. When they picked him up, there were three bullet holes in his body.

There were no arrests.

Was he guilty? Did he know? My own opinion is that he did know. There has always been a local belief that the night of the explosion his voice in the yard had been recognized. Anyway, the now-desperate Boys were not taking any chances. Life was closing in. There had been easy, carefree days on Uncle D. W.'s ranch in California, but those were gone. Would they ever return? And the two wives, what did they think? How did they feel? What kind of life stretched ahead of them?

The country was immeasurably shocked by the Pinkerton attack and murder. Sympathy went to the James Boys, dangerous and bloody as they were. People in this Middle West section felt the Jameses were a product of the savagery of the Border Warfare, and were willing to overlook some of their acts. And although they didn't say it openly, there was that private and personal feeling about the uncontrolled banks and greedy railroads.

At this point the State of Missouri got up as weird a document as could be found in a day's ride on a dogsled. It was proposed, in the state legislature, that if the 'James Boys and their associates' would come in they would be pardoned by the governor of the State of Missouri for all acts that had occurred before and during the Civil War, and would be given a 'fair trial' for all 'incidents' that had taken place since. What it shook down to was, 'Come in, boys, and we'll treat you right.'

It came within a hair of passing.

Even if it had passed, the Boys would not have come in. The best they could have hoped for was life imprisonment, and I think they would have passed that up.

But no matter who was after them and with what means, the Boys had to live, and by now they knew only one way. Four men rode into Huntington, West Virginia, the first day of September, 1875, and rode out with $2000.

There was the old familiar thing of the posse. But this time one of the gang was killed—not by a member of the posse, but by two farmers who thought the men looked suspicious and ordered them to throw up their hands. The robber killed was Tom McDaniels, a recent recruit. The detectives, who had been doing such a sugar-and-water business for so long, finally accomplished something. They arrested a suspect known as Keene and sent him to prison in West Virginia for twelve years. The other bandits had been Frank James and Cole Younger. Neither got a scratch. Jesse—so far as is known—was not one of the riders.

Next the Boys looked around and decided that Otterville, Missouri, would be a good place to accomplish something they had in mind. Otterville was a small town near Sedalia. Trains passed that way. The date was fixed for July 7, 1876. And scheduled to be tied up inadvertently in the Otterville affair (according to the talk that arose later) was a young boy who was still alive when this book came to be written.

I was told that Asbury Good-Knight knew a great deal about the Otterville robbery—'If he will talk.' I found he was a farmer living three miles south of Sedalia, eighty-nine years old. But I interviewed him at the Missouri State Fair in Sedalia, not at the farm, where I had missed him. First he warned me about the spelling of his name.

Yes, he had known Jesse James. And that was about all he said, despite energetic probings. He did, however, add one detail about the Otterville robbery that had not been known. In the express car was a 'through' safe; this meant it was locked, with no key for it. The safe was only sheet-iron, but heavy enough to serve ordinary purposes. It gazed defiantly at the intruders. A fireman's coal-hammer was brought, and one after another the robbers banged away at the hinges. The safe bounced and shook but remained faithful to its trust.

Then Cole Younger, who was the biggest and heftiest among the visitors, took the fireman's hammer and gave the hinges—so said Mr. Good-Knight—hell. The safe bounced a little more, but surrendered not an inch. A sharp-pointed pick was found and Cole mounted a box to get the necessary elevation. A piece of chalk—used for marking a bulletin board—was discovered. On top of the safe Cole proceeded to draw a circle, then gave it everything he had. The safe withstood the onslaught a few moments, then gave up the ghost. Cole put his hand into the hole. Someone brought forth the trusty grain sack, and into it went the safe's treasures. Later they were found to total $14,000.

Jesse James and one of the other robbers went to the smoking car to call on the passengers. The other man walked ahead, holding the bag out enticingly. Jesse came behind, holding out his pistol, also enticingly. Into the grain sack went the contributions.

One of the passengers, when he saw the aisle-workers come into the car, got under his seat. But arrange himself as best he could, one foot still extended out into the passageway. Jesse, who was closely following his fellow worker, did not see the foot and stumbled over it. Immediately the owner sat up, quaking with fear.

"I didn't mean to trip you, sir," he quavered. "Honestly I didn't. Please don't shoot me. I beg a thousand pardons."

"Make it two thousand and I won't," said Jesse James, and then, still laughing, walked on down the aisle.

During the course of our talk, Mr. Good-Knight said, "There's one other Jesse James man in Sedalia. You ought to go to see him. He was Jesse James's last letter-carrier." And then he gave me his name.

Jesse James's last letter-carrier! I padded off as fast as I could go.

I found Jacob Dirck in his home at 407 North Summit Street, Sedalia. He was eighty-four. The letter-carrying had taken place when he was a boy living on the Warsaw Road, east of Browningtion, Missouri. He said that, when pressed, Jesse James hid his horses and men in the timber; no one could approach without being seen or heard, and there was always more than one way out of the timber. Jesse met him one day on the road and asked him if he would like to carry letters for him. He said he would pay well.

At this time Jesse was being hunted by the detectives and did not dare use the mails. Dirck agreed to help, for no one would suspect him. The boy would stroll along the road, give a whistle, then go into the thick timber. There Jesse would hand him a letter and tell him where to find the man addressed. Then Jesse would give him $2.50. Whenever Jesse was in that section he would call on the boy to carry letters and would ask him the news.

"I found him a fine man to deal with," said Jake Dirck reminiscently. "I never attached any wrong to it; lots of people had a secret sympathy for him and would have done the same if they had a chance, especially they would on account of the banks. Nobody liked banks. I mistrust banks to this day. . . .

"Did Asbury Good-Knight tell you about him and Jesse? He helped Jesse hold up a train! I guess that will make a good item for the book you say you're writing. One evening he was walking along the railroad cut, just a lad, when all of a sudden he saw some dark figures approaching him. They approached close and looked at him carefully. Then one of them said, 'Boy, you turn a hand here.' So saying they began to pile crossties on the track. When the job was done, one of them lit a lantern, handed it to Asbury, and said, 'You mount the ties and flag down the flyer.' Asbury mounted them—with considerable trepidation, I reckon—and waved the lantern. Of course it wasn't all due to him, for the rest of the gang had secretly boarded the train at a watertank down the line, and now climbed over the tender with their guns pointed at the engineer and fireman. . . . I always understood that Jesse gave Asbury some money for his help, even if it was against his will, but on that score I don't know of my own personal knowledge. I hold, in similar circumstances, anybody would have taken the money. I know I would."

The Otterville robbery wasn't a complete triumph for the outlaws, for, later, one of the members was arrested and sent to the penitentiary for four years. This feat was accomplished not by the Pinkertons, but by a member of the St. Louis Police Department; and the man tucked away in prison was Kerry Hobbs, who was not exactly the brains of the gang. His contribution had been to hold the horses. For the others, it was the same old story that runs with a comic hoofbeat through these pages: a hastily formed pursuit returning with imaginative tales but no outlaws.

E. Price Hall told me a story which reveals the cunning the Boys had when being pursued by a posse. Mr. Hall said that, as well and as long as he knew Frank and Jesse, Frank had never talked but once about his career. (Mr. Hall named his son in honor of Jesse James: Jesse James Hall.) This is the one story Frank James told.

Once Frank and Jesse were being pressed in western Kansas by a hard-riding posse. "What will we do?" Frank asked.

"Kill a wild hog," said Jesse.

There were many wild hogs in this section and presently they found one and shot it. Then Jesse took a rope and tied one end around the neck, and, getting back in the saddle, dragged the carcass over the wild grass, leaving a trail easy to follow.

He dragged it about half a mile, then left the animal lying

on the ground, the rope still attached, as if they had suddenly had to abandon it. But they had dragged it far enough to establish the direction they were going.

Then, instead of continuing in the same direction, they turned and rode off the opposite way. The ruse worked completely and ended the unpleasantness Frank and Jesse were having with the posse.

IX

JESSE AND THE WIDOW

ONE of the marked characteristics of Jesse James was his humor. He liked to play pranks; rarely did he go through a robbery without doing or saying something that had an element of humor in it. A good illustration of this is something that happened in the foothills of the Ozarks. One day the James-Youngers were taking a back road when noon came upon them. It was their custom to go to a farmhouse and get the wife to prepare a meal for them. And they always paid well. (I have not been able to find a single instance where they rode away without paying, or offering to pay.)

They came to a humble cabin, and one of the group went to the door to ask the question. A woman answered the halloo, a bit startled to see two other mounted men. She didn't know whether she could cook the meal or not, she said, as there wasn't much to eat in the cabin. But finally she was prevailed upon. She watched the men dismount and seat themselves in the yard to wait till the meal was ready.

As the men waited they were more and more impressed by the poverty of the cabin and by the hard struggle the woman had to live. Then they noticed that the woman was weeping, and asked her if she was frightened. She said she wasn't, but that seeing men in her cabin made her think of her husband. It developed that her husband was dead and that she was having to face her problems alone.

The men were appreciative of this and, glancing at each other, decided to be liberal with her. Sensing this friendly sympathy, the woman choked up; she tried to hide her emotions but she was so wrought up that she was unsuccessful.

Jesse said, "Won't you tell us what's the matter?"

The woman hesitated, but at last the trouble came out. The cabin and her little farm were mortgaged to a heartless skinflint who had been pressing her for the money. He had warned her that if she did not have the mortgage money ready when he arrived, he would take her property.

"He's coming today," she said, again beginning to weep.

At last dinner was ready and the men sat down. Jesse, for the most part, ate in silence, now and then glancing at the poor widow in her humble surroundings. Finally he said, "How much do you owe this man?"

"Eight hundred dollars."

Jesse ate a few moments.

"When did you say he was coming?"

"This afternoon, about four."

Jesse took a few more bites.

"What does he look like?"

She told him.

"How will he be traveling?"

"In a democrat wagon, drivin' one horse."

At the end of the meal Jesse pushed back in his chair. "What road does he usually take?"

The woman told him.

"It so happens," said Jesse, "I have that much money with me and I'm going to loan it to you."

The woman looked at him in amazement. Was he joking? He wasn't.

"You remind me of my mother," said Jesse, "and I want to do something for you."

The woman began to weep afresh. "I'll work my fingers to the bone, but I don't know when I can pay you back," she cried.

Jesse patted her shoulder. "Don't you worry about that. I'll stop by some time, then if you have it, you can pay me back."

The woman sobbed anew at her guest's splendid generosity.

"Now you want to do this in a businesslike way," said Jesse. "He sounds like a hard man to deal with, so you ought to protect yourself. This gentleman here"—indicating Frank James—"will write out a receipt. Then you copy it in ink in your own handwriting. Before you pay over the money, you make the man sign the receipt. That's the proper way to conduct business. He'd make you do the same. And don't tell him anyone has been here. Now, will you do as I say?"

"Yes, sir," cried the weeping widow. "I think you're wonderful."

"I wouldn't say that," Jesse answered modestly. "I like to help deserving people when I can."

"He's a very kind-hearted man," explained Frank.

Finally the men mounted their horses. In the door the widow stood, her face alight, and waved goodbye to them.

That afternoon the skinflint called on the woman, signed the receipt, and left. After he had driven about three miles away from her cabin, on his way home, an unfortunate incident occurred. Suddenly three mounted men popped out of the timber; one seized the horse's bridle and all leveled cruel-looking weapons at him. The man chanced to have $800 . . . but not for long. The horsemen appropriated it, then they whipped up his horse and sent it spinning down the road, leaving the mortgage-holder alone and on foot with the problem of catching his horse as best he could.

Then the three men rode away. No one knew where they went.

X

THE NORTHFIELD BANK ROBBERY

JESSE continued to face the problem of getting good men—good for the kind of work he expected of them. No more Kerry Hobbses. So great had become the fame of the James-Younger gang that men wanted the honor of riding with it. He could get them in plenty, but when the pinch came they might, and often did, fail him. Just natural lack of temperament for the work . . . yes, but he could never forget, also, that hard and heavy on his head lay a $10,000 reward, a prodigious sum in a day when a dollar was a dollar. All one of his followers had to do was to shoot him, then claim he had been working for the law all along.

The way Jesse got his men was simple. One of the gang would announce that a certain man wanted to 'talk' to Jesse, Frank, or Cole. A meeting would then be arranged. Many of the volunteers were neighbors, or their families could be identified, or they came from some adjoining county. Three counties furnished most of the men: Clay, Ray, and Jackson. Two of the gang, later, came from Kentucky; but they were Jesse's cousins. Kerry Hobbs was an outsider, and his work showed it.

But if Jesse's increasing fame brought him troubles, nevertheless he reveled in it. When he met new people, he would discreetly ask about the James Boys. Sometimes he would say, "What would you do if you met one of them?" He was especially amused if a person told how he would shoot them down like mad dogs. Now and then he would actually divulge that he was Jesse James; but it was always when he was leaving, or when he felt it would not endanger his organization.

Things had been going well; his confidence was growing. He had become the best-known outlaw in America, yet he had never felt a posse's bullet or spent an hour in jail. And, bit by bit, he and Frank had organized the best robber band ever gathered together in America. Every man had been fire-tested. There were eight of them; besides the James brothers, they included Clell Miller, Charlie Pitts, Bill Chadwell, and the three remaining Youngers—Cole, Bob, and Jim. Never in American outlaw history has this band been equaled for daring; yes, and for ability. There was not a Kerry Hobbs among them.

Moving into his second decade of banditry, Jesse James found that he had to range farther and farther afield. The banks and trains in his section were growing more and more alert. The old days when one of the gang could go in and ask to have a $100 bill changed, and then bring out a pistol, were vanishing. Horses and strange men on the street now attracted attention, especially when they appeared to be cattle buyers. (One reason the James-Youngers assumed this role during their excursions was that cattle buyers wore long, loose-flowing linen dusters to keep the dust off when driving herds to market. These male Mother Hubbards were exceedingly well adapted for keeping the gaze of the curious from any personal hip-jewelry a man might chance to be wearing—and the James-Youngers did not always carry just one holster of two guns, but sometimes far exceeded this. They stuffed them in their pockets; once Jesse had six pistols on him at one time. In addition, he wore belts containing extra rounds of ammunition and carried cartridges loose in his pockets.)

Now Jesse and Frank and Cole Younger began to look about them for a new place to open up. They had operated in Missouri, Kentucky, West Virginia, Iowa, Kansas, Arkansas, and Texas. Now where?

Bill Chadwell, a recent recruit, came forth with an idea. Although born in Missouri, he had lived in Minnesota, and he said that the banks in that state had more money than they knew what to do with. The men answered that if they could get their hands on it, they would know what to do with it.

But Jesse counseled against the idea. It was northern country, they had no friends there, no old ex-guerrillas they could bed-down with, no letter carriers, no knowledge of streams and back roads, no friendly blacksmiths to shoe their horses in a hurry. But Bill painted such a land of milk and honey—with not a single bee—that the others persuaded Jesse to fall in with the idea. And he did, hesitatingly.

Chadwell said that Mankato, Minnesota, was a hive of vast opportunities, so the eight rode north in that direction on the finest horseflesh obtainable. But not together. They never rode together. Usually it was in pairs; sometimes, however, three of them would jog along in a group, gazing at the dull farmers plodding away in their fields and feeling sorry for them. There was no money in following a plow; the rewards went to saddle work. The hours were shorter. A person never knew where he was going to sleep that night, and meals were irregular—but then, nothing in this world is perfect. They figured they still had the best of it.

The men were feeling fine; the air was surcharged with success. An example of how confident they were took place in my Nodaway County, in the town of Graham. Jesse and Frank arrived one evening about sunset and went to the hotel run by Mr. Freytag. The latter's son, Frank Freytag, was later postmaster of St. Joseph, and it was he who passed the story along. Jesse (as it turned out to be) told young Frank that he had been riding hard and wanted his horse watered and rubbed down. The boy led the animal to Brown's Springs, a short distance from the hotel, and took care of it. When Frank came back, Jesse was so pleased that he gave him a silver dollar, an immense sum of money. Mr. Freytag asked the men to sign the hotel register. They looked at each other, then Frank James with great good humor said, "We're queer. We never sign a hotel register until we're ready to leave."

The next morning the two had breakfast and were ready to go to their horses when Mr. Freytag reminded them of the register.

"Oh yes," said Frank James, "where is it?" And he signed, with a great flourish, 'Frank and Jesse James, Kearney, Clay County, Mo.' Then, mounting their horses, the two rode gaily away. They felt safe; no one was going to chase them; they were bold, confident, assured.

The eight converged upon Minnesota.

Cole Younger and Charlie Pitts, who had been teamed together, rode into the town of Madelia, Minnesota, and registered at the Flanders House. Cole Younger signed his name as 'J. C. King,' a play on 'King Cole.' Charlie Pitts signed himself 'Jack Ladd,' a joke in Charlie's estimation, for he did not know that Jack Ladd had been killed the night of the bomb explosion.

The proprietor, Thomas L. Vought, welcomed the cattle

buyers with fine Minnesota hospitality. Mr. King wanted to know about the roads he would later be driving his cattle over, and especially he wanted to know if any of the roads were closed, for he did not want to get his cattle in a cul-de-sac. Mr. Vought told him, as a proprietor should.

The next day J. C. King and Jack Ladd rode away on their quest for cattle. They had on their linen dusters to keep off cattle grime.

The gang finally got together in St. Paul, Minnesota, where they engaged rooms at the Merchants Hotel and at the European Hotel, and then went out to see a baseball game between the St. Paul *Red Caps* and the Winona *Clippers*. It was the last of August, 1876—the year of the famous Philadelphia Centennial.

The men pretty well knew the country now—the principal roads, the marshes, and the timbered spots. They were all in good humor. They would have another Otterville. (Its success was still upon them, for it was only two months away.) Off they jogged for Mankato.

They went to the bank that Bill Chadwell had proclaimed as overflowing with milk and honey, and the first bee appeared. When they got there a number of people were standing near the bank, gaping. The outlaws thought word had got out that something was afoot, so they withdrew. They came back the second time; the gapers were still there. The gang rode away, defeated. If they had only known that the crowd on the street was merely watching the construction work on a building next door, after the immemorial way of busy men . . .

But they didn't and so rode away. None of the cattle buyers knew how this would change history.

Now they had to find a new place to fulfill their ambitions. They rode through Janesville, Cordova, and Millersburg, as uncertain as a drove of bees that had lost its queen.

Some days before, two of them had scouted Northfield, Minnesota, a one-bank, two-college town. It wasn't 'choice' but it would do. (The two colleges were Carleton and St. Olaf; and there they are today. But *three* banks now. Another thing worth noting is that the town today is the 'Holstein Center of America.' However, on September 7, 1876, it was no place for cows or college students.)

The outlaws met in the woods five miles west of Northfield. They decided to join up, so five of them rode into town and calmly had lunch in two of the restaurants. After lunch they strolled about, then rode back and joined the three waiting in the woods.

Things now began to happen. The gang approached the town, breaking up so as not to arouse suspicion. A river runs through the middle of Northfield, by name of Cannon. Across it was a wooden bridge. Three mounted men rode slowly and casually across this bridge and tied their horses to a hitchrack near the First National Bank. The three were Jesse James, Charlie Pitts, and Bob Younger. Drygoods boxes lay in front of a store, and on these the men lazily sat down, pretending they had nothing better to do than stare at the passersby. If the passersby had known that the men had enough artillery to subdue the Sac and Fox, they would have jumped out of their skins.

In a few moments two other tourists rode up the street, gazing at the interesting sights. They were Cole Younger and Clell Miller, sightseers from Missouri.

Just at this moment Cole Younger's saddlegirth went wrong,

at least he pretended it did; getting off, he essayed to fix it, pulling and hauling at the stubborn article, meantime strategically managing to keep in the middle of the street where he could see both ways. The three loafers on the drygoods boxes got up and sauntered into the bank. Clell Miller went to the door and shut it, walking rather rapidly.

And now the first thing went wrong. While Clell Miller was still standing by the door, a local man came up to go into the bank. He was J. S. Allen, a hardware merchant. The last thing in the world that Clell Miller wanted was for some local person to go into the bank during rush hour, so he grabbed Allen by the shoulder and yelled, "Keep away from that door!"

Then something happened that Clell wasn't expecting. Allen jerked away and started to run down the street, shouting at the top of his voice, "Robbers! Robbers! Get your guns!"

Until now there had been only five men, but at this moment three new horsemen appeared: Frank James, Bill Chadwell, and Jim Younger. Seeing how the situation was developing, they began to ride up and down, shooting and yelling like Indians. Clell Miller had gotten back on his horse, and he and Cole Younger joined in too.

The innocent bystander had to suffer, as so often happens. Nicholas Gustavson was a Swede who had just arrived in this country and knew little English. "Get inside!" one of the men yelled; Gustavson shook his head to show he didn't understand, and started on down the street. It was a fatal decision, for he was shot and killed.

Another unexpected element entered. A young medical student at the University of Michigan was home for a vacation. His father had a drugstore and the young student was sitting idly in front of it, thinking of nothing in particular. But all of a sudden he discovered he had a great deal to think of. He knew that in the Hotel Dampier he could find a gun, and in a moment he was on the second floor of the hotel, a carbine in his hands.

But this was not all the unfortunate luck that was befalling the visitors. At exactly the wrong time another hardware merchant came along, Northfield, it seems, being supplied to the hilt with hardware stores. This hardware merchant rushed back to his own store and got a breechloading rifle.

And now one medical student and two hardware merchants were out to do all the damage they could.

Nor was this all. Three of the good citizens began to throw rocks. They might as well have thrown corncobs. Not a single robber was hit; one horse had his hip skinned.

But what was going on inside the bank? As soon as the acting bookkeeper saw that the three men who entered were robbers, he got down on his knees and began to pray for deliverance. The cashier himself was at the Centennial Exposition in Philadelphia, the most fortunate trip he ever took. His substitute stepped forward.

"Are you the cashier?" one of the robbers asked.

"No."

Which was strictly true.

The robber then pointed his gun at the bookkeeper and said, "Are you the cashier?"

"No."

The same question was asked of the assistant bookkeeper, who gave the same answer.

The robbers seemed beaten. But not quite. One of them turned back to the first man they had addressed, Joseph Lee Heywood, and said, "I know you are the cashier. Open that safe."

"The lock is set and it can't be opened now."

This was only half-true, for the safe was actually unlocked; the door happened to be closed and the bolts were in place, but the combination dial had not been turned. The door could have been pulled open.

The safe itself was in a vault which was large enough for a person to enter. And this Charlie Pitts tried to do. Heywood, thinking he saw an opportunity, dashed forward and tried to slam the door, hoping to entrap the robber. The other two bandits grabbed the cashier and pulled him back, again insisting that he open the safe. Once more he refused, which was a foolish thing to do. "Robbers! Robbers!" he shouted, very foolish.

One of the men struck out with his revolver, knocking the brave but shallow-thinking cashier to the floor. Charlie Pitts fired, not to kill him but to frighten him. The bullet entered the vault and went through a tin box containing papers and jewelry left there by a customer for safekeeping.

The third man in the bank, A. E. Bunker, tried to dash out; he went through the directors' room to the rear door of the bank and through that, too, taking the blinds with him. Charlie Pitts followed his flight with two pistol balls, one of them going through his collarbone but not killing him.

The three robbers in the bank knew that things were growing desperate, for they could hear the shooting outside. Worse than that, they heard one of their gang shout, "Come on out, boys. They're killing our men."

And at this crucial moment occurred the cruelest and most foul deed ever perpetrated by Jesse James. The brave and foolish cashier was on the floor, trying to get up, blood running down his face from the pistol-butt blow. Then and there the frustrated Jesse shot him dead.

A great deal was happening on the street. Bullets were still flying through the air, rocks too. And two of the outlaws lay dead: Bill Chadwell and Clell Miller. In addition, Bob Younger had been shot in the elbow, the bullet shattering the bone. But he was cool; in fact, they all were, except Jesse, who had shot in anger. Bob Younger transferred his pistol to his left hand and continued to fire. He had no horse to ride, his own had been killed. "Get on behind me," yelled Cole, and that is what Bob did, the enraged citizens popping away at them all the while.

Jesse came out and mounted what later was called the 'dun horse,' and, with the others, rode away in a loose, free-riding, weaving-in-and-out band. Cole and Bob Younger soon trailed, for Cole was heavy and the two constituted a burden for the horse.

Four were dead: the poor Swede who did not understand English, the courageous cashier who had acted so unwisely, and, on the streets, two of the bandits.

Their haul: nothing.

But the trouble had only begun.

In a few minutes the church bells were ringing and the whistles blowing. The robbers must be taken.

XI

THE INCREDIBLE RIDE OF THE BANDITS

THE outlaws set out on the kind of flight they knew so well. But now it was a bit different; six men were on five horses, and one of the men wounded. Not good.

The initial pursuit amounted to nothing. Two Northfield men caught the horses of the dead bandits and mounted them. The horses, eager to join their companions, flew down the street. Then the Northfield men thought it over; maybe the idea wasn't so good after all, two chasing six of the most desperate men in America. They decided to go back and get reinforcements.

Word was telegraphed to St. Paul and Minneapolis; soon the whole state was aroused. The towns began to organize posses; every hour the scope of the manhunt widened.

The first thing, for the bandits, was to get Bob Younger off Cole's horse. They met a farmer jogging down the road with a team; before he knew what was happening, he had a one-horse team.

They rode on till they came to a farmhouse. They explained to the farmer that they were officers of the law chasing horse-thieves, and could they borrow a saddle for one of their men who had joined so hastily he hadn't had time to get a saddle?

The farmer said he hated horsethieves and would be pleased to lend a saddle. The officers galloped away hot on the trail, the farmer smiling with satisfaction at the helpful contribution he had made.

But Bob Younger's farm horse was all feet, and fell, pitching Bob over its head and painfully jolting his arm. The fall broke the saddlegirth, and, to make matters worse, the horse galloped away, leaving Bob exactly where he was when he started. Up again behind Cole.

Soon they came to another farmhouse where they used the horsethieves story successfully again and got a new mount. But this animal balked; with all his spurring, Bob could not move him. Up again behind Cole.

Now, grown desperate, they went to a stable and grabbed a horse and saddle without any noble talk about horsethieves.

As the afternoon wore away, the county became alive with posses; every farmer who had a squirrel rifle was out, plopping along on a plowhorse looking for six men he was going to plug.

One of the first towns to leap to action was Faribault. It had been warned by wire, and a posse of ten started out, determined to have the robbers. They became hungry and went into a small family hotel at Shieldsville, leaving their rifles and muskets outside. While they were eating away, the outlaws rode up to the same place. They dismounted and started to water their horses, then suddenly began to stare exceedingly hard at the array of artillery leaning against the porch railing. They looked in the windows at the diners, who were keeping as silent as mounted butterflies. There would be no point in trying to shoot an entire posse, so the bandits leaped back on their horses and dashed off as fast as they could.

The possemen came out, looking pretty sheepish, reclaimed their weapons, and galloped after the bandits. It was becoming evident the six men were exceedingly skilled at the job of flight and meant to sell their lives dearly.

But reinforcements were steadily coming. Squads were everywhere, mistaking each other for outlaws and having to halloo it out. This was not all: the chiefs of police in St. Paul and Minneapolis sent men. Sheriffs everywhere—realizing it must be the James-Younger gang, with money on them, dead or alive—joined in. The Pinkerton detectives—who, in all the years they had hunted them, had never seen the Boys—also joined in, curious, no doubt, to find out what they looked like.

The Jameses always, in time of stress, traveled in the direction of home. They did not know this country, they had no friends—the very difficulties Jesse had originally suggested were being realized. But they kept going in the general direction of Missouri, and soon this fact became evident to the pursuers.

Always too, when he had outdistanced a posse, Jesse went into the timber to rest his horses and his men. There was, in this section, a swampy place in the 'Big Woods.' The men had planned on this and now made for it. And so did the searchers, who were increasing hourly. Many arrived by train and set out on foot, ready to take a potshot at anything that moved. Farmers drove along back roads with rifles beside them on the seats of their buggies. By nightfall two hundred armed men were on the trail of the six. The news had been flashed that the James gang had committed another robbery and was now being pursued; the whole country followed it breathlessly. Surely, this time, they would be taken.

As if things were not bad enough for the outlaws, it began to rain. Bob Younger's arm was paining him more and more. Truly the situation was desperate.

Fresh horses! They must have them. They found a farmer

and traded with him, leaving two and taking two. By luck they were able to capture a horse in pasture, and with it pressed on as best they could. They took the blankets off their mounts, spread them over bushes in a kind of tent, and tried to get some rest. The dismal rain continued. Instead of getting better, conditions grew worse. Bob Younger's arm was now inflamed.

They held counsel and decided to do something they had never done since the gang had come into being—travel by foot. Leaving their horses tied, so as not to inform on them, the six started through the almost impassable swamp. But it was too dangerous to travel by day, so, after going a short distance, they waited on a fairly dry spot until night, then started to wade. The next morning a piece of good luck befell them. They found an old abandoned house and thankfully fell on its floor. Here they remained two days, while food became more and more of a problem. They couldn't go and get a farmer's wife to cook dinner for them. They saw rabbits but didn't dare shoot.

Five days had passed. Now there were nine hundred manhunters on their trail, and they were only fifty miles from where they had started.

The courage of the outlaws was almost unbelievable. Nothing was so heartbreaking, utterly discouraging, that they did not continue to try. Another piece of bad luck occurred: the horses they had left tied broke away and were come upon by one of the posses. This changed everything. Instead of looking for men on horseback, the word went out to search for men on foot.

A Civil War general was secured to organize the army of chasers. He was General E. M. Pope of Mankato, Minnesota. "We'll soon have them," he said.

It became apparent the bandits would have to do what they

usually did when the law was upon them—split up. When the pinch came, Jesse and Frank always stuck together. Cole, Bob Younger, Jim Younger, and Charlie Pitts went one way and Jesse and Frank another. It was not long before the latter two had a piece of good luck, or so it seemed. They found a horse and Frank was helped up on it; he had been wounded in the right leg at Northfield.

Suddenly, in the night, they heard a terrifying sound—the challenge of a picket. "Halt! Who goes there?"

Instantly Frank spurred the animal. Instantly, too, the picket shot. Off went Jesse's hat; when it was picked up the next morning there was a bullet hole in it. It had been that close.

Worse luck, the horse got away.

Jesse and Frank started to plod on again.

Again luck appeared to turn their way. They heard horses in a farm lot and crept quietly among them, catching two. Thankfully they mounted and started desperately on. Then the horse that Frank was on began to act queerly and stumble. He lashed it and prodded it, but it only stumbled more.

He discovered it was blind.

On top of this, it was found that Jesse's horse had only one eye. The farmer had had a blind team and had matched them, as farmers sometimes do.

Never had anyone had such laughable, heartbreaking luck. Turning the horses loose, they again set out on foot, Frank limping.

The three Youngers and Charlie Pitts were desperately plodding on, Bob Younger's arm even more inflamed. In the early morning they came upon a Norwegian farmer industriously milking away. They spoke to him and successfully passed on. But the farmer had a seventeen-year-old son. No one yet has ever been able to dodge the curiosity of a seventeen-year-old boy.

"Pa," said the boy, after the men were out of hearing, "I believe that was the robbers."

The boy's name was Axel Oscar Sorbel.

"You go on with your milking, Oscar," said the father.

After the milking was finished, the boy discovered, at the house from his mother, that the men had stopped there and tried to buy food. They were hunters, they said; one of them had been wounded in an accident.

"Pa, I'm going in and tell the authorities," said the boy.

"You eat your breakfast, Oscar," said the father. "Why do you always try to think up ways to get out of work?"

But the boy did ride in—and rode into fame in bandit history.

It was about eight miles to the town of Madelia, where Cole Younger and Charlie Pitts had registered just a few unworried days before. Oscar Sorbel was there in no time. The first place he saw anybody was at the Flanders House, and there he drew up.

"I've found the bandits!" he gasped.

"What did you do with them, son?" asked Landlord Vought.

"Well," said the boy, a bit put back, "they're still there. They're four of them."

"That's a big haul. Have you had breakfast?"

But the boy was so confident—so sure of what he had seen—that Vought began to believe him. At this moment James Glispin, the sheriff of the county, arrived, and he too became convinced. A body of Madelia citizens was made up, mounted, and started for the Sorbel place.

The robbers, not realizing that fate was closing in, pushed on, without anything to eat, into an almost impenetrable morass known as Hanska Slough. Cole, who had also been wounded, limped along on a staff. Bob Younger, his arm in a crude sling, plodded behind him. They were all dirty and disheveled and weak from hunger and fatigue.

The pursuers, knowing shortcuts and dry paths, followed their sorry trail. At last they caught sight of the bandits, who had sunk down on a dry hummock to rest.

"Surrender!" shouted the sheriff.

The bandits struggled on.

The sheriff gave word to his men to fire. A bullet struck Cole Younger's staff, knocking it out of his hand.

The bandits turned and fired feebly. They had seen some horses hitched to a wagon. They started to run toward them. but just at this moment a farmer came up.

"We want those horses," shouted Charlie Pitts. "We're officers after the Northfield bank robbers."

The farmer leaped into the wagon and whipped his team in the opposite direction.

The outlaws waded across a murky stream and saw something on the public road they could hardly believe: two teams —four horses—jogging serenely along. They started to run toward them.

But the drivers bent over and each picked up a shotgun. They were going duck hunting.

Had ill fate ever pursued four men so faithfully? With groans of despair they turned back into the tangled morass of the slough.

Thomas L. Vought and the sheriff and their manhunters came toward the outlaws. Slowly they advanced, firing from time to time. The bandits, rearing themselves from the mud and water, fired back. The men of law and order came relentlessly on.

The end was inevitable. Charlie Pitts was killed.

And now the three Youngers were alone.

The end soon became inevitable for them, too.

Bob Younger got slowly up from the ground, his wounded arm in its muddy sling.

"All our men are down but me. I'll surrender."

It was soon over. It was found that Charlie Pitts had five bullets in him.

In addition to the wounded arm, Bob Younger had a bullet in his breast.

Jim Younger had five wounds.

Cole Younger had eleven. He got unsteadily to his feet—and saw something that made him gape. It was his landlord from the Flanders House!

Weak from loss of blood as he was, Cole Younger still had command of himself. "Hello, Mr. Vought. I didn't expect to run across you out here."

Vought looked at the body on the ground. "Who is that?"

"That's your other guest."

A farmer was summoned with his wagon. The corpse was lifted in, and the three men got in and sat on the floor. It was not long before Cole was back at the Flanders House, this time non-paying.

A doctor was called and the wounds of the three were dressed, and food was brought for the almost famished men. The word was flashed everywhere. Soon a Pinkerton detective arrived and saw members of the James-Younger gang for the first time. He wanted very much to see them, for he had been pursuing them six years. General Pope, who had said 'We'll soon have them,' came and looked, too.

At last the nine hundred manhunters had killed one of the bandits and captured three.

Frank and Jesse James hadn't yet been captured. They would have them next.

XII

THE END OF THE MINNESOTA MANHUNT

FRANK and Jesse pressed on in the general direction of Missouri, sometimes with good luck, sometimes with decidedly bad. They were in pursuit of the men who had robbed the Northfield bank, they said; sometimes they added that it was the James-Younger gang which had robbed the bank. They never made any pretense it was any other gang but the James-Youngers.

There is no complete record of this saga of the saddle, but the following incidents will give an idea of how the men traveled and how they tried to solve their problems.

One morning a farmer named Rolph, living near Luverne, Minnesota, was out in the yard washing his face from a pan on a bench, when he heard a sound behind him. Two travelworn men were riding up. They called from their horses, "Can you give us breakfast?"

Mr. Rolph looked at them doubtfully.

"We're officers of the law," one of the men explained. "The James Boys have held up the bank at Northfield. We think they are in this section and we are riding to Sioux City to get help."

Mr. Rolph was glad to assist the law, and soon the men sat down.

One took out his pistol and laid it on the breakfast table. "I'll have it handy in case I see one of them," he explained.

At the end of breakfast each gave Mrs. Rolph a silver dollar.

"Don't say anything about us having been here," one of them cautioned. "We don't want them to find out about it."

Then the two officers rode away.

Nels A. Nelson of Valley Springs, South Dakota, was sitting by a well on his farm when two men approached and asked if they could get a drink. Nelson said yes. A pail of water was on the platform, and before Jesse could dismount the horse thrust its nose into the pail and began to drink. Nelson got the bucket away from the horse and said he would draw fresh water.

Jesse was moody and bitter and said broodingly, "I reckon I'd rather drink out of a pail used by a horse than by some men I know."

The two rode on, using first one dodge, then another. Once they stopped to inquire their way to Sioux Falls, South Dakota, and asked, "Is there a telegraph office in Sioux Falls? We want to send a telegram to the federal authorities about the desperadoes we're chasing."

When told there was no telegraph office in Sioux Falls, the two looked thwarted, but after a moment revived enough to proceed on their way.

Their flight is usually crowned by the 'Devil's Gulch' story. Devil's Gulch is a chasm about twenty feet wide not far from Garretson, South Dakota. It is told that Jesse—hard-pressed by a posse—leaped his horse across the abyss. It's still shown to popeyed tourists who promptly whip out their cameras. A thrilling story, but—*alas!*—there's not a word of truth to it.

Jesse and Frank got what horses they could—farm plugs, for the most part; they could not have jumped a hog trough. They did not have any good riding stock after they lost their own horses following the raid.

Dr. Sidney P. Mosher, 2211 Kellogg Street, Sioux City, Iowa, was fourteen at the time of the raid. When he was eighty-six I sat with him on his porch and talked about the great manhunt, and it became a vivid and personal thing to me.

Dr. Mosher's father was also a doctor; his nameplate is on the front porch of the present Dr. Mosher's house. The latter also has a letter from Frank James. On the letterhead is printed, 'Frank James Who Never Broke a Promise.' But now the story.

On Sunday, September 17th (ten days after Northfield), the elder Dr. Mosher went to Broadbent's Livery Stable, in Sioux City, and told them he wanted the best riding horse they had. Procuring this, he set out for Kingsley, Iowa. It was a ride of about twenty miles, but the horse was a good one and the two clopped along.

He did not know the exact location of the place where he was going, and so, that afternoon about four, he cast around for someone to get directions from. The region was sparsely settled and for some time he met no one. Then, outlined on a hill, he saw two horsemen. He shouted at them, expecting they would wait, but they did not stop.

He put spurs to his horse and went hurrying toward them. The two men rode on, but kept looking back over their shoulders.

"Stop!" yelled the good doctor.

The two riders continued on their way.

"Wait! Stop where you are!"

When he came up he saw two grim-looking men with sacks

for saddles. One had a beard; the other had a handkerchief tied around his right trouser-leg.

"Why didn't you stop when I told you to?" demanded Dr. Mosher.

"What do you want?" asked one, gruffly.

"I want to ask a direction."

The two glanced at each other.

"What do you want to know?"

"Where does Robert Mann live?"

The two glanced at each other again, then one said, "Who are you, anyway?"

"I am Dr. Mosher," he replied, realizing there was something significant in their manner.

"What are you doing here?"

"I am going to see a woman who has a goiter."

"What's her name?"

"Mrs. Robert Mann."

Dr. Mosher was a short man with a heavy beard. The pair studied him carefully, and one said, "We know who you are. You're that St. Paul detective. Read that letter again, Frank."

The taller of the two got out a letter which he said was from his wife. It described the detective as a short man with a heavy beard. Then the spokesman announced, "We are the James Boys and we hate detectives. We are going to kill you."

The thoroughly alarmed doctor knew they meant it and repeated that he was a doctor and known in Sioux City.

"Prove you are a doctor."

The only thing Dr. Mosher had to show was a small scalpel in a little wooden box, with which he was going to lance the goiter.

The two conferred again. "Do you know of a robbery in Northfield, Minnesota?"

"Yes."

"How do you know of it?"

"I read it in the papers."

Jesse was still suspicious. He rode to the nearest farmhouse and asked where Mrs. Robert Mann lived; then asked if she had a goiter. This was confirmed. He rode gloomily back, as if disliking to give up an idea he had established in his mind.

Again the two conferred, at a little distance from Dr. Mosher, each with a pistol in his hand.

"Suppose we change horses," suggested Frank.

Dr. Mosher got on the gunnysack.

"You're going with us," said the dour Jesse.

They came to a house and the pair rode up with Dr. Mosher between them. A farmer named Wright came out.

"This is Dr. Mosher of Sioux City," said Frank. "He was in a cart but it broke down, so he had to get on his horse. Can you lend him a fresh horse and saddle?"

Farmer Wright was glad to help a doctor who had had such a bad piece of luck, and in a few minutes the three horsemen rode away, profuse in their thanks to the kindly Mr. Wright.

When they were out of sight of the house, Jesse said, "Suppose we change horses, Doctor."

This was agreeable to the doctor.

So now Frank and Jesse, on good horses equipped with saddles, rode along in the direction of Missouri with the doctor, who was forked on a feedsack.

With conditions improved, Frank became cheerful and talked to Dr. Mosher about the Civil War. But Jesse remained gloomy and rode silently. When he spoke it was bitterly.

For five hours the three rode along. Darkness came. Then Frank said, "Doctor, let's exchange clothes. Mine have seen some rough usage."

There was a clump of high grass near and they rode to it and Dr. Mosher peeled off his clothes. "They look nice," said Frank, putting them on.

In the distance could be seen the lights of a farmhouse. "Doctor," said Frank, "suppose you leave your horse here and go to that farmhouse and stay overnight?" He drew his pistol. "Run, Doctor, run."

The doctor ran.

I asked 'young' Dr. Mosher if his father had dressed Frank's wounds and he said no. They were only slight, anyway, and it had been ten days since they were inflicted. I asked him if his father had kept the suit, and he replied that his father had for years, then it had disappeared. But he still had his father's scalpel. "It saved his life," he said.

An illuminating part is the old doctor's statement that Jesse was bitter and gloomy. Well he might have been, for he had found out that six of his men were lost, and he had not taken in a cent. But at least he had escaped nine hundred pursuers, was still alive, and was on the way back where he had friends.

They crossed into Nebraska, but here their trail becomes dim and confused. Evidence would indicate that somewhere in Nebraska they disposed of their horses and came back to Missouri on the train. How confidently they had ridden north! And now how defeated they were. One wonders at their thoughts. Did Jesse consider giving up banditry, as he had so often? Did Frank want to settle down as a small-town politician, with horses of his own entered in the county fair races?

Now that we have come to the end of the Northfield robbery, I want to add some footnotes that did not fit into the general narrative. The first is about the seventeen-year-old boy, and shows quite well how greatly the James gang was feared. At the time the newspapers gave out that the boy's name was Oscar Oleson Suborn. If avengers had come looking for such a person they would not have found him. Later the young man went off to a veterinary college, and then moved to Webster, South Dakota, where it was not known for almost fifty years that he was the farmboy who had made the famous ride. He died in Webster on July 11, 1930.

Charlie Pitts. He was killed in the swamp, with five bullet holes in him. Strange things were to happen to him, as I will bear witness, for I have seen his ear! It reposes in the 'Hobby House' of William F. Schilling, in Northfield. The Hobby House is an amazing private museum, and Bill Schilling is the 'oldest columnist' in the United States. He does a weekly column for the *Northfield News*.

The ear is withered, but there it is in a glass cage. It's not just whacked off, but is surrounded with a patch of dry and crinkly skin about the size of a child's hand.

The unfortunate loss of an ear is not all that happened to Charlie Pitts. It was the law at that time in Minnesota that unclaimed bodies would go to the surgeon general of the state, who, in turn, could parcel them out to the medical schools for dissection. And thus in a short time Charlie Pitts found himself (with the exception of one ear) in St. Paul.

It so chanced there was a young medical student just home from Rush Medical College in Chicago. He went to Dr. Frank W. Murphy, who was the surgeon general of the state, and asked if he could have all that was left of the late Charlie Pitts. Students, meanwhile, had whacked away at Charlie; he was pretty cut-up-looking.

Young Dr. Henry F. Hoyt wanted Pitts's skeleton for his

office. At this time it was the custom for doctors to have skeletons in their offices to scare the daylights out of children. But first he wanted to whiten the bones, and the way it was done then was to put them in water. He procured a box and placed Charlie's guilty bones in it, loaded it with rocks, and alone one night he rowed out on the south branch of Lake Como, just inside the city limits of St. Paul. There he sank Charlie Pitts and rowed silently away. Charlie was supposed to stay there a year, growing whiter every day.

Then young Dr. Hoyt got a job in Las Vegas, New Mexico, leaving Charlie Pitts in soak. This was in March, 1877.

That winter young August Robertson thought he would go out muskrat-hunting; he took with him a hatchet to open the ice and a spear to finish the job. As he was walking over the ice he saw something that certainly wasn't a muskrat. He looked more closely. It was far, far from a muskrat. It was a box. The stones had worked to one end, and the other end was nosed up against the ice.

The young muskrat hunter was thrilled. Buried treasure! He whacked open a hole and got the box out on the ice. With trembling, excited hands he pried off the top—and out rolled a human skull.

After a moment he looked deeper into the box. Only bones.

Leaving his treasure on the ice, he got to the sheriff as fast as he could. The sheriff and the coroner got back with him as fast as *they* could. It was exactly as the young muskrat hunter had said. The marks of five bullets were found.

In no time at all the newspapers were telling about the foul murder. People were shocked through and through that such a thing could take place in their quiet city.

Days passed; the ghastly murder was unsolved.

The newspapers began to demand police action. They dug up all the other murders the police hadn't solved and wanted to know what they were going to do about this one? The police announced they had clues and would soon make arrests. But they didn't make them, whereupon the aroused citizens demanded a new police administration. The police said, "The matter is near solution."

At last a friend, thinking the story would interest young Dr. Hoyt, sent him a clipping. The story interested him.

He came home as fast as he could and went to see the chief of police and told him the story. Details were checked and the story found to be true.

At last the matter was settled and Charlie Pitts's bleached bones were given to a doctor who took them to Chicago to put in his office. Where they are now I don't know.

Also in Bill Schilling's fabulous museum is the safe which was the undoing of poor Joseph Lee Heywood. Mr. Schilling keeps his own papers in it. It was made by Evans & Watson, Philadelphia.

Now to Clell Miller. A young medical student named Wheeler, a senior at Ann Arbor, Michigan, was given Clell's corpse, and he shipped the body off to be used for his personal dissection, as was done at that time in medical colleges.

The body arrived late one day and was delivered by an express wagon. As young Wheeler was struggling alone to get the box in, a freshman passed. "Here, help me," commanded the senior.

The freshman laid hold, a bit frightened at being in a dissecting laboratory.

"What is this?" he asked nervously.

"It's the cadaver of a man."

"Oh . . . how did you get him?"

"I shot him," said Wheeler.

The freshman's mouth flew open and he got out of the dissecting room with a record, they say, that stood for years.

Dr. Wheeler took the skeleton to Grand Forks, North Dakota, where he kept it in his office. One day, some years later, an elderly man came to see him. He was ill at ease. He asked the doctor selfconsciously if he were Dr. Wheeler, and then, finally, inquired if he had a skeleton in his office. Dr. Wheeler told him he had.

"Could I see it?"

It was not unusual for country people to ask to see a skeleton, so Dr. Wheeler, giving it hardly a second thought, took him along in. The old man stood looking at it intently, without speaking; finally he said, "I'm glad you let me see it, Doctor . . . that's my son."

The doctor asked for some of the details. The man said: "When his mother read in the newspapers, after the Northfield bank raid, that you had his skeleton, she asked me to come and see if it was true. Now I'll have to go back and tell her it's our boy."

As to the reward money. The governor of Minnesota had offered a reward of $4000. But, as usually happens, the state delayed payment, the politicians now being at work on the case. The Youngers were safely in prison, but the men who captured them hadn't received a penny. They finally had to go to court. The posse which actually laid hands on the Youngers got $240 each.

Thirty-nine others who had participated got $56.25 each.

Eight got $15 each.

Seventeen-year-old Axel Oscar Sorbel got $56.25.

They received the money January 15, 1878, about a year

and a half after the capture. During the chase, if anybody had said, "Let 'em wait a year and a half for their money," he would have been stoned in the streets.

The First National Bank is not where it was when the James-Youngers visited it, but has moved across the street. The president of the bank, John D. Nutting, when asked if he had any souvenirs answered, "A few." They proved to be Jesse James's spurs and a pistol picked up in the street; the latter is an ivory-handled Colt .45, made in Hartford—'Pat. July 1872,' which would seem to indicate it was the latest model. The James-Youngers always wanted the most improved and up-to-date in firearms.

When asked if many tourists came in to look around, Mr. Nutting said, "In summer about two a week."

The only plaque in town is a brief and noncommittal one on the outside of the bank:

IN THIS ROOM
Joseph Lee Heywood
refusing to betray his trust
was shot by bank robbers
September 7, 1876
Faithful Unto Death

The room itself is now the insurance office of Ed F. Berg.

On the corner of the old bank building is the Jesse James Cafe—lots of postcards but only one authentic souvenir: the lock and handle from the outside door of the bank. Not very thrilling, but it seems to impress the tourists.

XIII

JESSE GOES FARMING IN TENNESSEE

AT LAST Jesse James reached home. By the extraordinary good luck that was so long his, he was the only man in the Northfield robbery who was not dead, captured, or wounded. But everything else had gone wrong. Here at home people were still his friends, largely understanding and sympathetic friends; everywhere else, however, he was confronted by an outraged and furious Middle West. Too many innocent men dead. Robbing the local bank might be pardonable, but not shooting down one's neighbors. And, assisted by this wave of popular indignation, the detectives and the sheriffs were on his trail hotter than ever before. The Pinkertons, who had broken up the Reno gang, who had a long string of successes in the field behind them, were *bound* to get the James Boys. The best-trained and most relentless manhunters in America had a reputation to think about.

Jesse had one important protection. No sheriff or detective as yet had his picture. Never once did he try to disguise himself; he lived as much like the average person as he could. He rode trains freely; he went to county fairs and races. One might think that some of the people he had held up in banks, stages, on trains, on the road, would sooner or later encounter him and recognize him. But they didn't. Who knows, maybe he looked different viewed over a pistol barrel.

Where were the Boys to go now and what were they to do? Examination of the available evidence shows that Zee James was living in Kansas City, and that there Jesse joined her. But Kansas City was only thirty-five miles from his birthplace. The Boys could not retreat to Paso Robles, for Uncle Drury James in 1868 had sold his interest in the ranch and hot springs. The best thing seemed to return to farming. But where? They could go to Kentucky: many relatives there, but also many people who knew them by sight. Finally they made an important decision: they would go to Tennessee, where no one knew them, where they would try to get land and start their lives anew.

It has long been a mystery how they got there, and I take quite a bit of satisfaction in helping to clear this up. They decided to drive, so they obtained two covered wagons, hitched a span of horses to each, and started eastward overland, just as their father had once started west. And, like him, they started from Liberty. What a picture—the most famous bandits in the world decamping in covered wagons with their families.

Frank engaged Tyler Burns to drive his wagon and Jesse got his half-brother, John T. Samuels, to drive his. The wives sat in the wagons, Zee holding little Jesse Junior, who was just two years old, while Jesse and Frank rode horseback. They would plod along with the wagons until they came to a town; this they would bypass, and join the wagons later. At night they camped together. Their movements attracted little attention, for everywhere people were on the go. It was a changing America and they were part of it.

When they reached Kentucky they felt they were out of danger, and the two drivers left them. In August of 1877 they reached Humphreys County, Tennessee, and came to the town of Waverly. There Jesse rented a farm from Banks Link. This farm has been in the same family for more than a hundred years. It is now the property of Hugh Link, grandson of the man who owned it when Jesse set down his plow. Water from the Tennessee Valley Authority now backs up to it. It is in a section known as 'Big Bottom'; and it was so known then.

On the Sunday afternoon I spent at the farm, Hugh Link showed me something that touched me—two little gravestones in the back yard. The stones had evidently been carved and shaped by Jesse's own hands. They were the graves of twins. No names are on them; they died, according to the older people who live in the community, when they were about a week old. As I stood looking at the stones I thought what a tragedy it must have been for Jesse's wife. At last, when after all the dangers had been safely surmounted they could add to their family, now this.

Mr. Howard was a good farmer, according to the local stories; no one suspected his shocking past. But they did notice that, in addition to his farm horses, he had an excellent riding animal named 'Red Fox,' which he entered in the local races, always winning.

One of those who dropped in to the Link farm that Sunday afternoon was James Crockett, who had been Jesse's nearest neighbor; he was a boy, then, light of weight, and he was engaged to train Red Fox. "Jesse certainly knew horses," said Mr. Crockett reminiscently. Then, sitting in the very room where Jesse had lived, he told this story.

A township election was being held and the men met at a schoolhouse to cast their votes. Jesse could vote and he was there with his neighbors. It was a hot day, and suddenly that aggravating after-effect of his surrender wounds made itself felt, and he fainted.

The men opened his collar, threw back his coat—and got a shock, for under the coat was a shoulder holster. It seemed a trifle odd for a man to attend an election thus equipped, and especially odd for a farmer.

But the thing was to revive him. They threw water in his face; his mind went in and out, then suddenly he came to his senses. Instantly his hand whipped over.

"Where is it! Where is it!"

The holster had been placed on the schoolhouse steps; one of the men held it up. Jesse's hand weakly moved out and rested on it; then he swooned again.

After a time he came to completely, and, without a word of explanation, buckled on his holster. The thing was unusual but not enough so to make people pay special attention. That is, until later. . . . But it shows how deep in Jesse was the instinct for self-preservation. Even with his mind reeling it was the deepest thing in him.

Harris W. Hooper lives in Waverly, Tennessee. He was ninety-one when I talked with him and heard this anecdote. There was a racetrack at Waverly, and one opening day Mr. Howard showed up with Red Fox, which he called his 'Four-Mile Horse' because it was capable of running that far in a race. He made bets on Red Fox and got ready for the start. Red Fox went like the wind, according to Mr. Hooper, but, a few yards from the finish line, fell. Jesse himself was on Red Fox but was unhurt.

The judges awarded the race to the next horse. Jesse—volatile as always—grew excited and protested. Such was his pleading power that the judges decided to run the race over; this time Red Fox and Jesse won, as might have been expected. "No one had ever heard of anything just like it," said Mr. Hooper, still a bit mystified.

Jesse got his mail at a post office called Box, named after a prominent family (it's now Denver, Tennessee). The postmaster, William K. Jackson, and Jesse became friends. Jesse became so hard up he had to borrow $60.

It takes time to get established as a farmer, and Jesse was making little. He decided to try his hand at raising cattle, and bought a load from a farmer named Mark Cooley for $900, on credit. For some reason or other, not now clear, the two had trouble. Cooley began to press him for the money. Discouraged by his attempt to farm and aroused by Cooley's attitude, Jesse suddenly decided to pull stakes. He loaded his wife and household plunder into a two-horse wagon and disappeared in the direction of Nashville, a distance of about seventy-five miles. He left under a cloud, for the sympathy was with the local man.

But before leaving he went to his friend the postmaster and paid him every cent he owed. The story illustrates both Jesse's hotheadedness and his loyalty.

Jesse James—the most famous bandit in the world—had quietly farmed two years while, all over the country, detectives had been hard at work hunting him. During this period, so far as it is possible to tell, he had not even looked in the direction of a bank. Now he was on his way to Nashville to join his brother.

One thinks of his wife; in some ways she is the heroine of the story. After the years on the farm they were as poor as when they had arrived, and they were moving on again, their troubles unsolved, leaving behind them two headstones.

The exposure from his days and nights in the swamps after Northfield had injured Frank James's health. It was a weary, hard-pressed man who in the fall of 1877 had arrived at Nashville in his wagon, driving two horses and leading one—his fast one. He made inquiries as to where he could rest, and was directed to a farmer named Ben Drake who lived a few miles out of town. Mrs. Drake nursed him, and for this he remained, all his life, deeply grateful.

Next he moved to the house of Ben Drake's sister, a Mrs. Ledbetter, and there he continued to improve. Meanwhile he was on the lookout for a farm where he could work. He finally found one, the Josiah Walton place on White's Creek, a few miles outside of Nashville. The house stands much as it did when Frank James moved in. It is still in the Walton family. I talked to the grandson, E. B. Walton, who is a prominent Nashville businessman. He told me a story which had come down from his grandfather.

One day Josiah Walton's son started out to see Frank, who was plowing corn. He hallooed and got the answer, "Who is it?" Unthinking, the young man continued to plod through the corn. Again came the demand, "Who is it?" Still he plodded on. Suddenly he heard a sound and found himself looking into the barrels of two pistols.

"Son," said Frank, "when people want to know who you are, they're liable to mean it." Then he lowered his pistols.

When crop season was over Frank began to team for the Indiana Lumber Company, driving four mules. At noon he would draw up beside the road and eat the lunch his wife had prepared. The outdoor work and freedom from acute worry were returning him to health. On his leg there was still the Northfield scar.

For a while he worked for the Prewitt-Spurr Lumber Company, making cedar buckets. He kept a horse saddled and bridled near the mill. People thought this a bit queer, but still it wasn't unusual enough to make them pry into it. There was an organization called the 'Blood Horse Racing Association,' with a track in what was called 'The Flats,' in North Nashville. Frank raced there, and sometimes acted as starter.

He had a log house in the neighborhood (it no longer exists) and a son was born there. The child was named after his grandfather, the preacher, and after Frank himself, thus becoming Robert Franklin James. But he was dressed as a girl and called, first, 'Mary Ledbetter,' and later 'Mary Woodson,' the idea being that some day Frank might need to switch his child's sex for alibi purposes.

Frank thought he saw a better opportunity, so he moved to the Jeff Hyde farm on the old Hyde's Ferry Road. That farm, too, is still in the hands of the family who owned it when Frank moved in. I talked to Mrs. A. W. Stephens, whose mother had known the Jameses.

"They were a quiet, hardworking family who paid their rent promptly. Once our renter—Mr. Woodson—quoted Shakespeare to my mother. That surprised her, for it wasn't often a farmer mentioned Shakespeare. She noticed something else unusual but did not think much about it at the time. Our renter kept a fine horse saddled and bridled, day and night, standing in the stable. We couldn't understand it either, but it was his business and we did not mention it. He was a good tenant and the people in the neighborhood hated to see him go."

Frank moved a third time. He rented the Felix Smith farm on White's Creek. This house is owned today by Emerson B. Smith, the grandson. I asked him if there were any James souvenirs and he said, "Yes, the hanging shelf." He took me to the basement and there, suspended from the ceiling, was the 'hanging shelf' used for 'vittles.' I discovered, on inquiry, that the Jameses had put up these shelves in all the houses they had lived in. They were a sort of trademark, as was the grain sack in another line of work.

Mr. Smith took me to a bedroom on the first floor and said, "That's where Jesse James's daughter Mary was born."

Frank's financial condition began to improve and he did what was so deep in him—bought a racehorse named 'Jewel Maxey' and entered it in the local races, riding it himself. He also began to raise pedigreed hogs—so successfully that he took first prize for Poland Chinas at the Nashville fair. Meanwhile the detectives were hunting him high and low.

He became a registered voter and went to the polls and voted. The detectives never thought of waiting at a polling booth for a questionable character. In addition, he made friends with the sheriff of Davidson County. It seems doubtful that the detectives ever thought of dropping in at a sheriff's office to pick up one of the Boys. He acquired other influential friends, among them Judge Cantrell, who was judge of the Eighth Circuit Court.

Frank lived among the people as a Northerner. Now and then this raised a problem. One day he went to Dude Young's blacksmith shop to get his team shod. Dude was an exceedingly powerful blacksmith with large and sinewy arms as strong as iron bands—Longfellow would have loved him. This day, however, he was intoxicated, not at all like the smith that children adore. When Frank James ventured to make a suggestion about the way the horses should be shod, Dude resented it, raging, "You're a damyankee. A carpetbagger, that's what you are. Get out of my shop." This to a man who had fought under Quantrill!

Frank protested that he had a right to specify how his own horses should be shod, whereupon Dude became doubly abusive, calling him vile names and again ordering him out. Frank was armed, for he never relinquished his protection. Goaded by the bellicose Dude, he reached for his pistol. Then, at the last moment, he controlled himself and left. If it had been Jesse, it would have been the end of Dude Young.

It is said that when Dude found out who the damyankee was, he missed his stroke and bent three nails in succession.

Jim Cummins turned up. He had been a member of the gang, was none too bright and was of little consequence. Furthermore, he was about the last person in the world that Frank wanted to see just then. He hung around for some time, Frank wishing to God he would clear out. He thought of a dozen ways of getting rid of Jim, without result, until one day he took him down to Warner's Restaurant to buy him a meal. There, standing outside the door, was a detective named Watson. Frank knew the detective was in Nashville but it didn't worry him, as he had little respect for Watson's ability.

When Frank got Jim inside, he told the latter who Watson was, and said: "Jim, come on out and I'll introduce you under another name. You'd like to say you'd met and shaken hands with a detective, wouldn't you?"

"Of course not," declared Jim indignantly.

He got as far back in a corner as he could and ate one of the fastest meals ever known in Nashville. Then he proceeded out of Davidson County.

A person who brought Frank James back and made him a living reality was an ex-slave woman ninety-four years old —Betsy McGavock. She sat on the porch of her shack in Nashville, and when she got up to move she used a staff instead of a cane. Some colored children came up and began to romp on the porch; suddenly she gave a swipe with her stick.

"You-all clear out so I kin hear the gennelman."

She said that before the Civil War she had been the slave of a white family whose mistress would not let her go barefooted. This she considered a mark of high distinction. The other colored children had gone barefoot, but not she.

She had worked as a hired girl for Frank James. But to her the name 'B. J. Woodson' meant more than Frank James.

"Yes, sah, I reckon I can 'member wukking for Mistah Woodson; tall-like and scrouged in the shoulders, with a thin hawk nose. He wasn't a complainer, like everything I do, both him and his lady. Never begrudged me my pay. He had a racehorse he was mighty proud of. One time he take me out and get on and ride and ride around to show me how good he could ride. There wasn't any doubt he could ride good. . . .

"He wasn't the famous Frank James to me," she said. "He was Mistah B. J. Woodson. I liked to wuk for Mistah Woodson."

Then she rose, her stick grasped in her hand, and walked to the edge of the porch. "You say you going to write a book about Mistah Woodson? Well, you tell 'em he was a fine man to wuk for."

These were the happiest days Frank James had ever known. He was farming and teaming, and he had ease of mind. The nights of riding and days of terror were over. He was a part of the community (listed in the city directory), was respected and liked by his neighbors, and he had his racehorse and his prize hogs.

Then something happened. A two-horse wagon drove up; in it were Jesse and his wife.

XIV

BACK TO THE OLD WAYS

THOUGH Jesse's arrival must have been highly disturbing to Frank, there was no question about what to do. They had always stuck together. Jesse and his family moved in with the Woodsons, and for a time things continued smoothly. Jesse helped Frank with the farming and hauling; he joined the Methodist church in Nashville and once again could be heard singing his well-loved hymns. He had separated himself from the men with whom he had ridden, and none knew where he was.

Trouble raised its head briefly when Mark Cooley followed him to Nashville and sued him for recovery of the $900 debt. Cooley won the case, but so cool and assured was Jesse that he appealed to the Tennessee Supreme Court. The appeal never came to trial, because Jesse soon had business elsewhere, but it indicated how 'settled' he felt himself at the time.

He acquired a horse named 'Jim Malone' and began to race it. On March 17, 1879, he was treated by Dr. W. A. Hamilton for a return of the malarial fever he had contracted in the Big Woods swamp after Northfield. And we know something else about what Jesse did in this year of 1879, the last year of peace. He took a second western trip.

Jesse thought that, if farming was not making a living for himself and his family, ranching might. He had seen something of the latter with Uncle D.W. at Paso Robles. The question was, where to try it? He had gone to school with a boy named W. Scott Moore who was now running a hotel at Las Vegas, New Mexico—the Old Adobe Hotel it was called. Jesse appears to have written him, for he went to Kansas City and got on a Santa Fe train for Las Vegas. He chose this train in preference to others because he had a friend who was the conductor.

It was not long before he was at the hotel. The Old Adobe was famous for its Sunday dinners; ranchmen came in from miles around to gorge on Mrs. Moore's Sunday spreads. The men waited in a kind of lounge, and here Mr. Moore introduced Mr. Howard. Jesse sat listening rather than talking, as was his custom when he was among strange people. Mrs. Moore gave the word and the men marched in.

Jesse, being new, waited for the others to be seated; when he sat down himself there proved to be a vacant place beside him at the end of the table. As he was eating silently and listening to the conversation, a man younger than himself came in and sat down next to him. The two began to talk casually. Finally the stranger asked Jesse his name.

"Howard, from Tennessee."

At last dinner was over and the men went into the yard and began to lounge about.

As soon as Jesse came out, Moore nodded to him and took him into another room with a great air of suppressed excitement. "Do you know who that was beside you?"

Jesse said he didn't.

"That," said Scott Moore, almost bursting with the intelligence, "was Billy the Kid!"

It was Jesse's time to be astonished.

"Why don't you two really get acquainted?" asked Moore. He got permission to tell who Jesse was, and, taking Billy the Kid off by himself, conveyed the exciting news. And now, indeed, it was Billy the Kid's turn to be astonished.

The upshot of it was that the two went into one of the rooms and began to get acquainted. At last Billy the Kid said, "Why don't we join up?"

Jesse had come west for an entirely different purpose, but here was something interesting. He began to size up the Kid. Jesse was twelve years older and an entirely different type. Billy the Kid was contemptible in comparison to Jesse James. He robbed no bank, he held up no train. He stole horses or cattle and shot unarmed men, and ambushed or killed Mexicans and Indians. The more Jesse talked to him, the more he became convinced he wanted nothing to do with such a miserable piece of flesh. At last Jesse told him he couldn't 'go in' with him, and the two parted and that was the end of it.

It was not known Jesse had been in the vicinity until the *Daily Optic* of Las Vegas published the following:

Jesse James of Missouri was a guest at the Las Vegas Hot Springs from July 26 to July 29, 1879. Of course it was not generally known.

The paper very carefully gave no secret away, for it didn't print the item until December 8th.

Jesse had found that getting into ranching would take more money than he could hope to get together. He got on the train and returned to Nashville, and a last chance to avoid returning to the old ways disappeared down the rails.

While he had been away, in July, his daughter Mary had been born. Four mouths to feed now. He made his decision.

Bits and pieces of the old gang had begun to float in. Buck-toothed, watery-eyed Jim Cummins was around again. Bill Ryan, a good man who had a dangerous liking for spirituous liquids. And Dick Liddil, another weak member. Jesse got his men around him and rode away and back to the country they knew so well—their old home in Missouri. Here they could always get protection. The matter turned out quite well. On September 7, 1879, they robbed the Glendale train, on the Chicago & Alton Railroad, of $9400. After the business was successfully concluded, Jesse James went up to the engineer and said, "I didn't get your name, but mine is Jesse James," then turned and walked away.

Frank had no part in the Glendale train robbery. Jesse was working on him, trying to persuade him, beginning to exert control over him, but he still would not be moved. Life was going too smoothly for him: Why risk it? So Jesse embarked on a little private enterprise of his own. Mrs. James Killebrew, 221 Carden Avenue, Nashville, tells the story. Her grandfather, Robert Burns Stone, was the manager and part-owner of the Cumberland Furnace in Dickson County. This was an iron-ore furnace, very profitable then, today no longer operating.

Everybody in the section knew when it was payday at Cumberland Furnace, for that loosed quite a bit of money in the community. And payday was always the same day of the week. Everybody knew this, too.

Christmas week, 1879, arrived at Cumberland Furnace, and so did a man on horseback who explained that he was a cattle buyer from the west and that he had made an engagement with Mr. Stone to look the next morning at his cattle. The time was the day before Christmas.

The well-mounted gentleman went to the inn and engaged a room. The inn was across the creek by foot-log from the office of the furnace, where the safe was kept; the latter was a large room and the employees of the furnace occasionally played poker there, at a big round table.

After dinner Mr. Howard, being in a genial mood, suggested they all have a friendly game. This was agreeable, and soon the men were in the office. Mr. Howard sat down first, choosing a chair that faced the safe; in a little while the men noticed that he was looking intently at the safe; in fact, he looked so intently that he attracted attention.

As the men played, they talked, as poker players have since time immemorial.

Suddenly Mr. Howard looked stunned, not at the hand he had drawn, but at a remark he had just heard. It was to the effect that, because of Christmas, payday had been advanced, and that the men had received their pay the day before, consequently leaving the safe as bare as Santa's sack at the end of Christmas Eve. When he heard this the visiting cattleman threw down his hand, saying he was very tired and would have to go to his room at the inn and go to bed so that the next morning he could get up early and look at Mr. Stone's stock. He left, barely grunting a word of goodnight to the puzzled players. He did not go to the hotel but to his horse, and departed, rather hurriedly people said, thus ending his career as a western cattle buyer at Cumberland Furnace, Tennessee.

Jesse began to absent himself from Nashville on private missions more and more frequently; once he was gone three months. On another occasion he took Bill Ryan with him, and the two rode away without mentioning where they were going.

Mr. Sam McCoy, driver of a stage plying between Mammoth Cave and Cave City, Kentucky, was swinging comfortably along on September 3, 1880, when two masked men stepped out and rudely commanded him to throw up his hands. He lost no time in doing so. On the stage were six men and a girl. One of the men was Judge Rutherford Harrison Rowntree of Lebanon, Kentucky, and with him was his daughter, Miss Lizzie Rowntree. At the suggestion of the bandits, the passengers began to put their money and jewelry in a grain sack, and one of the articles that went in was Judge Rowntree's watch, a prized possession that had been given to him by the governor of Kentucky. Joining the watch went the daughter's diamond ring, with her pet-name carved inside. The passengers made a cash investment of $803. The watch was valued at $200, and there were, in addition to the ring, other articles of jewelry generously contributed by Miss Lizzie.

When the ceremony of filling the sack was over, Bill Ryan removed a bottle from his pocket and drank to the long life and prosperity of the passengers. Then, wiping his lips, he mounted his steed, and with Jesse at his side the two disappeared down the road.

A posse rode forth and, as at Glendale a year before, accomplishing nothing. But later a man named T. J. Hunt was arrested for the robbery and imprisoned for eighteen months, then sentenced to three years. This became a famous case of mistaken identity and is still quoted in the lawbooks of Kentucky, for Hunt had nothing in the world to do with the robbery. His misfortune was that he looked a vague bit like Jesse James. The passengers, eager to make somebody pay, swore they recognized him and off to jail he went.

Jesse returned to Nashville better off financially than when he had left, and now his influence on Frank began to take its effect. Perhaps if Frank had been alone he would not have succumbed to the ideas Jesse was proposing. They involved Muscle Shoals, Alabama (later to become part of TVA), which lay not far away. A construction messenger plied between Florence, Alabama, and Muscle Shoals, carrying a goodly payroll. On March 11, 1881, the messenger was relieved of his heavy load by two men who rode off without a satisfactory account of where they were going. Again a posse was formed. After a time it came back, having just missed the thieves. Also missing was a $5000 payroll.

After the Muscle Shoals affair, a minion of the law came to question Frank James on the unfortunate matter. It was such an awkward situation that Frank had to engage a lawyer, Raymond B. Sloan, to point out that he was guiltless. Frank's alibi was that he had sat up with a sick friend. Investigation showed that Frank was right. The lawyer asked the sick neighbor as to what time of night Frank left, saying, "Could Mr. James have had time to reach Muscle Shoals by the time the robbery was committed?"

The neighbor thought it over carefully. "Yes," he said, "he just about had time to make it."

That ended the questioning.

The two brothers realized that a good and foolproof arrangement about alibis was going to be of considerable use to them, and they hit upon a novel method. Having teams and wagons, they made a deal with the road commissioner to haul gravel in their spare time. The careless commissioner did not pay any particular attention to the dates on the receipts the James brothers prepared for him to sign. It didn't seem important. But later, when mischief took place, it developed that the Boys could prove they had been hauling gravel like any two honest men.

Frank and Jesse had no more than settled down after the Muscle Shoals affair than Trouble again tapped. It had to do with Bill Ryan, the problem child. He was fearless and was to be depended on when people were being relieved of their money, but there was the matter of drink. He had been hiding under the name of Tom Hill. On March 26, 1881, he rode up to a grocery store with a saloon attachment at White's Creek, on the fringe of Nashville. Dismounting, he wove his way unsteadily in and managed to anchor to the bar. His eyes wandered here and there, seeing things denied to others. Suddenly he pounded on the bar and called for whiskey and oysters—an unusual combination. They were cove oysters, canned, and were considered a great treat in country districts (and still are, for that matter). It proved to be an ill-chosen combination, for soon he felt a desire to trounce the disagreeable people he saw around him. Suddenly he let off a mighty yip and said, "Stand back and give me room or I'll shoot you as full of holes as a sausage grinder! Do you know who I am?" His gaze wandered unsteadily over the customers. "Well, I'll tell you who I am," he roared. "I'm Tom Hill, the outlaw, thash who I am!"

It so happened that an ex-detective was on the street outside; a messenger sped to him and the detective entered the saloon.

By this time Bill Ryan was offering to fight Middle Tennessee.

The detective (not a Pinkerton) crept silently up behind and threw his arms around the oyster lover and pinned the latter's arms to his side. Others helped—willingly, now—and in a moment Bill Ryan was trussed up like a Christmas turkey. They sent word to the police department, in Nashville proper, and soon Bill Ryan was on the way to the cooler.

There they searched him and found he had two revolvers and a buckskin vest containing $1300 in gold. The police asked how he had gotten it. "By honest labor," said Bill. This immediately aroused suspicion. But they were not able to dig up a single clue as to his identity. The police telegraphed a description of the liquor-and-oyster lover to the police chiefs of the country; word came from Kansas City asking for details. These were telegraphed. Then word came. "We think he is Bill Ryan of Jackson County. Will send a man to investigate."

It wasn't long before Bill was on the way back to his native state, a distaste in his mouth for oysters.

The day of the arrest Jesse was away from home; he returned late that evening on horseback. When he came in his wife told him what had happened. He was thunderstruck. Bill Ryan had been living with him, he had spent the night there, he had eaten breakfast in the house . . . now he was in the hands of the police.

What would happen? Would he tell where Jesse and Frank were? Even if he didn't, the police and detectives might guess he had been with them. Something would have to be done.

Frank came to see Jesse and in Jesse's house they talked it over. Roughly speaking, Jesse had been in Nashville two years, Frank four. Here their children had been born. Here Jesse had joined the church and Frank had won first prize for his Poland China hogs. Now the pleasant, easygoing days were over. The two would again have to be on the move. Outlaws again.

"If only those men hadn't come back," said Jesse's wife bitterly.

It was a bitter moment for Jesse, too.

They decided to chance staying overnight. The next day their families would have to go, too—little Tim Howard and his sister Mary Howard, and little Mary Woodson—but the men must go fastest of all. In the morning Jesse and Frank sat on horseback in the back yard of Jesse's home. They talked a few minutes, then shook hands. "Goodbye. Frank," said Jesse. "Goodbye, Dingus," said Frank; and the two rode off in opposite directions.

XV

JESSE IN KENTUCKY

JESSE picked up Dick Liddil and the two started west. Now and then doubt came to him about Dick, who was shifty and none too bold. Bill Ryan had been the best man he had had . . . except for the drinking. Oh well . . . they were heading back to the state where they had friends.

But the war had been over some time; law was pretty well established in a land where it had been a stranger, and the ex-guerrillas hesitated to shelter old friends just because they had ridden together. They hesitated, too, at the idea of joining up with Jesse again. He had lost six men at Northfield; could he build up a new band? He had done so, briefly, when he had come back for the Glendale robbery. But it was not in a class with the old James-Youngers. He had to have something as good as that if he was to go on.

On his way back to Missouri he stopped at Samuels Depot, Kentucky, where he had an old Clay County friend—Donnie Pence. Pence had not only been a boyhood friend, but had also ridden with Jesse as a guerrilla. On top of this, he was the sheriff of Nelson County—the last place in the world where a detective would look. Here Jesse set about organizing a new band.

He got together some of his veterans, but he also had to put in green timber. He rounded them up by letter, writing them and receiving the answers addressed to Donnie Pence or through Miss Nannie Mimms, his wife's cousin, who also lived in Samuels Depot. The kind of letter he sent out ran like this:

> I will be at your house on [the date filled in].
> Respectfully,
> Joe

Translated, it meant: Meet me at Donnie Pence's on the date mentioned.

He moved south to Adairville, Kentucky, where his uncle, George Hite, lived, and enlisted two of Uncle George's sons, 'Wood' and Clarence. Robert Woodson Hite and Clarence Browler Hite: they were the only two cousins who ever rode with Jesse. If it has been written once it has been written ten thousand times that Bob Ford was Jesse's cousin; not true. The legend persists that the Youngers were also his cousins; not true. Just Wood and Clarence.

Now the band was beginning to shape up.

During this period while he was moving about Kentucky, Jesse kept playing tag with the law. There are a couple of good stories of how the grim game was played, always marked by Jesse's devil-may-care attitude and his extravagant sense of humor. One concerns Detective George Hunter.

Jesse knew that Hunter was after him. Once the detective had come close enough to find a warm bed that Jesse had just vacated, but he hadn't found Jesse, warm or cold. Jesse had an idea what the trouble was: Hunter didn't know what he looked like. So he wrote the detective a letter and explained this to him, and pointed out that he had an unfair advantage over Hunter, because *he* knew what Hunter looked like. To prove it, he described in the letter how, on a certain day at the gate of the Nelson County fair, he had walked right past Hunter, and he even gave the name of the man Hunter was talking to at the time.

Every word was true. It about drove the poor detective distracted.

An even better story involved the Pinkertons. Jesse got special pleasure out of taunting the renowned manhunters. One of the most famous of them was D. T. Bligh of Louisville, who had first gotten on Jesse's trail after the Russellville robbery in 1868, and joined up with the detective agency when the latter entered the chase. At this time he had just had a sensational success in apprehending a railroad robber, and now returned hopefully to the James Boys. He immediately began to have the trouble that all the Pinkertons were having; he didn't know what the brothers looked like. He believed, however, that they could be brought down through the routine of their daily habits. He interviewed people who claimed to know their ways and studied newspapers to establish their habits, but *alas!*, the Boys had no settled habits, so much were they on the move. In addition, Jesse and Frank took pains to know their pursuers by sight.

One day Jesse was in Louisville when he happened to see Bligh, no doubt hard upon his trail. Jesse spoke to him, a conversation sprang up, and Jesse invited him to have a drink; they went into the railroad station at Fourteenth and Main, and up to the bar. Jesse explained to him—with what must have been a private smile—that he was agent for a tombstone company. The conversation rippled along pleasantly.

There had been a recent robbery which the papers attributed to the Jameses. Bligh, hiding his identity, said, "I'd like to see Jesse James before I die."

They parted amiably and went their ways.

A few days later, Bligh received a postcard mailed in Baltimore (where Jesse had sent Zee) which reminded him of the drink at the railroad station, then continued, 'You have seen Jesse James. Now you can go ahead and die.' It was signed, 'Your friend, Jesse James.'

At last, three months after he and Frank had turned their backs on Nashville, Jesse felt he was ready. He gathered his band and made a quick foray into Missouri, where, at Winston on July 5, 1881, they held up a train. It didn't go so well. Two members of the train crew were killed and the take was small. The whole thing was badly handled and lacked the precision of the early robberies. Jesse was grim and there was no joking. It was a bad start—were his great days behind him? The men became difficult to handle; Frank seemed aloof.

He met Charlie Ford, who lived near Richmond, Missouri, in Ray County. Charlie wanted to join and Jesse accepted him. The Fords bore none-too-good a reputation, but he could no longer afford to be particular. Charlie might be just the man. And he began to hear about Charlie's younger brother, Bob, who was nineteen.

Without waiting for the cry to die down after the Winston robbery, without giving himself enough time to know the several new recruits who had come in or to plan properly, Jesse swept down on Blue Cut, Missouri. The day was prophetic—September 7, 1881, exactly five years after Northfield. Blue Cut, on the Chicago & Alton Railroad a few miles from Kansas City, was territory he knew well. The grain sack came out, passengers made their contributions, the men got on their horses and loped away . . . and, some time later, a posse thundered gently after them.

But only $1200 had been taken. On the whole, it was another botched job.

After the Winston and Blue Cut affairs the popular outcry went up once more, louder than ever. The James Boys must be captured. They were world-famous now; their very names struck terror, and anything that bore those names was news. Paperbacked books telling of their exploits tumbled off the presses. People tried to get into the spotlight by connecting themselves in any way they could with the Boys. One instance of this struck Jesse very close to the heart.

When, as a boy, Jesse had joined the guerrillas, one of his leaders had been George Shepherd. He had gone with Shepherd to Texas. Later, as Jesse rose in power, he had taken his former commander into the band and Shepherd had helped rob the bank at Russellville, Kentucky. But Shepherd had been captured and sent away to think it over. When he got out, after three years, Jesse had again taken him into his gang and Shepherd had participated in the Glendale train robbery.

One day Jesse picked up the paper and there, on the front page, was a news story telling how George Shepherd had killed him. Shepherd had given out an interview in which he told exactly how he had performed the deed. As the two were riding along a country road, Shepherd had dropped back, and when Jesse was a few feet ahead of him, he had fired and Jesse had tumbled off his horse.

Jesse could hardly believe his eyes, but there it was from his old guerrilla leader! Who could he trust?

Another and even more damaging result of their notoriety was that every train robbery, every bank holdup that occurred was being laid at their doorstep. Frequently robbers told their victims that they were the James gang. One day former Congressman Ben Johnson of Bardstown, Kentucky (who was ninety years old when he told the story for this book), went to Donnie Pence's home to hunt, as he did frequently. There he met a stranger and they were paired off together. The stranger was affable, and an excellent shot. Late afternoon the two returned to the house. In the meantime a newspaper had arrived; in it Mrs. Pence saw a news story. She handed the paper, with a significant glance, to her husband. He read, hesitated, then gave it to the affable stranger.

The news item told how, the day before, Jesse James had held up a train in Texas.

The stranger held the paper a long moment in his hand, thinking. Then he went to the window, took a diamond ring from his pocket, and scratched on the pane: *Jesse James, October 18, 1881.* Turning to the others, he said, "I want you to bear witness that I was here on this date and not in Texas."

After the Blue Cut robbery Jesse rode back to Kentucky, to Donnie's and to Uncle George's, where he felt safest. He had many friends in Missouri, but also enemies. In Kentucky he had both friends and relatives, but there were fewer people who knew him by sight. That reward was still on his head. And more trouble was on its way.

Clarence Hite was seized by the police (not the Pinkertons) at Adairville and brought back to Missouri, where he was accused of having taken part in the Winston and Blue Cut affairs. He confessed and stated that Jesse had been the leader in both cases, but this only harmed Jesse and did Clarence no good, for he was sentenced to twenty-five years in the penitentiary at Jefferson City.

It had always been felt by the James men that they had so many friends in Missouri that no member of their gang would ever be convicted. That no enemy would dare to testify against them. Now they realized how long it was since the Border days, how much times had changed. Bill Ryan finally came to trial, and joined Clarence Hite in the same place and for the same length of time.

The dark shadows were lengthening. Harder than ever to keep together and to control after the failures at Winston and Blue Cut were Jesse's men. The fear of being shot for the reward became more and more vivid to him, and he and his companions began to live in an atmosphere of mutual suspicion. One of these companions was Ed Miller, the brother of Clell Miller who was hanging on a hook in a doctor's office. Evidence shows that Ed had $600 stowed away and wanted to quit. Be that as it may, Jesse and Ed went out riding. Only Jesse came back. He had shot and killed Ed Miller and left his body beside the road. At such times he was hard and merciless; he felt Ed was turning traitor, so he shot him without compunction.

Now even Jesse could see that it was time for him to have a change of scenery.

XVI

JESSE JAMES MOVES TO ST. JOSEPH, MO.

JESSE had sent his wife from Nashville to Baltimore, but she apparently remained there only a brief time, for it is known that she was with him in Kentucky. She did not stay in Kentucky long, either; soon she and the two children left for Kansas City. It was there that Jesse joined them. For a while he conducted himself as he always did after a new move, becoming a member of the community and acting as any unhunted person would. One of his neighbors was a county marshal named Cornelius Murphy; he paid a call and said he was organizing a posse to hunt Jesse James and would Mr. Howard help? Mr. Howard solemnly asked what Jesse James looked like, then said:

"I don't believe I can go, as I had planned to stay with my family this evening. But I'll watch and if I see him, I'll let you know."

Marshal Murphy thanked the kindly Mr. Howard and went away. Mr. Howard watched very carefully for Jesse James but did not see him.

But Jesse realized that he was too near home and that somebody might recognize him at any time, so he gave up the Kansas City place and, putting Tim and little Mary in a two-horse covered wagon, started for St. Joseph, Missouri, about sixty miles away.

St. Joseph was a booming, prosperous city with a population of 40,000. In the old days the covered wagons had started from there to California; herds of cattle had been driven from St. Joseph by foot all the way across the plains. The place had been settled by Joseph Robidoux (pronounced by the people of St. Joseph 'Roobidoo'), who had thirteen children and had named a street for each one. It was here that the Pony Express riders, twenty years before, had leaped on their horses and raced to the Missouri River, where they were rowed across, and on the Kansas side had leaped on again and continued until they reached Sacramento, California. Jesse could crane his neck out his window and see the Pony Express barns where the horses were kept. It was an interesting, an exciting city . . . and it was soon to become even more interesting.

Jesse had been known in Tennessee and in other states as 'J. D. Howard,' but here he changed his alias to 'Tom Howard.' His wife called him 'Dave,' while he had a number of names for her—'Mary,' 'Kate,' sometimes whatever he could think of at the moment.

They arrived November 8, 1881, and rented a house on the corner of Lafayette and Twenty-first Streets. There they stayed a little over six weeks, then moved a few blocks away to a house at 1318 Lafayette Street, which was owned by a member of the City Council and for which they paid $14 a month. It was not much trouble to move, for all the household articles they owned were the ones they could carry in a two-horse wagon.

They moved in on Christmas Eve. Everywhere in town were signs of Christmas preparations, everywhere except in their house. Jesse looked at the children he loved so much. They must have some kind of Christmas Eve. But what? They could hang up their stockings, but there should be something more.

There was to be a Christmas-tree party at the Presbyterian church where toys, popcorn balls, and candy would be given away. Jesse went to the church to see if he could get some Christmas things, and, there in the basement, saw some suits to be worn by the Santa Clauses, and there, also, were whisker sets, made chiefly out of baling wire and bindertwine. An idea came to him. He took one of the outfits home, got the presents they had bought for the children, and then, dressed-up like a jolly Santa Claus, came into the room. The children were awed—Santa Claus had actually come to see them. Changing his voice to a deep note he said, "Tim, have you been a good boy this year?"

"Yes, Santa Claus," the lad quavered, trembling with excitement.

"Mary, have you been a good girl?"

"Yes, Santa Claus."

He pulled the presents from his pack and gave them to the delighted children, and a fine, lovely spirit vibrated in the room. Tim came closer and, boylike, wanted to know if there was anything else for him. He began to feel of the bag, hopping joyfully around; suddenly he stopped with a mystified expression on his face. His little fingers had come upon his father's revolvers.

"You're not Santa Claus," he wailed; "you're only my pa."

Jesse took him into his arms and tried to comfort him, saying he was just helping Santa Claus tonight, that Santa Claus himself would bring other presents and for him and Mary to go to bed and be good children. Then the father hurried back to the church and returned the suit and whiskers before the regular distribution of presents began.

The house was on the very crest of a sharp hill; anyone approaching it was laboring uphill. It commanded a view on all sides. It was known as the 'House on the Hill.' From this vantage point Jesse could keep an eye on approaching visitors. He had to be constantly on the alert.

One day, watching through the partly drawn blinds, he saw a man coming toward the house, followed by other men, all looking with close scrutiny. He recognized the leader as the chief of police in St. Joseph. In addition to his pistols, Jesse had in the house a rifle and a shotgun; he got the rifle and waited, silently peeping out the window.

The man stood for some moments at the board fence, talking to those behind him. Then he started on again. The decision saved his life, for if he had come into the yard he would have died—ironically, since he was merely showing some out-of-town visitors the city and had stopped to point out the House on the Hill with the wooden fence around. A close call.

In the rear of the house was a small abutment of the hill where a cave-stable had been dug, roofed over with boards. In this the new occupant kept two horses, one always saddled and bridled. Mr. Howard was a cattle buyer. The neighbors could understand this; the country was filled with cattle buyers and not too far away were the stockyards.

The record also shows that he thought of returning once again to farming, for he went to see a farm at Pawnee, Nebraska, and later received two letters from the agent. Since he was too poor to buy, he planned to rent; but he could not get around the fact that he would need a good deal of money for equipment. The project died. It was clearer than ever that, for Jesse, there could be only one line of business.

He preferred to hide in large cities because he could lose himself in the community, acting like any ordinary citizen. It is known that he joined the Presbyterian church, which was located near the World's Hotel. His name appears in the city directory for 1882; it was given as Thomas Howard and the address was the House on the Hill. Under 'occupation' he gave no information.

What else do we know of him during this period of marking time, of trouble and depression, of black moods alternating with lightheartedness? That he took increasing pleasure in his children, for one thing. Jesse Junior was seven, and little Mary three, old enough to be more than babes-in-arms to the lonely man watching from the house. He would never correct them and was inclined to let them do anything they wished. Their proper rearing and guidance fell on his courageous wife. Sometimes he told her she was too hard on them.

The stories that have come down reveal that during this trying time there still were flashes of the fun-loving, lighthearted farmboy. Once he had to go to the Union Depot in St. Joseph to make an inquiry of some kind. In the course of conversation, the station manager asked him what kind of business he was in and Jesse said solemly, "In the railroad business."

Later the man said he had noticed that the tip of Jesse's finger was missing and had believed what Jesse had said, for at this time it was the custom to give soft jobs to men who had been mutilated by the railroads.

Jesse liked to play pool. One night one of the customers said, "I've been reading about the number of robberies they've been having here in St. Joe and I'm kind of nervous tonight."

"Why?" asked Jesse.

"Because this was payday and I'm scary about walking home in the dark."

"Have you got your pay on you?" asked Jesse, instantly interested.

"Yes, I have," replied the man.

"Do you want me to walk home with you?" asked Jesse.

"I wish you would," said the man delightedly. "Then I would feel safe."

In a few moments the two started out—Jesse and his pay-packed friend—and the man got home safely, not losing a single penny.

Then Jesse must have heard the story that was running around the pool halls of St. Joe, and though he never told bawdy stories himself he wouldn't have been human if he hadn't enjoyed this one.

According to the tale, Jesse and his comrades held up a train in a rather remote section. They had taken care of the express car and were starting back to work through the passengers. Among the latter were a minister and an old maid.

Edging up to her so that the bandits could not hear, the preacher said: "Jesse James is coming. He is a bad man and will seize you and rape you. You have just time to get away. Go as fast as you can out into the weeds and hide."

The old maid delayed.

"Run!" ordered the minister.

"Stop," said the old maid sternly. "Jesse James is the one who's running things here."

XVII

THE BETRAYAL OF JESSE JAMES

AT LAST Mr. Howard, the cattle buyer and Presbyterian communicant of St. Joseph, Mo., began definitely to look for a bank to rob. First he decided to make a tour and examine the possibilities in the area, and he took along with him his friend, the ingratiating Charlie Ford, whom he liked.

In Graham, Missouri, lived a blacksmith named Uriah Bond, whose sons had gone to school with Frank and Jesse. Mr. Bond was a Northerner and in the guerrilla days his son John Bond had joined the Home Guards and done all he could to help capture the James brothers. At one point he returned home on a furlough, not realizing the mistake he was making. The Jameses learned he was in the neighborhood; they crept up to the house and killed John Bond.

The father moved away from Kearney and came to Graham, and there established his blacksmith shop.

One day Jesse James and Charlie Ford stopped in the town and Jesse asked where he could get a shoe for his horse tightened, a comparatively simple matter. He was told where the blacksmith shop was and rode up to it. Uriah Bond, in his leather apron, came to the door, then stared at his customer in bewilderment. Here was Jesse James, the leader of the gang that had murdered his son.

"I want a shoe tightened," said Jesse, finally.

Mr. Bond proceeded to do this, neither speaking during the time.

Jesse paid him, then said in a cold, hard voice, "Mum is the word for you."

He went back to Charlie Ford and the two rode away.

So dangerous was Jesse James that Mr. Bond never mentioned the incident until—as he phrased it—"Jesse James was on the cooling board."

Jesse and Ford visited the following towns to see about opening a bank: Humboldt, Nebraska; Forest City, Missouri; Oregon, Missouri; Sebetha, Kansas; Hiawatha, Kansas; and Troy, Kansas.

At Forest City the situation looked so inviting that Jesse said they would rob the bank that very day. But Charlie Ford didn't at the moment feel well enough to take part in it, so the robbery had to be given up.

At Troy the two tied their horses behind the building of Boder Brothers, bankers, then walked up and down the streets getting an idea of the town. Jesse himself went into the bank; laying a hundred-dollar bill on the counter, he said, "Can you oblige me by changing this?"

Louis Boder cast one glance at the bearded face. "I'm sorry, but our funds have been locked up for the night."

Jesse hesitated, trying to determine whether or not this was true; then, deciding it was, he walked out. A few minutes later the two got on their horses and rode away. The bank had come that near to being robbed; only Louis Boder's quick thinking had saved it. Several people, before he left, recognized Jesse, but so greatly did they fear him that none felt the urge to get on horses and clamber after him.

And now there came into his life a boy whom he hardly knew.

You have to go back a little way to get a true picture of Bob Ford's relations with Jesse. He was fifteen years younger. He had been born in Virginia, but when still a boy had moved to Ray County, not far from where the James family dwelt. (He lived for a short while at the Seybold Tavern, about a mile and a half from Excelsior Springs, which during the Gold Rush days had been a favorite stopping place for California-bound travelers; it still stands.)

Bob Ford heard the James Boys talked about constantly, and he became obsessed with the idea of capturing them. Other boys in the neighborhood liked to play 'stick horse,' but he wanted to play 'capturing robbers.' He envisioned himself as a great hero. And while he was growing up there occurred an incident which prevented this boyish ambition from disappearing in the natural course of time.

Jesse had discovered that Jim Cummins was proving untrustworthy, and decided to deal with him as he had with Ed Miller. He thought that Cummins was at the home of Bob Ford's father, and there he went. Albert Ford, a fifteen-year-old cousin of Bob, was there. Jesse asked him where Cummins was. Albert didn't know, but Jesse thought he was withholding the truth and slapped and knocked the boy roughly about before he rode away.

Young Bob Ford seized on this. To killing Jesse for glory

was now added the element of killing to satisfy a grudge. And in time, as Bob grew older, he began to think, too, about that huge reward on Jesse's head.

In the summer of 1881 Charlie Ford joined Jesse's band. From time to time he would mention he had a younger brother who was anxious to ride with the Boys.

Then, during the first week in December, 1881, occurred something which turned the paths of Bob Ford and Jesse still more sharply toward each other. Bob had a sister, Mrs. Martha Bolton, whose reputation was not as white as a heavenly dove. In point of fact, she was living with Dick Liddil. The two of them were together on Martha's farm near Richmond, Missouri, at the time, which was three months after the Blue Cut robbery. Also there were Wood Hite, who had come from Kentucky, and Bob Ford.

On the morning of December 4th Dick and Wood began to quarrel over the way the Blue Cut money had been divided. Dick said that Wood had grabbed off $100 too much; Wood said he hadn't and called Dick a liar, something that should be done only after prolonged thought. Breakfast was soon a feast of lead, Dick and Wood serving each other. But they fetched only wounds. Then Bob Ford, who had nothing to do with the matter at all, hauled out his gun and killed Wood Hite.

Killing a cousin of Jesse James could not under any circumstances be thought of as a prescription for attaining great age. Bob, however, got out of the difficulty with the help of an older brother (not Charlie); the two of them carried the body, wrapped in a horse blanket, into the woods about half a mile from the house, and buried it in an abandoned well with rocks thrown on top of it. Then Bob calmly went his way.

The killing remained a secret from Jesse. The only other

people who knew about it were Dick Liddil and his mistress, and the effect of the incident was therefore to draw Dick and Bob close together. The former had always been a weak link in the gang. Now the link snapped. He made a deal with Bob, and threw in with the latter's plan to murder Jesse.

The ambitious young killer set about his task in earnest. He went first to Kansas City, where he saw the police and got himself appointed a detective. This would protect him and put the intended killing in the proper legal line of duty. Then he cast about for some way of assuring himself that what he was to do would also receive a proper reward.

Missouri had a governor who saw the political possibilities of cleaning up the Jesse James gang. It'd elect him to a later term, he figured. A fashionable ball was being held in Kansas City in honor of Craig's Rifles, a carryover from the Civil War. Governor T. T. Crittenden attended. Then, after the ball, he had a secret meeting with Bob Ford, at one o'clock in the morning at the St. James Hotel in Kansas City, and there gave what amounted to official sanction of the murder of Jesse James. Hard words, but true ones. The date was January 13, 1882. No one was present at the meeting but the two; later, however, Ford on the witness stand swore to what had been said.

During the talk, Governor Crittenden promised to pay $10,000 dead or alive for each of the James Boys.

Bob Ford had a favor to ask for putting Jesse away—pardon for Dick Liddil. And Governor Crittenden promised it. What a horse-swapping that was!

Governor Crittenden then told Ford to report to the chief of police in Kansas City and to the sheriff of Clay County, advising them of the situation.

Ford had everything set now, except that he didn't know where Jesse was. He might as well have been a Pinkerton. Then the final stitch in the pattern was taken.

Jesse was planning another robbery, but he had only one person to help him and that was the weakling, Charlie Ford. So he asked Ford where he could get another man and Ford suggested his brother Bob.

The two decided to ride to Richmond and see Bob, but when they got there they found that he was at the home of his uncle in another county, so back to their horses went Jesse and Charlie. They finally reached the place at night, and shouted for Bob to come out. He knew his brother's voice and realized Jesse must be with him. He trembled . . . had Jesse found out? But still, his brother was with Jesse.

He came forth frightened and shaking—and heard fine news indeed. Jesse was there in front of him, and was asking him if he would help rob a bank.

Bob said he would be glad to help.

When he had a chance he took his brother aside and told him that he intended to kill Jesse. Charlie was shocked, but there was the reward money and the honor of doing what the detectives had failed to do; finally he told Bob he would come in with him.

Next Jesse and the plotting brothers rode to Jesse's mother's at Kearney, where they found strange horses in the barn. John Samuels had just been shot at a party and was near death; friends of his had come in to sit up with him, as was then the custom. So Jesse and the two Fords hid in the barn until the others left at daylight.

Then Jesse brought his fine friends in.

They had breakfast, then Bob went upstairs to bed in the

room with the grim loopholes. Charlie slept in the same bed with Jesse in the big room downstairs. The bed is still there . . . it gives one a grisly feeling to look at it.

His mother, who was more astute as a reader of character, warned Jesse against Bob Ford. "I mistrust him," she said.

Jesse thought she was prejudiced. He knew more than she did about Bob Ford—wasn't Bob going to help him?

Premonition hung over his mother that all was not well, and some of her feeling must have been communicated to Jesse, for when the moment of parting came, he looked at the house where he had played as a child and said, "Mother, if I never see you here again, we'll meet in Heaven." He meant it, for his religion never deserted him.

The three left at night; the next morning they moved into a patch of timber. That evening they had supper at the farm of Jesse's half-sister, Sallie Samuels Nicholson, then started on again. The following night they stayed in a church eighteen miles from St. Joseph.

Jesse's wife had been waiting for him in the lonely, forever fear-ridden House on the Hill. She was thunderstruck when she saw Jesse ride up with a new bandit. It was always happening—these terrible men who came so suddenly into her life.

He introduced the new man. He was a brother of Charlie's and was all right.

The house had two bedrooms and the brothers were put into one; she and Jesse had the other. Jesse locked the door, kept the windows down, and slept with a revolver under his pillow.

The next morning Zee prepared breakfast and the three men sat down. Jesse treated the children affectionately, as he always did. Charlie Ford, looking at the little family scene, had such thoughts of his own that he could not eat. Jesse laughed at him and twitted him for having a small appetite, but could not rally Charlie into eating. Bob Ford ate stolidly on.

There was a problem about having three able-bodied, unemployed men around the house, and Jesse said they must not all be seen in the yard at one time. So Zee had them in the house with her, except sometimes in the evening when Bob Ford would go out by himself. Jesse read the St. Joseph, Kansas City, and Chicago papers; also, sometimes, one from Jefferson City. Often there was news about himself . . . where he had performed a robbery, or had been seen; also news of where the police were searching for him.

To make it safer for the Fords, they were to be called Johnson. Bob and Charlie Johnson.

Bob Ford complained that his revolver wasn't good enough. Jesse gave him another.

Charlie Ford said that his horse was skittish. Jesse turned up a couple of days later with a horse and gave it to him.

After his first revulsion at the foul deed they were planning to do, Charlie Ford had fewer and fewer qualms. Bob Ford's confidence grew. He sent word to the chief of police in Kansas City he would have Jesse inside of ten days. The word went on to the governor and the governor rejoiced.

There were constant little dramas in the House on the Hill. Before Bob Ford had joined Jesse he had gone to Kansas City to confer with Police Commissioner Henry Craig. They had slept in the same room and their drawers had become exchanged. One day, to help Zee out, Bob washed his underclothes; after they had dried he spread them on the bed in his room. Jesse, coming in, gave them a glance, then came back and looked again, for on them were the initials 'H. C.'

"What does that stand for?" he asked suspiciously.

Ford was stunned. He did some quick thinking. "Why," he said, "I found them in a hotel."

"Oh!" said Jesse, satisfied with the explanation.

Later on Ford stated, "It made me exceedingly nervous."

Time was moving along. Jesse decided on the bank at Platte City, Missouri, only a few miles from St. Joseph. A murder trial was in progress; the people would be in the courthouse. And he further decided to do something he had never done before: to kill the cashier whether or not he offered resistance. Coldbloodedly he told Bob Ford to get him a butcher knife. When they got to the town, Bob was to hold the horses, Charlie was to guard the streets, and Jesse himself was to go in, seize the cashier, and cut his throat. It was horrible. It was a new and desperate Jesse.

In the meantime Dick Liddil, who had heard through Bob that if he turned state's evidence against Jesse he would be pardoned by Governor Crittenden, had surrendered. The news of his arrest had not been published; it was being suppressed until Jesse could be taken.

Then it came out anyway. Jesse was reading one of his newspapers when he ran across the startling news. Bob Ford was in the room at the time, and Jesse asked him casually, "By the way, Bob, where is Dick Liddil?"

"I don't know."

Jesse knew that Bob had Liddil's confidence; he realized now that he had a traitor in his home. Bob caught his look.

Bob at once became afraid to go on the bank expedition, for he believed that as soon as it was over Jesse would kill him. Later he said, "I think Jesse would have killed me, then and there, but he did not want to in front of his family."

After a few moments they began to talk about the robbery and how they would carry it out. It was Sunday; on Monday Bob Ford would buy the butcher knife and that afternoon they would ride toward Platte City. Monday night they would hide in the woods. Tuesday morning, when court was in session, the three would descend on the bank.

That night the three men sat around talking as if nothing had happened; finally Jesse went to bed, locking the door to his room. The house was peaceful and quiet. It was Sunday night.

The time was the first week in April. Sometimes, in this part of the Missouri River Valley, there is a kind of rehearsal of spring, and so there was this year, 1882. Monday morning was balmy and there was the lazy feel that comes with this first promise of summer.

Zee James served breakfast in the kitchen. Jesse and Charlie went to the stable and fed and curried the two horses, which had stood all night bridled and saddled. Bob remained with Jesse's wife, playing with the children.

The two came in from the stable, talking casually. Charlie stopped in the kitchen, but Jesse walked on through to the front room, which faced on the street. In the room was a bed, really a cot.

On the wall was hanging the picture of a racehorse named 'Skyrocket'; picking up a featherduster, Jesse started toward it. "It's awfully hot today," he said, and taking off his coat and vest, tossed them on the bed. Then he opened the street door and started to mount the chair to dust the pictures. "If anybody passes they'll see me," he said, so he unstrapped the holster in which he carried two .45-caliber revolvers, one a Smith & Wesson, the other a Colt, and put it on the bed. Then he went back, mounted the chair, and raised both hands above his head to take hold of the picture frame.

From the kitchen the two Fords saw him. This was the moment they had been waiting for. Charlie winked at Bob, who casually strolled in and managed to place himself between Jesse and the bed. He was now behind Jesse. He drew his revolver and cocked it. Slight as the sound was, Jesse heard and started to turn to see what had caused it. Bob was about five feet away; he extended his arm with the revolver in his hand until it was about three feet from Jesse. It was the revolver Jesse had given him.

Jesse was knocked forward by the impact but regained himself; he began to weave back and forth. Then he fell on the uncarpeted floor.

The two Fords stood over him a moment, each with gun in hand, to make sure the deed had been accomplished. Then Bob seized his and Charlie's hat and the two ran out into the yard.

Zee came in and saw the body of her husband on the floor and the two men fleeing. "What have you done?" she screamed. "Bob, have you done this?" she cried in agonized tones.

Bob paused in his flight. "I swear to God I didn't."

"A pistol went off accidentally," explained Charlie.

The two men leaped over the wooden fence and ran down the street as fast as they could, leaving her alone with Jesse.

She picked him up and held him in her arms. He tried to speak, but the effort was too great. The children came in, and at sight of their father began to scream. Leaving Jesse on the floor, she went to the kitchen and got a cloth and with it tried to wipe the blood away, but it was running too fast.

The two Fords hurried to the telegraph office and sent three telegrams announcing the good news. The first was to Governor Crittenden in Jefferson City, another was to the chief of police in Kansas City, and the third was to the sheriff of Clay

County. Then they went to City Marshal Enos Craig's office to surrender, but found him gone, so they went to a deputy marshal, Frank M. Lovejoy, and gave themselves up. Soon they could collect the reward.

Word had gone out that 'a man' had been killed at Lafayette and Thirteenth Street. The coroner left for the house, accompanied by a reporter. When he arrived he found curious neighbors collected in the yard, silently looking at the house and asking each other what had occurred. He opened the front door and went in and there, lying on the floor, was the body of an unknown man. In the next room the coroner could hear the wailing of children; opening the door, he came upon a woman and two children. When the woman saw the coroner and the reporter, with notepaper in hand, she began to sob, saying, "Please don't put it in the paper."

At first she refused to tell anything about the shooting. "What is your name?" asked the coroner.

"Howard."

"Who is this man?"

"My husband."

"Who killed him?"

"Two boys named Johnson."

"Where are they?"

"They jumped over the fence and ran away."

"Had your husband and the Johnson boys had trouble?"

"No. They have always been on friendly terms."

"Why did they kill him?"

"I don't know. . . ." She began to weep and the children, seeing their mother crying, joined in.

The coroner asked her to tell exactly what had happened, and she began to describe the dreadful events of the morning.

As they were talking, the Ford boys reached the house and gave themselves up. "Do you know who the man is?" asked the marshal.

"It is Jesse James," one of them said.

"My God!" said the marshal, "do you mean this is the famous outlaw?"

"Yes," said both boys at once. "We have killed him and we won't deny it. We feel proud we have killed an outlaw known over the whole world."

Leaving the Fords standing in the yard, the marshal went in and said he wanted to talk to Zee alone. Taking her into a bedroom he said, "Your name is not Howard. That man is Jesse James and you are his wife."

She began to sob afresh, saying over and over her name was Howard. "I can't help what they say, I have told the truth," she sobbed.

"Come to the window with me," said the marshal, and led her through the room where Jesse was lying; he took her to the window and pointed to the Fords.

"Oh, have they come back?" she cried. She began to call them cowards.

"Is it true that he is Jesse James?" the marshal pressed.

"What will become of my children?"

"Is that Jesse James? You must answer."

"Yes," she choked, "and a kinder-hearted and truer man to his family never lived."

The reporter went out into the yard and interviewed the two Fords. "Why did you do it?"

"We wanted to rid the country of an outlaw. You never expected to see Jesse James's dead body in St. Joe, did you?"

The men still had their arms and now these were taken from

them. Bob Ford handed over the revolver that Jesse had given him less than a week before.

By this time the Ford brothers were tired and worn out from the morning's activities, so they were taken to the marshal's headquarters where they were given a hearty dinner.

XVIII

HIS WIDOW TESTIFIES

THE murder was a sensation. People were stunned. Would his friends come to reap vengeance on the killers? Was any home safe? Where was Frank James? What would he do?

The morbid and curious filled the yard, trying to peer in the windows, asking each other over and over, "Is it really Jesse?" Many were doubtful. They had believed Jesse had been killed by George Shepherd, only to find later that he was very much alive and kicking. Furthermore, on that same day, April 3rd, there was a dispatch in the papers telling how Jesse James had robbed a stage in Texas.

The coroner, his inspection completed, notified Undertaker Sidenfaden, who came shortly after ten o'clock and bore the body away in a black hearse. Crowds followed it.

Those who caught a glimpse of the dead Jesse saw a man of thirty-five with a pug nose and high cheekbones. The blue eyes, which had become larger and deeper-set with age, were now closed. He was neatly dressed, as he always was; in fact, according to the standards of the day, he was a dandy. His hair was black, but his beard was sandy-colored. It was neatly trimmed. Many, commenting on his appearance, said he looked like a doctor, for at this time it was a common practice for doctors to wear trimmed beards.

At the undertaker's the coroner ordered a medical inspection. It was revealed that Bob Ford's bullet had entered the head behind the right ear, had ranged upward, and had passed out over the left eye, near the temple, and on into the wall. The examination further revealed two old bullet holes in Jesse's right breast and one in the fleshy part of his right thigh—the only wounds he had ever received in the course of his nearly twenty years of guerrilla fighting and banditry.

Young James W. Graham had just gotten a job as photographer for a firm in St. Joseph. On the second day of his job, the startling word reached the studio that Jesse James had been killed. It seemed improbable, but he would see what he could get in the way of pictures. He obtained an order from the city marshal and went to the undertaker's. The coroner was still viewing the body. When he had finished, Graham went into the back room and set up his camera on a drygoods box. He had a photographic dry plate in a studio camera, 8 x 10, but there was only a single plate-holder, for the double plate-holder had not yet come onto the market.

The body was carried into the room on a board, but it could not be photographed in that position, so the young photographer and the undertaker's assistant put a rope around the body, under the arms, and tied it to the board. They then stood the body as nearly upright as they could and the picture was made. It now is famous.

When he was through, Graham started to the studio to develop the plate. People were so eager to get a picture of Jesse James that they followed him there and waited while the plate was developed and the prints made.

(When Jesse's picture was published, Judge Rowntree, who had been robbed on the Mammoth Cave stagecoach, stared very hard indeed; here was the man to whom he had entrusted his watch. T. J. Hunt had just been tried and given three years in the state penitentiary. Judge Rowntree stirred himself and a motion for a new trial was entered, with the result that the governor of Kentucky granted Hunt a full pardon.)

At three o'clock that afternoon the inquest testimony was begun in the old circuit courtroom in the courthouse. Two juries were prepared. There was a good deal of wrangling among politicians and petty officials, but finally one was selected, and the widow, who had left her children with a neighbor, was brought in. She was rather goodlooking, with blue eyes and brown hair and had a nice figure.

The Fords—armed—were brought in and placed opposite her. At sight of them, she began to weep. The coroner waited until she had possession of herself again, then began to question her. Here follows, in part, the official record as taken down in shorthand:

Question. What is your name?
Answer. Mrs. Jesse James.
Q. How long have you lived here?
A. Since the 9th of last November.
Q. How long have you lived at the place where your husband was killed?
A. Since Christmas Eve.
Q. Where were you born?
A. In Kentucky.
Q. What is your age?
A. Thirty-five years.

Q. When were you married?
A. Eight years ago, April 24th.
Q. Whereabouts?
A. Kearney, Missouri.
Q. Well now, Mrs. James, begin when you were married and tell us where you first went to and where you have been, up to this time.
A. We first went to Texas.
Q. How long did you live there?
A. About five months.
Q. Where did you go after that?
A. Kansas City.
Q. How long did you live there?
A. Until the next November. From the time I went there it was about a year.
Q. Mrs. James, what year was that?
A. I don't remember.
Q. About what date?
A. I can not remember the date.
Q. Where did you go after that?
A. Went to Nashville, Tennessee.
Q. How long did you live there?
A. Until last March.
Q. Where did you go then?
A. Went visiting friends in Kentucky.
Q. Who was the party that married you?
A. William James.
Q. Who was he?
A. A Methodist preacher.
Q. Where did he live?
A. In Kansas City.

Q. Were you married in Kansas City?

A. No, sir, in Kearney.

Q. Did he come from Kansas City to marry you?

A. Yes, sir.

Q. What induced you to come to St. Joseph?

A. We came here to live as other people do.

Q. Has he always been at home?

A. Except two weeks he went to Kearney to see his half-brother, then went up into Nebraska.

Q. How many brothers has your husband?

A. One full brother and one half-brother.

Q. Where was he at the time you speak of his being away from home and what was he doing?

A. He was in Nebraska looking to see if he could get a place. He wanted to go to farming. Wanted to find some place to work to make a living.

Q. Had he ever been wounded before?

A. Yes, sir.

Q. Whereabouts on the body?

A. On the right side. Two on the right side, I believe, and one in the leg.

Q. Where was he wounded at, what place and where?

A. Well, some time during the war. I don't know where.

Q. Was he disfigured any way?

A. No, sir, I believe not.

Q. In his hands, I mean, any wound?

A. Yes, sir, he had one finger shot off. I don't remember which one; it was some one of the middle fingers.

Q. How was his mail directed?
A. To Thomas Howard.
Q. Where was this mail from?
A. He never received any except from Nebraska. From an agent in regard to a place he wanted to get.
Q. What was the object in killing your husband?
A. I don't know, sir, unless it was for the reward, that is all I can think of.
Q. At the time your husband went to Nebraska, did these boys go along?
A. Charlie went.

The strain began to prove too much and the coroner, seeing how she was suffering, told her she could step down. She was helped out of the room by Marshal Enos Craig.

Bob Ford was brought to the witness stand. He entered it confidently, feeling certain of the sympathy of the crowd. He was short, with blond hair and blue eyes, and wore a gray coat and vest and green-striped trousers.

Question. What is your name?
Answer. Robert Ford.
Q. How old are you?
A. Twenty years old.
Q. Where do you live?
A. Two miles north of Richmond, Ray County, Missouri.
Q. How long have you lived there?
A. Four years.
Q. When you left Richmond where did you go?
A. I joined the detective force and had a conversation with Governor Crittenden.

Q. When was that?
A. The 13th of January, 1882.
Q. What was the conversation?
A. I told him I was willing to look for the James outlaws, and he referred me to Captain Craig of Kansas City and Sheriff Timberlake of Clay County.
Q. Were you to look for them as a detective?
A. Yes, sir.
Q. Did you know anything about them?
A. I had known him for about three years.
Q. Did you know where the Jameses were when you were talking to Governor Crittenden?
A. No, sir.
Q. You offered to go in as a detective?
A. I knew them when I saw them.
Q. When you had this conversation with Governor Crittenden, what was said?
A. He asked me if I thought I could assist the officers to catch the outlaws. I told him I thought I could. I was also trying to get a pardon for Dick Liddil. He promised to give it to me.
Q. What did you tell Jesse you were with him for?
A. I told him I was going in with him.
Q. What arms did he have?
A. He owned a .45 caliber Colt and one .45 caliber Smith & Wesson.
Q. Any other arms?
A. One breech-loading, double-barreled shotgun and a Winchester rifle.
Q. Is there any doubt about this being Jesse James?
A. I think not. He told me himself that he was Jesse James.

Q. Did you hear any of the Samuels family calling him by name?
A. They called him Dave. That was his nickname. They never called him anything but Dave.
Q. Do you know anyone that can identify him?
A. Yes, sir. Sheriff Timberlake can when he comes; he was with him during the war.
Q. Have you any arms on your person now?
A. Yes, sir, by permission of the policeman.

While Ford was on the stand, two telegrams addressed to him were received. One was from the commissioner of police in Kansas City—his old underwear friend. It bubbled over with enthusiasm: 'Will come on the first train. Hurrah for you.'

The second was from the chief of police in Kansas City: 'What time did you get him, and where?'

The crowd had had time to study Ford and now seemed to realize what a traitorous thing he had done, and as he withdrew from the witness stand there were mutterings of disapproval.

After she had revived, Zee James got the children and took them home with her; they did not stay overnight in the death house, but at a neighbor's.

She had sent a telegram to Jesse's mother. Twenty-four hours after the murder Mrs. Samuels arrived by train. The word had spread and a great crowd was at the depot. They saw a large woman with blue eyes, high cheekbones, and a lined, careworn face—this woman who, so many years ago in Kentucky, had been a tobacco bride. She was greatly agitated and she was indignant, for she was a warrior and had the hot temper that had gone straight down to Jesse.

She was taken to the undertaker's and admitted to what was called the 'cooling room.' (At that time undertakers did not have preservative fluids; bodies were 'iced.') She swayed rather than walked to the slab, and stood silently gazing at the body. Then she began to sob so convulsively that it shook her entire frame. "Yes, it is my son," she moaned. "Jesse! Jesse! They have taken you from me. The miserable traitors!"

She was led out, still sobbing, and put in a carriage and taken to the courthouse where the coroner's jury was waiting. "Hold up your right hand and be sworn," said the coroner. She held up the stump.

Question. What is your name?
Answer. Zerelda Samuels.
Q. Where is your residence, where do you live?
A. Clay County.
Q. In this state?
A. Yes, sir; three miles from Kearney station.
Q. What is your age?
A. Fifty-seven years.
Q. Are you the mother of Jesse James?
A. I am. Oh God!

She began to sob and it was some moments before the coroner could continue.

Q. Do you know where he is now?
A. I just saw him—his body.
Q. When?
A. A few minutes ago.
Q. Whereabouts?
A. In the undertaker's place.

Q. Did you recognize that he be the body of your son?
A. Yes, sir.
Q. There is no doubt about it?
A. Would to God there was. [Sobbing.]
Q. Mrs. Samuels, who is the lady by your side?
A. That is my son's wife. Jesse's wife and his poor little children. Oh God! [Sobs.]
The court. That will do.

Mrs. Samuels stood up to go, taller than any man near her. Suddenly she saw Dick Liddil and her face became inflamed with feeling. Raising her empty sleeve she started toward him as if to strike him, crying out: "Oh you coward! You did all this; you brought all this about. Look at me, you traitor. Look upon me, the broken mother and on this poor wife and her children. It would be better if you were in the cooler where my boy is, than here looking at me. With the coward you are, God will have vengeance."

So violent was she that Dick Liddil—the train robber—cowered away from her, whining, "I did not kill him. I thought you knew who did it." Covering his face with his hat, he slunk down in his seat.

The officers, taking her by the arm, got her out—still shrilly protesting—and into a carriage.

Zee, Jesse's mother, and the children went to the house. Mrs. Samuels stood in the room where the cowardly deed had been committed and looked at the spots on the floor and at the hole in the wall. But there were many things to do; souvenir hunters had been busy. The following articles had been taken: two revolvers, a rifle, and shotguns; two watches, two chains, a diamond ring, a gold ring, a breast-pin belonging to Zee, a pair of cuff-buttons and a coral set of shirt studs used by Jesse, and a tiepin with his initials on it. In addition, Zee had a set of earrings. One was gone.

The two women moved a wooden box into the middle of the floor and began putting the household articles into it. Jesse was so poor that their possessions would have to be sold at public auction—that is, everything the police and souvenir hunters hadn't got. During the packing Mrs. Samuels stopped, wiped her eyes, and cried, "The traitors! Why did they murder him? Ten days ago he was alive and at my home."

The children had been taught to call Charlie Ford 'Cousin Charlie.' Jesse Junior found a pair of blue spectacles that Ford sometimes had worn as a matter of disguise, and brought them to her and said, "Grandma, Cousin Charlie used to wear these."

"Don't call him your cousin!" she cried. "He was a traitor." Seizing the glasses she threw them angrily into the box.

By six o'clock the work was finished; the two women got supper and put the children to bed in the house with their father's blood on the floor. The following day they moved into the World's Hotel, where they waited until the body of their son and husband could be returned to them.

The police of St. Joseph and Kansas City began to quarrel over the body. Each set said they ought to have charge of it and began to give out interviews denouncing the absurd claims of the other. It about sickens one on the human race.

At last the governor telegraphed that the body was to be turned over to the wife and mother. Then he started by train for St. Joseph. On the way he gave out interviews about how he had cleared the state of the worst band of outlaws ever known in American history. Not to be outdone, the police chief and police commissioner of Kansas City and the sheriff of Clay County told how hard they had worked on the case. It was soon apparent that about every official in the state had contributed in the breaking-up of the desperate gang. Especially those moving up toward re-election.

But there were two sides. People were beginning to sympathize, more and more, with the betrayed bandit. His friends began to speak up openly for him. He was not guilty of all the robberies heaped on him; and he had robbed only banks, railroads, and express companies who could afford it and who delighted to grind down the common man.

A host of people began trying to see the widow; had important business with her, they said. An item from the *St. Joseph Herald*, April 4, 1882:

> Mrs. Jesse James stated yesterday that Alex Green represented to her that she was liable to be arrested and urged her to retain him as her attorney. He wanted $500 in advance. Alex's modesty will be the ruination of him yet.

And all was not going well with the swaggering Fords. The people were not calling them heroes at all, as the Fords had expected, but something far removed from that. The feeling became so intense, and so many rumors were going around, that the governor telegraphed, ordering out the state guards.

Never in all its history had the river town of St. Joseph had so much excitement; all wanted to see the body and nearly all did. People waited in line for hours at the undertaker's to catch a glimpse of that strangely calm, bearded face. The body had to be identified officially, for there was the matter of the reward. About twenty identified it: Mattie Collins, Dick Liddil's wife; Dick Liddil himself, who remarked, "That's Jess all right. I'd know his hide in a tanyard"; Harrison Trow, who had ridden with Jesse in guerrilla days; Thomas M. Mimms, Zee's uncle; Prosecuting Attorney William H. Wallace of Kansas City, who had grown up in the same county with the Boys; William J. Clay, a farmer from Clay County; Jim Wilkerson, a longtime friend, who said, "I ought to know him; I soldiered with him."

Four of them drew up and signed the following:

> St. Joseph, Mo., April 4, 1882. We, the undersigned, hereby certify that we were well acquainted with Jesse James during his lifetime, that we have just viewed his remains now in the custody of the coroner at this place and have no hesitation in saying that they are unquestionably his.
>
> Harrison Trow
> William J. Clay
> James Wilkerson
> Mattie Liddil.

I went to see the Sidenfaden ledger. It is a tall, narrow, oldfashioned journal, the day-by-day chronicle of the Black Angel. This is what is written by pen on one yellowed page:

> Apr. 3.
> Mr. Jesse James killed. Number 11 S. casket with shroud, $250. Shroud $10. Paid.

I asked Mr. Sidenfaden, the grandson, why Jesse was called 'Mr.,' and he said possibly it was to show that he was a man. The 'S' after the number of the casket meant 'State casket.'

I began to compare the cost of funerals as shown on the same page. The one immediately above was $14 and the one below was $27. The $250 paid for the casket was considered, at the time, very expensive. The papers carried stories that it had cost $500.

Since the family was not able to pay that much for the casket, it has always been a bit of mystery where the money came from. As a matter of fact, it was paid for by the police commissioner of Kansas City, Henry Craig, and by Sheriff Timberlake of Clay County, whose shoes must have been pinching.

XIX

JESSE IS BURIED IN HIS MOTHER'S YARD

CROWDS stood all night in the streets, talking and looking at the undertaker's. At seven in the morning of April 6th, a pine box was wheeled out and put into a two-horse spring-wagon and started for the depot, the crowd walking along with the wagon.

Jesse's mother, wife, and children arrived by carriage; instantly the crowd surged out. While attention was directed to them, a man with a knife in his hand rushed up to the pine box and began to whittle off souvenirs.

The box was put in the express car. Jesse's family got on, along with some police officials who had suddenly become extremely attentive, having seen which way sentiment was blowing. The train, without the usual call of 'All aboard,' drew silently out.

At Cameron Junction, Missouri, a change of train had to be made, and again Jesse's mother watched the pine box wheeled sadly out. About ten o'clock that morning the funeral train reached Kearney, and the coffin was carried to the Kearney House, where the lid was opened. The body lay in what might be called 'state.' So great was the interest that the passing trains—both freight and passenger—stopped for twenty minutes to allow passengers and crews to see Jesse. The hotel was about a block from the depot, so that they could view the body and get back within the time. Almost since dawn farmers had been arriving, and now men who had gone to school with Jesse—old friends and neighbors—marched steadily past, looking down at the bearded face.

Mrs. Samuels, with the widow and children, had been driven to the old farm. A reporter followed, and she said to him from the depth of her feeling: "I am proud of my children. I am proud to be the mother of Jesse James. He was generous to the needy and he was never a traitor. Two of my sons have been murdered—one in this house—and another lies at the point of death. Thank God, Frank is beyond their reach! They can't shoot him in the back."

At a quarter past two the coffin was taken out of the hotel and carried down the street to the church where Jesse had been converted sixteen years before. The casket was placed on wooden supports in front of the pulpit. Jesse's mother and family sat near it. An out-of-town pastor assisted; when he began to pray a fresh burst of tears came from Jesse's mother, and she repeated over and over, "Oh God! Oh God!" The minister of the church conducted the services, choosing ironically as his text, 'Therefore, be ye also ready, for in such an hour as ye think not the Son of Man cometh.'

After the first few words the minister made no further reference to the dead man. The sermon was stilted and advised the congregation to 'prepare to meet thy God,' as was the custom of the time. At the end he requested the audience not to go to the grave, saying that Mrs. Samuels' son was seriously ill and the excitement of seeing so many people might be too much for him.

But many people who could not get in the church had already started for the house. They did not hear the request.

The pine box was loaded into a four-horse wagon. The roads were rutted from the recent rains and from the unusual amount of driving back and forth to the James farm, and the casket began to slide back and forth. A boy named Gale C. Henson, the brother of the driver, was put in the wagon to keep the box from sliding around. When a rut came he braced his feet and hands, but sometimes the load was too much and the box knocked against the sides of the wagonbed.

The wagon turned in at the James gate and went up the winding road that Jesse had galloped over so many times. The box was opened and the lid of the coffin pulled back; then friends and neighbors carried it into the house. John Samuels was propped up in bed. It was a pitiful scene. Mrs. Samuels wept louder and more distractedly than ever, saying, "John, here is your poor brother they killed."

Now the casket was carried to the grave. Neighbors had dug it in the yard under the edge of the coffee-bean tree where Dr. Samuels had been hanged by the Federal soldiers. Because Mrs. Samuels was afraid of vandals she had ordered the grave to be dug seven feet deep. Some dirt had fallen in, and one of the men got back into the grave to throw it out; his head was below the level of the ground.

Jesse's mother and widow put their heads down on the casket and began to weep bitterly, both saying over and over, "Oh, the traitors!"

The two ministers led the pitiful group in singing 'We Will Wait Till Jesus Comes.'

Jesse's mother sobbed harder than ever, crying out: "They

drove him from the plow when he was a boy, and for money they betrayed him—my generous, noble-hearted Jesse. I call for vengeance upon the traitors. I ask eternal God to look down on me, his mother. All for money! They call him a robber, but he never betrayed a friend. Oh, why did they kill my poor boy who never wronged anybody, but helped them and fed them with the bread that should go to his orphans?"

At last the funeral was over. The neighbors stayed awhile, doing all they could do to comfort the mother and widow, then started home in their wagons and buggies.

After the news of Jesse's death a reporter from the *Kansas City Journal* went out to look for the man who had killed him three years earlier. He found George Shepherd working as a night watchman in a Kansas City lumber yard. The substance of the interview was published on the day after Jesse was buried.

The reporter asked if he had heard about the death of Jesse James.

Shepherd answered promptly, "I have, but I don't believe it."

"Why don't you believe it?"

"Because he would be too smart to be caught napping. Nobody was as quick on the draw as Jesse was."

"Do you really believe you killed Jesse James at Joplin, Missouri, in 1879?"

"I am positive."

"If you shot him, why is it you never had any trouble about it?"

"Jesse was afraid to tackle a man who could shoot as straight as he could."

Jesse would have liked that story.

The aftermath for Zerelda Mimms James was sad and bitter. She was so needy that she had to hold a public auction of her household goods. While the sale was going on, people slipped into the room where Jesse had fallen and cut splinters of the bloodsoaked wood from the floor. Some of the items bid in were touching. The morning his father had been shot, Tim had been in the kitchen playing with the coffee mill. With this high recommendation, the coffee mill was sold for $2. The day before he had been killed Jesse had carried coal into the kitchen. The scuttle he had used went for $1. Little Mary's high-chair brought 75 cents. Jesse's pocket-knife $3. The family dog brought more than any piece of furniture—in fact, a higher price than anything sold: $15. The sale totaled $117.65.

The sum was so pitiful that Zee James entered into a contract to do what was very popular then—'Go on the lecture platform.' But she found she was too distraught to talk herself, and arrangements had to be made with a professional. She was to sit on the platform with her two children and, at the end of the lecture, answer questions from the audience. At the last moment the idea was abandoned.

Many people, believing that Jesse James must have buried great sums of money away, approached her with crackbrained get-rich-quick schemes. All the while she was trying desperately to raise money. A St. Louis publisher named Chambers, according to the papers, got her to agree to write the life of her husband; this she did verbally, relating the story to the man. When he had put it into written words and words into printed pages, he would allow her to see only ninety-two pages out of two hundred and twenty. She refused to let him have a picture of herself to use, so he sent an artist to her hotel, who put his drawing paper on top of the piano and proceeded to sketch her. She ran out of the room and ordered him to leave. Things got so bad that she had to hire a lawyer to protect her from the human beings who wanted to make money out of her.

In an interview she said this about Jesse: "He was always fond of our children and his home, kind and affectionate to all. While in the house he was always playing with our boy and telling him that he must be a little man. Jesse was quiet and mild in the house and affectionate to me."

In the end she went to relatives in Kansas City who were willing to take her in.

And what of the cocky, confident Fords? A big cloud fell across their sun. The day after the shooting of Jesse James, the body of Wood Hite was found on the Bolton farm. Bob Ford was arrested. He looked more serious now, for this killing hadn't been 'arranged.'

The Fords were to be removed to Richmond, where Bob would be tried. By this time the popular feeling against them had grown to such an extent that armed guards had to be placed on the train with orders to shoot anybody who tried to interfere. At Kansas City there was a silent, watchful mob. Here the brothers were scheduled to leave the train and stay overnight, before going on to Richmond. The matter of getting them from the train to the hotel was a considerable one. So the sheriff put two handcuffed men between two deputies and started them out of the train. The crowd rushed forward, then discovered the men were not the Fords at all. The latter had been slipped out the back way.

In their hometown of Richmond they were met by a muttering crowd. Bob Ford was promptly arraigned on the charge of killing Wood Hite, but was let out on a bail of $2000 furnished by his father.

Feeling continued to mount. When the brothers were brought up for examination, they had to be surrounded by armed deputies. They came almost jauntily, in spite of the armed guards, and when the question was put they answered promptly, "Guilty." The judge sentenced them to be hanged a month later. Then they were led back to their cells. There was no other trial. Their attitude was that they had done something fine and noble.

When the verdict had been announced, they had smiled. They were depending on the governor's promise. Well they might; two hours after he received word, he sent a pardon freeing them.

The last word in any tale like this has to be about the reward, that big $10,000 for which, among other considerations, the deed was done. Well, nobody knows exactly. Its payment was in the hands of politicians and the various police officials who had a greater or lesser part in the plan of Jesse's death, and during the handling, I imagine, some of it stuck somewhere. Governor Crittenden proudly announced that the State of Missouri had not paid out a single cent. What evidence I have been able to turn up shows that Bob Ford got about $1200.

XX

THE SURRENDER OF FRANK JAMES

FROM the moment of Jesse's death people had asked, "Where is Frank? Will he kill Bob Ford? Will he organize a new gang?" There had been wild rumors that he had come to the undertaker's parlor, that he had attended the funeral in disguise. The newspapers sprouted headlines: he had been seen here, he had turned up there; he was everywhere. Actually, he was in Baltimore.

His wife saw the news in a Baltimore paper and handed it to him. Frank read it and said, "I think this time it's true. I think they've got Jesse."

He wanted to see his mother and try to comfort her, but this was too dangerous, with the whole country looking for him, so he did not come back to Missouri. Nor did he try to organize a new band. One by one the members were gone or going. Jesse had been their natural leader; he was more truly a bandit than Frank, and Frank made no effort to get in touch with the remnants.

The summer went by and so did a thousand rumors. When would Frank strike?

Fall came. The governor of Missouri got a letter asking whether, if Frank James came in, he would be given protection and a fair trial. The governor wrote to the go-between (who was Frank R. O'Neil, a reporter on the *St. Louis Republican*) that Frank would be assured a fair trial, but, if found guilty, would have to pay the penalty.

Frank's wife went to see the governor and extended the plea. Frank had been living quietly, she said, and wanted to give himself up, stand trial, and if freed live a normal life. The governor could only give the assurance that Frank would get a fair trial.

Six months had passed since that fateful day in St. Joseph before Frank really did start back. He went to an old guerrilla friend near Lee's Summit, Missouri. Seventeen years since the end of the Civil War, but the Missouri Bushwhackers still hung together. There was something fine about it, the loyalty the old fighters had for each other. There he stayed overnight. What stories must have been retold . . . what adventures relived!

The next morning Frank and his friend went to the depot; they shook hands and Frank mounted the steps of the train. No one knew that one of the famous men of America was entering the ancient car.

At Sedalia, Major John N. Edwards got on. The two arrived in Jefferson City at one o'clock in the morning, went to the hotel, and there registered as John N. Edwards and B. F. Winfrey, the night clerk never realizing that a bit of history was being made under his eyes. They slept in the same bed; next morning they had a leisurely breakfast, for Frank knew that from now on his breakfasts would be entirely different. They went out for a stroll. Everybody knew Edwards; he introduced the tall, silent, bearded Mr. Winfrey. The people hardly glanced at him . . . they wanted to talk to the famous newspaperman instead.

At noon the two went back to their room, where Mr. Winfrey lay down and slept. Then, at five that afternoon, they walked down the street and turned into the capitol building and went to Governor Crittenden's office. Half a dozen political catchalls were waiting in the reception room. They hopped to their feet and palavered with Mr. Edwards.

Mr. Winfrey went to a vacant chair and sat down alone, no one noticing him.

When the secretary announced that Mr. Edwards and his friend could now see the governor, the two went in. Seated with Crittenden were some state officials and political odds-and-ends. They were pleased to see Mr. Edwards. Mr. Edwards plowed through them and shook hands with the governor.

"Governor, allow me to introduce an old friend of mine, Frank James."

The political odds-and-ends smiled pleasantly.

Crittenden extended his hand. "I'm glad to meet you, Mr. James."

And now the politicos stared very hard. Was this some kind of hocus-pocus?

Frank reached under his coat and took a six-shooter out of a holster. He extended it butt-first.

"I want to hand over to you something that no man except myself has touched in twenty-one years. I've taken the cartridges out so you can handle it safely." There was a glint of humor in his expression.

The eyes of the hangers-on popped.

Frank showed a well-worn leather belt studded with cartridges. In the middle of the belt, arranged to snap the ends together, was a big bronze buckle in the form of a 'U.S.' The governor looked at it in surprise.

"Yes, that's a Union belt. I got it off a dead Federal soldier in Centralia, Missouri. We had killed him."

All these years Frank had worn that Union belt as a bit of defiance against the hated North. And at last he too had come in to surrender.

Now that the State of Missouri had him, what was it going to do with him? To the governor's chagrin he found there wasn't a specific charge against Frank James. He had offered a reward for Frank, but the courts had to have a charge before they could proceed. At last somebody remembered there was some kind of charge against him, not in Jefferson City but in Independence, Missouri. After a great deal of pother, Frank was kept overnight, then the next day put on the train and started for Independence. Meantime the newspapers had it. It was a sensation of the day—Frank James had come in.

People flocked to the train as if he were a President. He had to appear on the back platform and wave.

When he got to Independence his mother was there in the station waiting, and so were his wife and their son Robbie, and his wife's father and mother. Mrs. Samuels threw her handless arm around his neck. "Buck! Buck!" she cried. "Home at last. They can't do anything to you. Oh Buck!"

The charge the authorities thought they could support was the murder of the Pinkerton detective Witcher, but when they examined the evidence carefully they realized it could be seen through as easily as a bride's veil. After a great deal of confabulating, they decided to switch the charge and try him for the murder of the railroad man who had been killed in the Winston robbery about a year and a half before. A man named McMillan.

Preparations lasted until the following August (Frank had

surrendered October 5, 1882). There must be no slip-up. Frank James would have to pay. But what the prosecution hadn't counted on was the way popular opinion was running in Frank's favor. More and more it was realized how dastardly had been the killing of Jesse. Frank must be given a fair deal; no legal shooting in the back. Feeling against the banks and railroads and express companies had not slacked off; and the Pinkertons were rat poison. The James Boys had done a great deal of good; on everybody's lips was the song of how they had robbed the rich and given to the poor.

Frank was to be tried in the famous old courthouse at Gallatin, a few jumps from the Croy home. The courtyard began filling almost at dawn, and when the door to the courtroom was opened, grim armed men rushed in and plunked themselves down on the long wooden benches that served for seats. More and more came, all to see Frank and defend him. The judge, alarmed by what he saw, announced that court was adjourned and would be resumed again at the opera house. He further announced that admittance would be by ticket and that the tickets would be supplied by the sheriff of the county. The men bore down on the sheriff like dogs on a bone, but he issued the tickets as he saw fit. Firmly at the door was a deputy sheriff who stated that no guns could be toted inside; they must be checked. At this news arguments began to go off like popcorn in a kettle; men who had packed guns ever since the end of the Civil War said they'd be damned if they'd give them up: a gun was a man's private property and he could do whatever he wanted to with it. Wasn't this a free country? But after no end of hot words, the men were finally talked out of their guns and went into the makeshift courtroom feeling half-dressed.

So grave, so serious was the matter that Frank had eight lawyers; one of them, later, was in President Woodrow Wilson's cabinet; another became a federal judge. They were the biggest potatoes in the bin. When Frank entered, under guard, silence fell on the courtroom; men who had never seen him before looked on him and liked what they saw. He was one of their own. Aligned against him were the State of Missouri, the railroads, banks, and the express companies; and the State of Missouri, through the devious ways of the governor, had caused Frank's brother to be shot in the back. Also lined up against Frank was Dick Liddil; and there came into the courtroom a flood of Fords, ready to bury the hatchet . . . in Frank's back.

William H. Wallace was a spellbinder who had been elected prosecuting attorney on the platform of 'Break Up The James Gang.' His record was one hundred per cent. That very moment Bill Ryan was languishing in the penitentiary at Jefferson City, sent there by Mr. Wallace. He wouldn't send Frank there; Frank's would be the simple rope ceremony.

Wallace had eighty-nine witnesses to prove that Frank was guilty as a dog.

Frank had thirty-nine to prove he wasn't.

However, among Frank's witnesses was the most popular man in Missouri—General Jo Shelby. What Robert E. Lee was to the South, Jo Shelby was to Missouri—that is, to the Southern part of Missouri. When he saw Frank, he started toward him, saying, "There's a hand I'm proud to shake." The judge hit the gavel so hard that pigeons on the roof blinked.

The trial began. It turned on as curious a point as you will ever come across—the identification of Frank James. He had to be placed at the robbery. Wallace found a preacher who testified Frank had stayed overnight with him the day before the robbery, and the way he identified him was that Frank quoted Shakespeare. Never before in all outlaw history had a bandit been accused of quoting Shakespeare. Not only that, but the preacher told exactly what Frank had quoted. Frank hung his head, whipped. It just showed what Shakespeare could lead to.

Frank's sister Susie, who was now Mrs. Allen H. Parmer, testified that on the day of the robbery Frank had been with her and her husband on a ranch in Texas, but that couldn't offset the Shakespeare taint. The simple farmer jury looked at Frank questioningly . . . there was something intrinsically wrong with a person who would accept another's hospitality and then sit around quoting poetry. Why didn't he damn the railroads like a man ought?

That night the men got their arms back and slept in the yard; next morning, when court opened, they checked them again and went into the opera house. It was a privilege to be there and see that a Southerner got a fair deal.

Eight days this went on. The newspapers said that the trial attracted more interest than had that of Charles Guiteau, the assassin of President Garfield.

Wallace was famous as an orator. As the trial drew to a close he soared to heights never before approached even in Missouri. Pointing dramatically at Frank, he said: "Farewell, Frank James, prince of robbers, you are going to your death. You are the cruelest horseman who ever wore a spur, or held a rein. You seemed like Death itself mounted on a pale charger. Thou foul blot on the escutcheon of the fair State of Missouri—farewell!"

The jury went out. But it was hardly away long enough to turn around; then it brought back the verdict—Not Guilty.

It liked the escutcheon just as it was. People shouted; the judge grabbed his gavel; pigeons went fluttering away.

But the end wasn't yet. Frank was out, but only temporarily, for the State of Alabama grabbed him and hustled him down to Huntsville to stand trial on the charge of having robbed the government paymaster at Muscle Shoals. This would settle his hash. No prejudiced Missouri jury.

The Alabama jury listened to the evidence and brought in its verdict—Not Guilty.

While Frank was being tried, a mysterious man had arrived in Huntsville, had asked some questions, then had gone to a hotel and registered. He said he was from Versailles, Kentucky. He waited a day or two, until the jury pronounced Frank not guilty, then revealed his true identity. He was Frank Rogers, a former captain in the Confederate Army and now sheriff of Boonville, Missouri, and he had a warrant for Frank's arrest for the Otterville train robbery eight years before. Soon Frank was on the train, a prisoner once more, bound for Boonville. Once more his mother was on the depot platform and again put her handless arm around his neck—this amazing mother who believed so deeply and unshakingly in her wayward sons. The people on the platform were so glad to see Frank that it practically amounted to a reception.

I saw hanging on the wall in the law office of Roy D. Williams at Boonville the bond that Frank James put up. It was signed by seven men who, at that time, were prominent in Missouri: 'Good, substantial citizens.' Popular sentiment was against another trial. After all, the gang was gone; besides Frank only Jim Cummins was left, and what was the use of trying that old horsethief? The days that had brought about banditry—the Border Warfare days—were over; a new life and a new way of living had come to the Middle West. Let the thing go! And the state did. The case petered out and was officially dropped on February 21, 1885.

And so at last Frank James was a free man.

XXI

FRANK AS A FREE MAN

AFTER Frank James became a free man, the first thing he did was to go to see his mother on the old farm. She was growing old, but she was still the same fierce, hot-tempered, son-defending, enemy-hating woman she had always been. Her sons had always been right; they had never been understood; they had been betrayed by their enemies. Only she understood them. Now she and her oldest son talked over what he would do. It was, for Frank, the beginning of a new life.

He had practically no money. Those eight lawyers had gnawed it away, and during his career, while he had made a fair amount, he had kept very little.

He made a promise to himself that whatever money he got from now on, he would come by honestly. Inherently he was an honest man. There is no evidence that he ever stole a dollar in his life . . . except in his professional work. Now he had given that up. Would he live up to his high promise? Would the grind of earning a meager living make him restless? What about seven-year-old Robbie, who had once been 'Mary Woodson'? He must be taken care of. He had grown into a bright, alert, winsome boy, the pride of his father's life. And what about Frank's wife, who had never complained of the kind of life she had had to lead?

He got a job in a shoestore in Nevada, Missouri. People came to stare at him as he fitted shoes; it took him twice as long to sell a pair of shoes as it did anyone else. But that was all right. It paid.

The winters were difficult, for he was not strong, so he moved south to Texas, where he worked for a time in a Dallas shoestore. Then, his health improving, he came back to Missouri and got a job as doorkeeper at the Standard Theatre in St. Louis. He received $70 a month; on Saturday night there wasn't much left. During this time he had offers to go on the stage (as Bob Ford had done), but refused. He became assistant starter at the Fair Grounds racetrack in St. Louis; he attracted more attention than the horses. Politics! He liked politics and followed them avidly. He tried to get a position in the state legislature as sergeant-at-arms, but failed; this cut him deeply.

At about this time Cole Younger came back from Minnesota, having done all the inlay work the state deemed necessary. What a reunion that must have been! The two hadn't seen each other since Northfield. Cole brought back with him seventeen bullets, all carried inside. He had been wounded twenty-six times, but had only the seventeen in him; the others had gone through, or been cut out. Cole went to the old family home at Lee's Summit, where he made talks in church and at Sunday school, expostulating with rare discernment on the theme 'Crime Does Not Pay.' He also proposed to Frank that the two join up in a Wild West show. Their most valuable asset was their notoriety, so they decided to cash in on it.

Pious Cole had promised the governor of Minnesota that he wouldn't take part in any performance where he would have to exhibit himself, so he became business manager. The outfit was owned by professional showmen from Chicago; Frank and Cole were to be paid for being with it. The two didn't know what they were getting into, for it was about the cheapest, seediest combination of cow chasers and alleged Indian fighters ever to roam the fertile valleys of the Missouri. They came to our town August 29, 1903, and pitched in what we called the Prather pasture. I was not there at the time, but I looked up what the Maryville paper said. It was plenty:

> The show is without exception the poorest ever seen in our city. It was largely composed of toughs and jailbirds. Gambling games were run wide-open; some of our hare-brained residents allowed themselves to be drawn in and lost money to these travelling brigands. The 'short-change' racket was vigorously pushed. J. T. Hays was robbed of $12. Henry Neuens of $5. An altercation took place between the employees and our citizens which almost resulted in a panic, during which Merril Gingrich barely escaped serious injury. Before leaving town, the circus employees broke into a car of watermelons. That tells about all that is necessary. Cole Younger did not appear in the performance, but walked here and there in the tent, now and then waving a hand or speaking to the people he knew. Frank James took a prominent part in the exhibition. Finally the circus left town, there being no mourners except the gouged and cheated.

They returned in July, 1908. This time the paper exerted rare repression, for all it said was: 'Cole Younger is fat and bald-headed. He is advertised as the last of the famous Younger Brothers, which, it seems to us, is going in the right direction.'

The situation does not seem to have been quite as deplorable, as far as Frank was concerned, as the paper made it out. Frank and Cole protested to the management about the cheaters and swindlers who followed the circus like nits over a horse's head in a hayfield, but it did no good. They threatened to quit, but the management reminded them of the contract and bond, so Frank began to write ahead to the chiefs of police and to the mayors of the towns where they were going to play, informing them of conditions and suggesting they add to their police and marshal forces.

The grifters learned of this; they disliked Frank thoroughly for his attitude regarding what the swindlers considered legitimate prey—'suckers.' One day, after the regular performance, Frank went into a store. It so happened that several of the circus thugs were there, and, seeing that Frank was alone, they advanced upon him, declaring they would teach him a lesson. He had a permit to carry a pistol and he had one on, but above everything else he did not want to use it. Just at this moment he saw Cole passing by on horseback. "Cole," he called, "come in here. We've got to do a little cleaning up."

Cole saw their threatening attitude. "Hold them, Frank. I'll come in on them the back way."

The toughs got out and scurried down the street.

Frank grew to dislike show and carnival life more and more, especially the varieties of human offal that were drawn into it, so finally he gave it up and went back to the farm. The James farm was beginning to pay better and better—not from corn and wheat but from tourists. This crop was excellent. The farm had always been a magnet for the popeyed; it became an even more powerful one. Frank put up a sign that admission was twenty-five cents; as tourists kept coming, he raised it to fifty cents. After a time this became his chief source of income.

He put up a homemade sign which he printed himself: KODAKS BARED. After the sign had been finished and nailed to the wooden gate on the main road, he discovered he had missed a letter. So he lightly marked in a caret with the second R above it. This provided him with a quiet joke of his own. He would show the tourists through the house, explaining the exhibits and telling matters of general interest. Sometimes, at the end of the tour, somebody would remark that he had seen the sign about cameras, but hadn't Mr. James misspelled a word?

Frank would look mystified, then say, "Why, I reckon not. I spelled it just like they learned me in school."

"It's not right," the tourist would say.

A genial argument would start, then Frank would say, "I feel so sure of myself I'll just bet five dollars I've got the word spelled right."

Often the bet was made, then Frank and the other would march down to the gate. There—when one came closer—the other R could be seen. "I didn't say anything about the location of the letter. I just said it was spelled right. I guess I'm the winner."

Usually the tourist would pay. If he didn't, Frank would let the matter drop. In the meantime, a good many five-dollar bills found their way to him for safekeeping.

His interest in politics continued. The James family had always been Democrats; in him old ways died slowly. The other party he called 'Black Republicans.' But in 1904, when Col. Theodore Roosevelt was running for President, he switched over to the Republican party—which, in Clay County, was as astonishing as the Missouri River suddenly reversing itself and beginning to flow north.

This was the year of the St. Louis World's Fair—officially the Louisiana Purchase Exposition. Col. Roosevelt visited St. Louis, where a mighty spread was put on in his honor. George S. Johns, then editor of the *St. Louis Post-Dispatch,* told him that Frank James was now an ardent Roosevelt man. Col. Roosevelt was 'de-lighted' (remember that?) and asked to meet Frank. "Why, I'll invite him to the White House for lunch." But at the time Frank was in Montana and, for one reason or another, the White House luncheon was not kept, but it shows how far Frank had advanced in his effort to become an accepted citizen.

Frank was exceedingly chary about speaking of his earlier days, especially about his bandit experiences. Sometimes, however, when he was among close friends, he would mention his adventures, but always very briefly. B. J. George of 3 East 65th Terrace, Kansas City, told a story that brings this out. His father was Hiram George (better known as 'Hi' George), who, with Frank James, had ridden with Quantrill. He was, in fact, a pallbearer at the second burial of Jesse James.

"I remember an incident that took place about 1909 at my father's house at Oak Grove, Missouri," said B. J. George. "Frank James came to see my father and they had a talk reunion, with plenty of Mother's cherry wine and pound cake —y'know, a pound of this and a pound of that. The two men began to talk about a skirmish they'd had with Federal troops. The Federal troops were coming up a winding lane, the sun flashing on their buttons and buckles. They made perfect targets for the men on Father's side and they seem to have made the most of it. At the end of the story there was a pause, and my sister, who was two years younger than I, said,

" 'Mr. James, did you ever kill a man in the war?'

"Frank was momentarily stunned, then he replied, 'I can't rightly say I ever killed a man, but I sure shot at a lot of 'em!' "

XXII

THE GIRL WHO MARRIED FRANK JAMES

THE wives of the James Boys! What woman would ever have envied their lot? Forever moving, often deserted, always fearful; companions, lovers, mothers, homemakers, and comrades-in-arms; they were courageous women. We have told the story of Zee Mimms, but what about the girl who married Frank?

She was born in a log cabin (now replaced by a brick house) not far from the present home of President Truman in Independence. Her name was Ann Ralston. The Ralstons settled not far from the James farm, and the two families had much in common—both Southern sympathizers, both farming folk, and both were prominent in the neighborhood.

One day Ann and a girl friend were playing croquet in the yard when two young men rode up on horseback. One was a neighbor boy whom she knew. He introduced his companion under an assumed name. The stranger was Frank James, armed and with a reward on his head. The four played croquet, and when Frank rode away Ann looked lingeringly after him. He came back another day and the two began to meet regularly. Then he told her who he was; this was something of a shock, but she had become so interested in him that she let him continue his attentions.

When Samuel Ralston found out who was courting his daughter, he sternly told her that she was not to see the outlaw again, and was under no circumstances to have anything to do with him. That, of course, settled it. Ann began to see him constantly.

One night he came to visit. The two were in the kitchen when Frank heard a suspicious sound. He crept outside, and it was as he feared. Detectives. He did not even have time to return to tell her he was leaving. Again her father pleaded with her not to wreck her life.

Frank wrote her and the two began to have secret meetings. Samuel Ralston learned of these too. Frank took her to a dance; again he became suspicious and had to ride away into the night, leaving Ann to come home with her brother. Thus the courtship went on and the family opposition continued.

Then Ann packed a satchel and got on the train at Independence and started for Kansas City; her heart must have thumped, realizing what a desperate chance she was taking.

She was twenty-two. Frank was ten years older.

Kinfolks met her, and Frank and Ann went across the river to Leavenworth, Kansas, where a minister made her a bandit's bride. It was 1874, the same year that Jesse was married.

I wish I knew the details of the amazing marriage—how they lived one jump ahead of the detectives—but I have only fragments. (Maybe someone can supply me with a bit of information. I would appreciate it.) They appear to have gone to Texas, as Jesse and his wife had done. It was not long before Frank had to have money; and he got it in the way he knew best. What must she have thought? But she knew how he *had* been getting it. Did she try to get him to change?

Always, every minute, there was the dread that detectives might have him. At night every scratch of a twig might mean something. His very life depended on how quickly he reacted to danger. Once they were strolling together in Kansas City, near the Union Station. Just at this moment a policeman started to arrest a drunken man. The drunk put up a stiff resistance and the two began to struggle, the policeman getting the worse of it. He saw Frank and called to him to come and help. The last thing in the world that Frank wanted to do just then was to help a policeman, and run the risk of questioning afterward.

"Come and help me!" shouted the policeman.

Frank started to walk on, but the policeman, enraged, drew his pistol. "I tell you to come and help me!"

"I can't," said Frank. "I'm running to catch a train." Turning to a Negro, he handed him a silver dollar and said, "Take my place and help."

And then Frank began to do exactly what he had told the policeman he was doing.

The days of uncertainty continued, but the two really loved each other, and were drawn together by their common danger. They were constantly on the move. Usually Frank hid with his old war friends, or with relatives, but he began to like Baltimore and to stay there. The city had a Southern flavor, and it had a theatre where he could, from time to time, see a Shakespeare play. One day he was walking down the street when he noticed a police officer eyeing him. Frank pretended great innocence and strolled on, demonstrating to any fair-minded person that he had nothing on his conscience.

The police officer came straight toward him. "I want you," he said shortly.

Frank always carried a gun; he had it in a shoulder holster. It was a split-second decision. "What do you want me for?" demanded Frank.

"For the coroner's jury," said the police officer. "A man has been found dead in this house and I'm trying to get a jury."

Again Frank did the lightning thinking he was capable of when danger was upon him.

"I'm sorry, Officer, but I can't. I live in Washington, and am not a resident here."

He walked on, shaking, no doubt, a little on his pins.

Frank and his wife loved the soil. After his outlaw days and his show days and his wanderings were over, they settled down on the James farm. Old age came along and took them gently by the hand and led them down its descending path. On February 18, 1915, Frank died.

She was at his side; she stood for some moments looking at the face that had grown so calm. Then she said, "He is gone, the best husband who ever lived."

Frank had resolved that his body should not be exhumed like Jesse's, so he had told his family that he wanted to be cremated. This was done; when his will was opened, it was found that the ashes were to be kept in an urn until the death of his widow.

She loved the old farm and there she stayed, but she was an entirely different personality from Frank's mother. Mrs. Samuels had boldly shown tourists around, extracting every dime she could from them and giving them their money's worth in talk, but Mrs. Frank James would show no tourists through; when they came in sight, she retreated to her bedroom and secreted herself until they again started toward the highway gate.

She never talked of Frank's or Jesse's exploits. Sometimes neighbors would try to draw her out, but she had an answer. "That's all over and I don't care to think of it."

She liked to read, but her eyesight began to go. Her son Bob and his wife Mae read to her. These were her happiest hours. Sometimes she walkd in the yard, scooting back into the house at the sound of a tourist car approaching. There was no bitterness in her life; it was truly as she had said, "Those things are over. Life must go on." And it did for her, year after year.

When the First World War came she was sixty-four; she was especially interested in General Pershing, for he had been born nearby. The Second World War came. Now she had a radio and would sit adjusting the dial. Robert and Mae would come in and sit with her, discussing what they heard.

Only once did she come out of seclusion. This was when a current impostor arrived in Excelsior Springs and announced that he was Jesse James. She was so aroused that she went to see him, asked him a few questions, then denounced him in a sharp voice for a person usually so gentle.

She complained of the winters. At first she had gone to Texas, but now that was too far away and she began going to Excelsior Springs, where she lived in a small rented apartment and took the mineral baths.

At home, in the summers, her step grew slow; she could go out only on good days. But she never complained; that was the way life was and one had to accept it.

At last she could not go out at all, but Frank and Mae were there; that helped.

She had always—as she expressed it—'kept away from doctors,' but one day she said she thought they'd better send for one. He arrived too late. The date was July 6, 1944. She was ninety-one . . . this woman who had met Frank James when she was a girl playing croquet on the lawn.

She had told them she wanted to be cremated too. When her will was opened it was found that her ashes were to be placed in an urn, and the two urns buried side-by-side in the same grave. This was done, and there they lie today, Ann and Frank, in Elmwood Cemetery, Kansas City, not very far from the log house where she was born.

XXIII

THE DEATH OF BOB FORD

WHAT had become of Our Hero, Bob Ford? Feeling against him had continued to grow; more and more it was realized what sort of creature he was. He had been tried for the death of Wood Hite and found guilty; the governor had immediately pardoned him. Bob Ford had committed two murders but was as free as a cottonwood seed floating on the breeze.

He was living with his parents near Richmond. Even the people in his hometown could not stomach him. When he felt he was safe, he boasted how he had killed Jesse James. He sat with his back to the wall; his eyes were always darting; if a door opened, he looked up.

He got a job in 'The Outlaws of Missouri,' a sort of drama but hard to describe; between curtains he would come out in front and tell how he had killed Jesse James, holding a pistol at arm's length and bravely snapping the trigger. It's a wonder somebody didn't take a potshot at him.

One of the girls in the company was Nellie Waterson, a rather dizzy creature; soon the two were necessary to each other.

Two seasons he went out in the play, then its time was over

and he looked about for some other way to earn an honest dollar. P. T. Barnum offered him a job in a freak show. Ford accepted it, and seems to have given the show just the lift it needed.

A weakness began to develop: drink. And gambling. He drifted here and there, explaining to the boys at the bar how he had killed Jesse James. They would buy a drink, then he would explain another interesting detail. Sometimes he said that Jesse wasn't a very brave man. He was a dandy, affecting loud clothes, especially highly colored vests.

He and Dick Liddil concocted the idea of going into business together. They proceeded to Las Vegas, New Mexico, and opened a saloon on Bridge Street in the Old Town. They expected—because of Ford's notoriety—that customers would come tumbling in. But they didn't; Ford bore such an ill odor they came hardly at all. Business grew so bad that the two sold out. The contemptible Dick Liddil got a job taking care of a load of racehorses for J. W. Lynch; he shepherded them east and helped race them on the Eastern and Southern circuits, sleeping in the stalls with them, sensitive as the horses must have been.

At about this time an event seemingly unrelated to Ford took place in Colorado. A man named N. C. Creede discovered two silver mines; one he named the 'Ethel' and the other the 'Holy Moses.' So rich were they that they became known as 'King Solomon's Mines.' Immediately there was a stampede and a town sprang up overnight, named after the man who had discovered the silver.

Creede was the wildest, the most dissolute town in the United States. Everybody had money and craved to spend it. Ford got there in no time and opened a saloon and dance hall.

Miners would come down out of the hills, load up at the bar, then go on the floor and try to dance. The place would shake as if there'd been another blast in the hills. Ford was the 'attraction'; he would stand at the bar and tell the miners how he had killed Jesse James. He did a lot better than in Las Vegas. He was the most spectacular man on the streets in a town that was running over with flashy men. He wore a huge hat that he'd had made to order, with what was said to be the widest brim in the West. He was conceited, and when drinking became quarrelsome. Once he became so obnoxious that he was waited on by a delegation of citizens and given twenty-four hours to leave town. He went to Pueblo, remained a week, then wrote a letter saying that if they would let him come back, he would reform. There was no answer, so he decided that silence was favorable and returned. It proved to be favorable, for the committee did nothing about it.

On the occasion of another visit to Pueblo, fate stepped into Bob Ford's life for the last time. The town was crowded. On this particular day it had snowed. Rooms were hard to get; finally he found a landlady who said she had a room with an extra bed, but she would have to ask the man who had the room if she could rent out the bed. The other tenant said yes.

The room was occupied by a man named Ed Kelly from Harrisonville, Missouri. Cole Younger was from near there, and some of Kelly's relatives had married into the Younger family. Kin of kin.

When Kelly came in later that day, there, sitting in the room, was Bob Ford, who had killed one of the men who had ridden with Cole Younger. Kelly recognized Ford . . . what must he have thought? Anyway, the two began to drink together, thinking about each other and sizing each other up.

Finally they fell asleep. The next morning Kelly went out first; later, when Ford got up, he missed a diamond ring he had purchased for Nellie Waterson, whom he had brought to Creede.

About two that afternoon, when Kelly returned, Ford accused him of having stolen the ring. Kelly denied it; the two began to quarrel, growing more and more heated. Ford went to the landlady, paid his bill, and moved out. In a day or two the snow cleared and he went back to his dance hall in Creede. Kelly brooded.

One day fire broke out in a hardware store, roared up the canyon, and leaped into Ford's place. Girls ran screaming out. There was no organized firefighting equipment, so buckets had to be passed along by hand. Ford ran frantically in and out, trying to save what he could. The most valuable thing he had was a piano in the dance hall. He begged the men to rescue it, but no one moved. Finally he shouted, "I'll give a thousand dollars to anyone who will save my piano!"

Well, that was a lot of drinks. Two men rushed in and managed to get the piano into the street. Ford paid the money . . . if he hadn't, it would have been his last waltz.

He hastily built around the place a siding of boards about four feet high, then put up canvas walls and roof, and, three days later, opened up again—same piano, same girls; the only thing new was the suckers. The miners would come down out of the hills and gaze on the glamorous ladies—*bang!* another month's diggings would be gone.

Now and then word got down to Pueblo that Ford was telling people Kelly had stolen his ring. Kelly continued to brood about this, and about the great injustice that Ford had done Jesse James who had ridden with Cole Younger. He came to Creede and went to Ford's saloon and up to the bar. There he stood a moment, looking at the people and listening to the thump of the piano. "Where's Ford?" he asked the bartender.

The bartender was also Ford's bodyguard; he looked Kelly over. "What do you want with him?"

"I'll tell him when I see him," announced Kelly.

The bartender ordered Kelly to leave. When the latter refused, the bartender made a sign to the bouncer and the two seized Kelly. They found a six-shooter and a bowie knife on him. They rushed him into the street and told him not to come back.

Kelly stood a moment looking at the flashy front, then started on down the street. He came to the Major Mercantile House, went in, and bought a revolver.

Later that day he met an old friend—'French Joe' Duval from Missouri, a bandit. He took Duval into a saloon and the two began to talk earnestly.

The next day, June 8, 1892, Kelly again came down the street. At this moment Duval appeared on horseback, carrying a shotgun. Walking up to him, Kelly said, "All right, Joe. Hand it over."

In a moment Kelly was in Ford's saloon. The owner was standing in front of the bar talking to a customer.

"Hello, Bob!" called Kelly.

Ford recognized him instantly and reached for his revolver, but before he could get to it Kelly discharged both barrels full at him, catching him in the neck. Ford fell to the floor moaning.

Instantly the place was in an uproar; the piano stopped, the girls came running out. Kelly walked up to the prostrate body, felt in Ford's pocket, and took out Ford's revolver; then, shotgun in his arms and revolver in his hand, he walked out into the street he had left only a moment before.

A girl from the dance floor ran to Bob Ford's body. A

collarbutton had been blown into his jugular vein. The girl picked it out of his neck with her gory fingers.

Men lifted Ford up and placed him on a table, where he died without speaking.

The commotion was heard by a deputy sheriff, who came up and arrested Kelly. In a few minutes there was an ominous creaking in the street—the coroner's wagon. Ford's corpse was put into it, then the wagon again creaked on down the street.

In spite of its lawlessness there was no jail in Creede, so Kelly was taken to a cabin on the school land and placed inside, and a guard was stationed.

Two doctors examined Ford and found that Kelly's gun had been loaded not only with shot but also with slugs, for some were found in the wall. Ford was as dead as Jesse James. A coroner's jury returned the following verdict: 'We find that R. N. Ford came to his death by a gunshot wound inflicted by the hands of one Ed Kelly with felonious intent.'

Kelly was given a preliminary hearing, then taken to Pueblo where he was convicted of murder in the second degree and given a sentence of twenty years in the Colorado State Penitentiary, with ten days out of each year to be served in solitary confinement. Sympathy was with Kelly, even if the killing had been coldblooded, for no one liked the boaster and braggart.

Ford's widow claimed the body, Nellie Waterson fading out of the picture, and took it back to Richmond, where it arrived just eleven years after Ford had started out to get Jesse James.

XXIV

THE MAN WHO KILLED THE MAN WHO KILLED JESSE JAMES

AFTER two years Kelly was pardoned. With the apotheosis of Bob Ford as the Great American Villain, he became something of a hero. Among the rough set in which he moved, he was pointed out as the man who had killed the man who had killed Jesse James. He liked it; it gave him a sense of importance. He had always moved among people who held life cheap, so that the deed itself did not weigh on him.

He was alternately a miner and a marshal; most of all he was the man who had revenged the slaying of Jesse James. Physically he was almost six feet tall, with thick heavy shoulders; his hair was red and he had a stubby red mustache. He was sometimes called 'Red' Kelly. Bob Fitzsimmons was the hero of the day, and many pointed out how much Kelly looked like Fitzsimmons. He liked this, too.

Drink was his curse. He began to drink more than his uncertain salary could shoulder. He began to drift here and there, always known among the people he associated with for his one great distinction.

In December, 1903, a little more than eleven years after he had shot Ford down, he arrived in Oklahoma City and moved into a cheap rooming-house called the Hotel Lewis on West Reno Avenue. Oklahoma City at this time was a rugged place, which is as politely as one can phrase it. And West Reno Avenue was about the most rugged street in the brawling, blustering, tough young city.

Bars were as thick along West Reno as fenceposts on a Missouri road. Kelly's weakness became more and more apparent. He went from one to the next. They began to eat up his clothes and he became shabby. But he was a hero to the men holding up the bars. When he came in a little hush went over them. There he was!—the great man. They would buy him drinks to hear him relive the scene in Creede. He hardly ever had to pay for a drink.

One day he was arrested by a policeman named Joe Burdett as a 'suspicious character.' He was taken to the station house, where he soon proved who he was, but he had to stay two days to clear himself completely of the charge, for telegrams had to be sent. He was missed by his West Reno Avenue cronies. Then the word got out that their hero was in the jug.

When he finally did free himself of the charge and once more appeared among them, they began to twit him about allowing himself to be locked up—the great man who had revenged Jesse James. He tried to laugh it off, but the boys kept it up. He became sensitive and began to drink more and more. He had lost face; he had been arrested by a common pavement-pounding policeman. He began to brood over that as he had over what Bob Ford had done, and stayed more and more in his room at the hotel.

On January 13, 1904, he was going down the street, this big, thick-shouldered, red-faced giant, when he saw Burdett coming toward him. He hated the sight of the policeman now, and turned his face aside so he would not have to speak to him.

Burdett breezed on toward him. When he got almost abreast he sang out, "Hello there, Kelly!"

Kelly did not reply.

"I said 'Hello there, Kelly,'" repeated Burdett in a superior, amused voice.

Suddenly, enraged, Kelly drew a revolver out of his overcoat pocket and struck at Burdett. The latter's tune changed instantly; he seized Kelly's hand and the two began to struggle. Kelly, the more powerful, began to bring Burdett to his knees. The policeman called repeatedly for help. Some street loafers were there, but not one came to assist; instead, as the struggle grew in intensity, they ran away. Burdett called after them pleadingly, "Stop and help me! I'm a police officer." The men disappeared. The struggle went on.

It seemed about over. Burdett was licked. But as he was going down he managed to twist his hand so that the revolver pointed at Kelly. The gun went off; the bullet took effect. Kelly died on the sidewalk. His body, unclaimed, was buried in the potter's field at Oklahoma City. Thus came to an end the life story of the man who killed the man who killed Jesse James.

XXV

JESSE GOES TO HIS GRAVE A SECOND TIME

THE world had changed; the great days of banditry were gone. A few outlaws, such as the Daltons, rode briefly to early lead-filled graves. The new generation hardly knew what the Border Warfare was. Clay County itself had changed—Clay County which had been the hottest part in the bed of the Border coals. But even this had begun to cool; a little sputtering along the edges, that was all. Mostly it was from the old people; youngsters thought they were overdoing it and looked out the window. 'Aunt Zerel' had cooled; that was the final test. Frank had been at home now for years; grandchildren were coming along. And the body of Jesse James was no longer in peril of snatchers. Twenty years had passed since he had been buried in the yard of her home; she could look out the window of her room and see the grave and she could rock on the porch and see it. Now she gave orders that the body was to be moved and taken to Mount Olivet, the family cemetery at Kearney.

The farm was rented and, for the time being, she and Frank were living at a hotel in Kearney. It was June 29, 1902, a Sunday. Jesse Junior had come, the night before, from Kansas City to be with his grandmother; he was now a strapping young man, rather on the goodlooking side, with his father's blue eyes and high cheekbones. He bought a coffin and made arrangements with two grave-openers, and on this Sunday morning the gravediggers got into a spring-wagon and started out to the farm. Jesse and his uncle, John T. Samuels, followed. They arrived at five o'clock in the morning and went to the grave under the coffee-bean tree. Twenty years and two months! Thousands of visitors had come to gaze on the grave; hundreds had wondered if the real Jesse James were in it, for already men were exhibiting themselves as the real, the still-living Jesse James. What would the grave reveal?

The two gravediggers set to work. Seven feet down. At last one of the picks sent up a grating sound; there it was—the burial box. The sides of the grave, at the bottom, were widened, planks slipped under, ropes attached, and the men started to lift the coffin. There was a crashing sound—the bottom of the casket had fallen out and so had Jesse James's skull!

The box was lifted out as best it could be done with the rotting and decaying wood, and all that was left of Jesse James was scraped up and put into the new casket. It was a grisly scene.

One of the diggers got back into the grave, picked up the skull, and handed it to young Jesse. He turned it over, silently inspecting it. There, behind the right ear, was a bullet hole almost as large as a quarter. And little Tim Howard recognized the gold-filled teeth.

Jesse's decayed arms were arranged over his breast, as they had been in the original burial, and the coffin carried into the room where Jesse had slept with Bob Ford a few nights before Ford had shot him down, the room where Jesse had courted Zee Mimms, where his mother had lost her hand and his half-brother his life. How much of violence and gentleness that room had seen! And now Jesse was in it again, stretched out between two chairs.

Young Jesse and John Samuels drove back to Kearney, where Mrs. Samuels was waiting. They told her all that had happened. Frank was upstairs in his room and the two young men went to him. Meantime the pallbearers were gathering—all Quantrill raiders or men who had ridden with Jesse. Time was having its way with them; eyes were growing dim and hair gray. Why, the younger generation hardly knew who they were! these old coots who liked to gab of days that were no more.

They almost filled the dining room, and Jesse's mother came and sat at table with them. She had had made for her a combination steel knife and fork which she wielded with her left hand. Frank announced that, although he was sick, he was going with his mother. She told him what to wear and how to take care of himself, as she had so many years ago. Her son! Her wonderful Buck.

At last the hacks and spring-wagons and mounted riders arrived at the old farm; the gate opened, they went in, this strange, pathetic cavalcade.

Jesse's mother looked at the casket. Then she went to the old grave under the coffee-bean tree where she and Jesse's widow had flung themselves on the coffin, but now Jesse's widow was not there; she had died two years before. The decayed boards of the first coffin had been put into the grave and covered.

"He used to play here in the yard," she said.

The funeral procession arrived at the cemetery. A grave had been dug, and toward it the old Quantrill warriors came, carrying the new black coffin on which was a nickel plate with the words: *Jesse James*, nothing more.

Frank James took off his hat and put his arm around his mother. The coffin was lowered; as it touched the bottom, she gave an agonized moan and dabbed her eyes with her one hand. During the filling of the grave no one spoke; there was no religious ceremony.

When the grave was filled, they began to talk a little in low tones. She pointed: "When my time comes, I want to lay down beside him."

She and Frank and young Jesse went to the spring-wagon. Frank got in beside her and they started back to the hotel.

There the ex-guerrillas talked, laughing over their old exploits. At last the whistle of the engine was heard and they walked the short distance to the depot. As the train began to pull out, there was a flurry of goodbyes. Then Frank went back to his mother.

XXVI

THE PASSING OF THE TOBACCO BRIDE

FOLLOWING the reburial of Jesse, life on the James farm went on at an ever-slowing pace. Old Dr. Samuels had never quite recovered from the shock of his hanging forty years before. He was now a semi-invalid, and complained of being a burden on the family. The tobacco bride looked sadly upon the decline of her lifelong companion. In 1905 they had marked their golden wedding anniversary: a couple different in so many ways, but they had gotten along well. A good man and a good husband, and best of all, to a woman so ferociously proud of her children, a good father and stepfather. His mind began to go, he became more and more of a problem, and finally they had to take him to the Missouri State Hospital at St. Joseph, where he remained under state care. On March 1, 1908, the old doctor died. The rope burns were still on his neck.

After the loss of her husband she complained of being lonesome and began to make visits to Frank and to her kinfolks. But she still loved the farm, and, after each visit, came back as if it were a place set apart from all others in the world—this farm where she had plowed with one hand grasping the plow handle, the lines over her shoulder. Once, when she was walking in the yard, she stopped, looked about her, and said: "I came to this farm a bride. Most of my life has been spent on it. I have had three husbands; all have died. I have had eight children. I have had two of them betrayed and murdered. Out in that field, I saw my son Jesse beaten by soldiers. For weeks my son John lay upstairs at the point of death. In that room there my hand was blown off. I have spent endless uneasy nights here. But I still love the farm. I want to die on it."

Fear of want laid hold of her and she began to practice small deceptions, this woman who had always been so upright. One was to sell small stones from Jesse's grave; these she renewed from the creek. Another was to sell shoes from the horses Jesse and Frank had ridden; she sold enough to fill a wagonbed. Tourists always wanted to take her picture; she would tell them they could but they must send her a print. And this she sold to the next tourist who came along.

She never ceased to uphold her sons; over and over she said they had never been traitors, had done more good in the world than harm, and had had more friends than any two men in the state.

Her grandchildren became a consuming interest. Jesse Junior was doing well, a lawyer now in Kansas City, with four smart daughters. Frank's son Bob was working in St. Louis, so she had one grandson on one side of the state and another on the other.

When Frank was at home, his old ex-guerrilla friends came to see him; she welcomed them. They were fine men; they had ridden with her son. She liked to hear them tell stories of the old days and would sit entranced, a faraway look in her eyes. She complained of not having any 'get up and get' . . . the old lady who had always had so much driving force. Sometimes she would sigh and say, "I'm having one of my pore days." But no matter how badly she felt or how weak she was, if anyone reflected on her sons her eyes would flash and she would defend them as if they were children at her knee.

Railroads were allowed to give passes—chiefly to butter up politicians. The Burlington, which had transported the detectives the night of the bomb, gave her one. She accepted it—and went up and down the aisle denouncing the cowardly road.

Frank bought a farm near Fletcher, Oklahoma. As soon as he was settled she went to see him. It was nice to be with Frank and Ann, but she was, as she put it, getting to be a burden to herself. She enjoyed being with them, but the habits of a lifetime were hard upon her and she began to talk about wanting to go 'home'; things had to be taken care of; at last they put her on a train.

That night, on a Pullman sleeper, she began to feel badly; when she identified herself, the crew was surprised. They would do everything they could. But there was nothing they could do and she died on the train, on the night of February 10, 1911, eighty-seven years old—this woman who, so long ago, had left Kentucky as a tobacco bride to come to Missouri. How much of history had happened since then! And in how much of that history had she played a leading part.

The funeral was held in the Baptist church, just as Jesse's had been—the very church where Jesse had prayed for Frank. She was buried beside him. The inscription on the monument reads:

In Loving Remembrance of My Beloved Son
JESSE JAMES
Died April 3, 1882
Aged 34 Years, 6 Months, 28 Days
Murdered by a Traitor and Coward Whose
Name Is Not Worthy to Appear Here.

And there beside her, in final resting, are Dr. Reuben Samuels and Archie. Over her grave is a stone which reads MOTHER and over Dr. Samuels' is one which reads PAPPY.

XXVII

THE BEGINNING OF A LEGEND

HARDLY was Jesse in his grave before a song was composed and people began singing it. I remember the scholars at our country school used to sit on the wooden platform in front of the schoolhouse and sing that ballad as if the shooting were one of the greatest catastrophes that had ever befallen the human race. There were endless versions, but perhaps the best-known began:

Jesse James was a lad that killed a-many a man;
He robbed the Glendale train.
But that dirty little coward that shot Mr. Howard
Has laid Jesse James in his grave.

Jesse had a wife to mourn all her life.
Two children they were brave.
'Twas a dirty little coward that shot Mr. Howard
And laid Jesse James in his grave.

It was Bob Ford, the dirty little coward,
I wonder how does he feel,

For he ate of Jesse's bread and slept in Jesse's bed,
Then he laid Jesse James in his grave.

Jesse was a man, a friend to the poor,
He never would see a man suffer pain;
And with his brother Frank he robbed the Gallatin bank
And stopped the Glendale train.

I have not been able to trace down any of the authors except one. He was Billy Garshade, who lived in what was called the 'Crackerneck' section of Clay County, a few miles from where Frank and Jesse were born. This is the way his name went in:

It was on Saturday night
Jesse was at home,
Talking to his family brave;
Robert Ford came along,
Like a thief in the night,
And laid poor Jesse in his grave.

This song was made by Billy Garshade
As soon as the news did arrive;
He said there was no man with the law in his hand
Who could take Jesse James alive.

In fact, he worked too fast, for he did not get his facts quite correct; the deed had not fallen on Saturday night, but on Sunday morning. Nor was Jesse talking to his family, at least in the sense of the poem. But that was all right; the song did tell about a man who had been laid in his grave by what was considered a human monster.

Everywhere people sang of Jesse James who robbed the rich and gave to the poor. An example of how earnestly they treated the song is given by the story of the old blind woman who used to stand in front of the courthouse in Springfield, Missouri, and sing the ballad. People would drop coins in her tin cup and this was the way she made a living. One day as she was singing, a woman stopped and listened, and her face suddenly filled with indignation and resentment. She stepped forward and began to slap and push the singer until the blind woman fell sprawling into the street. Then she disappeared. Later it was found that she was Bob Ford's sister.

Even before he was killed Jesse was a legend, and novels about him and his exploits had begun to appear. (He used to read them to see how far they were from the facts.) The most prolific Jesse James author was John R. Musick, of Missouri, who wrote under the name of 'D. W. Stevens.' His stories—all pure inventions—and those of at least a dozen other writers appeared in these weekly publications: *New York Detective Library*, *Boys of New York*, *The Golden Weekly*, *Young Men of America*, *Wide Awake Weekly*, *Log Cabin Library;* there was even a *James Boys Weekly*. Richard K. Fox, publisher of the *Police Gazette*, brought out *The Outlaw Brothers, Frank and Jesse James*. Another publisher, Frank Tousey, made more money printing stories about Jesse James than Frank and Jesse made in all their lives as bandits, thus pretty conclusively showing that crime does not pay and that the big money is in telling about it.

Another writer was Frank Doughty, who wrote under the authoritative name of 'New York Detective.' No one seems ever to have doubted that he knew all about the Missouri boys. The Pinkertons experienced a little difficulty along this line, but New York Detective didn't.

Immediately Jesse was killed the so-called 'dime novels' began to pepper the newsstands with sensational stories. Here are some of the titles: *Frank James on Bob Ford's Track*, *The Mysterious Mr. Howard*, *The James Brothers Driven to the Wall*, *Frank on the Trail*, *Jesse James' Last Shot*, *Frank James' Mistake.* Old Cap Collier and King Brady told about the bloody exploits of the Missourians. Street & Smith, prolific publishers at the time, had a staff name, 'W. B. Lawson,' under which appeared the work of three or four hack writers including George C. Jenks and Robert Russell. They dished out Jesse James fodder right and left. One of the titles that appeared was *Frank Reade, the Inventor, Chases the James Boys with his Steam Man.* I never learned if the Steam Man was successful.

I. & M. Ottenheimer of Baltimore brought out a series of James books written by a certain Captain Kennedy. The influence of the Civil War still held; the dime-novel world was filled with 'Captains,' all writing furiously. One of the Ottenheimer books was *Jesse James' Daring Leap*, which was probably the source of the legend of his impossible leap across the chasm at Garretson, South Dakota. Other titles included *Jesse James' Cave*, *Jesse James Among the Mormons*, *Jesse James at Coney Island*, and *The James Boys and the Ku Klux.* They covered about everything. In Cleveland the Arthur Westbrook Company was turning out *The James Boys in Old Missouri*, *Jesse James' Ring of Death*, *Jesse James' Nerve*, and *Jesse James, Gentleman.* It was big business.

The first of the James thrillers appeared about 1880; they continued until 1904, then dropped off, for by that time the sensational dime novel was beginning to droop like a hog-weed on a farmer's fence. A contributory factor was that the Post Office Department threatened to withdraw second-class mailing privileges: stories too gory. For a while the publishers shed less blood, but the combination of waning interest and post-office troubles finally made them put the stories on the back of the stove.

Charles Bragin, 1525 West 12th Street, Brooklyn 4, New York, is a collector of dime novels, especially of Jesse James novels. He tells me that, in all, about 450 novelettes have been written about Frank and Jesse James. In the stories, with few exceptions, the James Boys are baffled and beaten and sent away to jail, but *alas!* in the last paragraph or two they manage to escape and to continue (next week) their low lives. Deplorable.

It was not long before stage plays appeared, to satisfy the popular demand that Jesse and Frank be actually seen and heard going about their desperate business. And, naturally, the playwrights permitted themselves as much dramatic license as the dime novelists. Some strange adventures were trotted out on the boards. But they were as nothing to what followed upon Mr. Edison's kinetoscope. In the motion picture the James *legend* was glorified for fair, and through that medium it has come down to the present generation as an increasingly preposterous and presumptuous distortion of the truth.

Six major movies have been made about the James Boys between 1927 and 1949, in addition to countless serials. They invariably have the following standard equipment: The bomb-throwing; the Northfield disaster; and the shooting in the back. From this point each picture proceeds as it chooses and in whatever direction it chooses, sparing nothing except the facts—which is perhaps a little difficult to understand, when the actual truth is so fascinating, so thrilling, so remarkable a bit of Americana.

At the time when possibly the most lavish of the James Boys movies was made, the studio was anxious to have members of the James family, then in Los Angeles, announce that it was fine stuff. They invited Jo Frances James, Jesse's granddaughter, to a private advance showing; and after it was over they asked, "How do you like it?"

"If he hadn't been named Jesse James," said the forthright lady, "and hadn't ridden a horse, I would never have known he was my grandfather."

That about sums it up.

XXVIII

MYTHS AFTER JESSE JAMES

IN ALL the vast James apocrypha the most persistent myth is that Jesse was not killed that day in St. Joseph. It sprang up immediately, chiefly because of the precedent established by George Shepherd's fake alarm, and it has been going ever since, for it would seem that the public does not want to believe that a person it has been interested in is no more.

For exactly fifty years Jesse James lay quietly in his grave. Then he rose and began coming back, and as I write he is still at it, although each year he gets a little older. Some day he'll have to give up. He first returned in 1932, rocking the country from end to end. He came boldly to Excelsior Springs, the newspapers whooping with delight. Eighteen people from Clay County who had known the living Jesse came to see his reincarnation. They gathered in the Royal Hotel—friends, neighbors, cousins; then Jesse marched in.

"I am Jesse James," he said calmly. "Ask your questions."

E. Price Hall said, "What time was the bomb thrown?"

"Just before dark."

"It was thrown at half-past twelve, midnight," said E. Price Hall.

"Hold up your left hand," said William Nicholson, an in-law.

The visiting Jesse held it up.

"When you were a boy you shot off your third finger on that hand, but it's there now. How do you explain that?"

"That was a mistake," mumbled Jesse.

Frank Milburn had made Jesse's wedding boots. "What size boots did you wear at your wedding?" he asked.

"Eights and a half."

"Wrong. You wore sixes and a half. You had an unusually small foot."

"I've forgotten some things," explained Jesse, with complete logic.

Undismayed, the old man went to St. Joseph and to the office of the *News-Press*, where he repeated the assertion that he was the original Jesse James. He said a man *had* been killed in the house on April 3, 1882, but it wasn't he and he could prove it. He said that on the day of the tragedy he had gone out in the yard and buried his six-shooter, and he'd go there now and dig it up. Arthur V. Burrowes, now the editor of the paper but then a reporter, went along to see the miracle. When they arrived at the house the old man walked around the yard like a water-witch, trying to get the exact location. Finally he found the spot and began to dig with a grubbing hoe. And there it was! But Burrowes was not as impressed as he should have been, for in his mind was the idea that something had happened to that lot. He got the grading contractor and, by use of photographs, proved that the whole top of the hill had in the intervening years been dug away, and that for the revolver still to be there Jesse would have had to bury it as deep as a dinosaur bone.

Jesse Junior wrote me: "This man was John James. He

was of simple mind. As a young man he went about the country trading horses; he would leave a note saying, 'Jesse James was here.' Later he began to use the name. He died in the State Hospital in Little Rock, Arkansas, December 26, 1947. His body was never claimed."

It was two years—1934—before another claimant turned up in St. Joseph. He had learned a lesson from the previous man. No gun-digging. He came to the Electric Theatre, where each night he talked thirty minutes, telling his life story and explaining how another man had been killed in his place. In his talk he kept repeating over and over, "If I am not Jesse James, who am I?"

He had them there.

But not forever, for one night a patron answered, "Clara Bow." (Duly noted in the *St. Joseph News-Press* for July 11, 1934.)

In 1936 a brand-new Jesse turned up in Tulsa, Oklahoma. He marked a great advance in the art of being Jesse James, for he had affidavits, newspaper clippings, photographs, and two scars to prove he was the real article. Scars was a tremendous step forward. He said he had been living in Colorado under the name of David Williams. Finally he took his scars and left.

The next year another claimant showed up—in a trailer. He went back to Columbia, Kentucky, to see the bank he had supposedly done business with sixty-five years before. Once he had ridden like the wind; now he had to bumble along in a trailer. It was very touching. However, the idea seems to have worked out all right, for he got a job with the Russell Brothers circus where he added a new touch; he told how, in disguise, he had attended his own funeral. No previous Jesse had thought of that.

Each year Jesse James had to be a little older. In 1948 the greatest of them all came to view—aged one hundred and one. He was discovered in a tourist camp at Lawton, Oklahoma, by alert reporters for the *Lawton Constitution.* Fearing they would be scooped, when the story was being set the men on the *Constitution* locked the building and would let no one come or depart. The story was released by all press associations. Frank O. Hall, city editor, wrote an article for *Editor and Publisher* which began:

" 'JESSE JAMES IS ALIVE! IN LAWTON!' I know that I will never write another eight-column headline that gave me the thrill the above headline did on May 19, 1948, and I am quite certain I'll never write one that created such a furore among the reading public."

The explanation of the new Jesse was unique. It seems the gang had made an agreement that none would reveal Jesse James's true identity until the last surviving member reached a hundred. Then, they had said generously, he could reveal all. And now Jesse had passed that age and could do whatever he saw fit. He saw fit to talk.

He told things no Jesse James before had ever thought of; he had not only attended his own funeral but had sung. That was a brand-new idea. It had been overlooked for twenty years. The way he had been able to disguise himself so successfully was quite simple. He dyed his hair; he had wide spaces between his upper teeth (he said), so he inserted gold wedges in such a way as to make him look as if he had a mouthful of gold. This completely fooled everybody.

Many people rushed into print to say they recognized him, although they hadn't seen him in sixty years. One was Al Jennings, the most overrated bandit America has ever known. His outlawry lasted exactly one hundred and nine days and his complete take for all robberies was $60. The two men came together in Oakland, California. The Associated Press, on July 3, 1948, said, "When Al Jennings saw the other man, his eyes filled with tears and he choked, 'It's him. It's Jesse.' " It must have been a touching scene.

Another identifier was an ex-slave one hundred and eight years old who had been Jesse's 'camp cook.' No record of any tears.

This latest Jesse said that he had been living under the name of J. Frank Dalton. Here are some of the unusual things he had done:

After he had been supposedly killed, he went to Rio de Janeiro, where he soon became a captain in the Brazilian cavalry.

He fought bravely in the Spanish-American War.

He went to Africa and fought bravely on the side of the Boers. For this he was made a colonel.

Then he went to another part of Africa and fought bravely against the Hottentots. "They are the only people I ever ran from," he said, lowering his eyes in shame; "they were not human."

He fought bravely in Mexico with General Pancho Villa.

When the First World War broke out, he went to Canada and, at the age of sixty-seven, became a captain of field artillery.

Then he went to England and became an air pilot where he flew for twenty-two months.

When the Second World War came along, all he could do was to sell war bonds. It seems to have been pretty humiliating.

I interviewed the old warrior at a hotel in Chicago. He was having a bilious attack, he said, and was living on whiskey and doughnuts. He said it was a sure cure for bile.

I asked him what 'Red Fox' meant to him.

"He was a scout for Quantrill. Real name was Solomon Strickland, he was part Indian, died in 1947 at the age of a hundred and eight."

I looked at his left hand. "I thought when you were a boy you shot the tip off the third finger of your left hand?"

He looked startled; apparently that question had never before been put to him. "What did you say?"

I repeated the question.

"No, I've got all my fingers. But look at the first finger on my right hand, no nail, see that black ridge down the middle? I'll tell you how that came about. I got into a fight with a Mexican in Mexico and he chewed it up. No, son, you got it wrong. Have a doughnut."

But he garnered plenty of money from his Return, for he has made personal appearances at rodeos, state fairs, and on the stage at the movie houses for Western pictures. He did so well that he carried a manager and a nurse. He turned Jesse James into big business. He also had a 'Message to the Youth of America.' It reads:

"The youth of today will be our citizens of tomorrow. Upon their shoulders will rest the responsibilities of guiding the destiny of our nation.

"Education is something you can always carry with you. It isn't heavy and no matter how you travel, you can always take it with you."

No one will ever be able to dispute *that*.

I asked Jesse James, Junior, if any of his fathers had come to see him. "Not one," he said.

I talked to Robert F. James at Excelsior Springs. I did not know him so well then and thought he would go off in a tirade. Instead he said: "Oh, that's my new Uncle Jesse. I've had five of them, but none of them have ever come to see me. I don't know why they haven't, because we're a good law-abiding family."

Another myth is that of the Buried Treasure. The treasure of the Jameses has been found off and on for forty years. It shifts around more than the Magnetic Pole; one year it's here, the next year it's gone off goodness knows where. On November 5, 1937, Robert L. Ripley had a thrilling 'Believe It Or Not.' The headline was: 'FRANK JAMES BURIED $2,000,000—THEN FORGOT WHERE HE BURIED IT.' The text told how Frank had buried the money in the Wichita Mountains in Oklahoma, and after his acquittal had come back to retrieve it, only to discover that new settlers had plowed up the ground so that he could not find the money.

Not a word of this was true. It derived from the following legend:

Frank and Jesse were hiding in Oklahoma. One day, after a rain, they were going along a back trail when what should they see but a queer-looking bar sticking from the side of a hill. They scratched it out. It was a gold ingot left by Coronado. They became interested and scratched some more, finally digging out two million dollars in Spanish ingots.

They had a problem on their hands. What should they do with the treasure? Since it was washing out, they'd better move it, so they did, hiding it where no casual horseman would see it. After Frank had finished his bout with the law, he came back but couldn't remember where he had buried it. He hunted for days, growing more and more provoked with himself. Finally he gave it up and went with a circus, where the money was less but more sure.

At first the loot was found by trappers. In 1913 a new touch came. An oil-pipeline worker named George Harsook found it while digging a trench near Claremore, Oklahoma. Shortly after this the Boy Scouts began to find it; they found it in a variety of places. The most advanced step came when men returned from the combat zone at the end of the First World War with their mine detectors; they would move here and there with the detectors, listening for the buzzing sound that hidden gold makes. In this way the treasure was dug up several times. Everybody found it except the James family.

Hardly ever does a summer go by without somebody finding the loot. Much of it is found in caves. I have one record where it was found in the fork of a tree. I have a clipping telling how the federal income tax people announced they were going to make a claim against a man who had just found it. I had to laugh when I pictured those tax collectors going out to get their money.

The truth of it is that there *was* no buried loot. There never was much money left, once the men divided their takings. So far as is known, Jesse never had in his possession at one time more than $6000. He farmed for two years, and God knows that anybody who had to make a living by farming would have gone off to his loot and yanked it out as fast as he could. He tried to purchase a farm in Nebraska but didn't have enough money to buy a bull calf. Jesse died poor; his widow had to auction off the household effects. Frank was poor and had small jobs all his life.

A favorite part of the legend is that the Boys had their horses shod backward, so that a posse or a group of irate farmers riding after them would go in the wrong direction. I have clippings from half a dozen papers recounting how some local blacksmith had shod the James horses with the ends of the shoes reversed. But no posse would have been fooled for long by that; farmers would have had to stop by the roadside to laugh. Furthermore, the Boys kept changing horses, and a horse shod backward would have thrown the rider into a millet field.

The best first-hand information on the subject comes from A. L. Maxwell, Route 2, Lexington, Missouri:

"The James brothers spent quite a bit of time in the hills of Sni-i-bar Township in Lafayette County, Missouri, where my father lived. A problem they faced was getting their horses shod. In February, 1876, a go-between for the brothers came secretly at night to the home of Bowdrey McHatton's father and asked if McHatton would shoe the horses of a 'friend.' McHatton agreed and the emissary slipped out into the night. Two days later two men arrived with three exceptionally good specimens of horseflesh. The men, of course, were Frank and Jesse James. Frank stayed in the shop and watched as the shoes were being fitted. Jesse stood guard half a block away, for the shoeing had to be completely secret. The animals were rough-shod. This means the shoes were calked and toed. [Smooth shoes were much lighter and were never calked.] When the shoes were in place, Frank paid the regular charge, then gave a tip of a dollar a horse extra. The shoes were not put on backward and, so far as I know, the James brothers never had their horses shod with the shoes reversed. It would have made a horse uncertain on his feet."

Then there are the people who played pool with Jesse James. They're thinning out now, but at one time no man in Missouri with any social pretensions would admit that he hadn't knocked off a couple of games with Jesse.

And then there are the people who owned one of Jesse's guns. If all those guns had been assembled and put in one place, they would have filled a corncrib.

And then the ones who saw Jesse on the street and recognized him but didn't tell on him. They made quite a respectable-sized crowd.

And those who were on a train that Jesse robbed. Carloads of them.

XXIX

THE JAMES FARM AND THE DEATH HOUSE TODAY

On the gate, at the main highway, a sign reads:

JAMES FARM
ADMISSION—ADULTS 50¢
CLOSE THE GATE

It is a short drive through the pasture along the private road that leads to the house. This is the road the Pinkertons took that dark and bloody night. Somewhere about in here Jesse killed the sheriff's horse. Along it the half-dying boy was carried on his way to Rulo, Nebraska. Jesse and Frank walked this path when they shot Askew. Here, looking at each other shyly, Jesse and Zee once strolled. And down it, following Jesse's body, upon a time passed the tobacco bride. . . . This winding semi-lane, semi-road had seen a great deal of bitterness and blood and tenderness.

I move along, and now can understand the peremptory order at the gate. Cattle.

I come to the house, where Mr. and Mrs. Bob James now spend their summers. It develops that tourists cause the family quite a bit of trouble. "We have to watch them like hawks or they will steal our souvenirs," says Mrs. James. "Once they carried off our spinning wheel." I enter and begin to look around. Perhaps she believes writers have no tourist blood.

In the living room of the 'new part' of the house are two things that seem the very epitome of the character of Jesse James. There they are, side-by-side on a table: his Bible and his revolver. He was always hesitating between them.

On the wall is old Robert James's graduation diploma from Georgetown College in Kentucky. Somehow it makes him seem more real. The minister; the Forty-Niner. Perhaps it was just as well for him he died young.

A voice at my ears suddenly booms, "Grandma was six feet tall and weighed two hundred twenty-eight pounds." I give a start. It is Bob James speaking of Zerelda Cole.

On the wall is an oldfashioned sampler. 'St. Catherine's Academy. March, 1840,' it says. How can it be possible that the girlish fingers which worked the pattern became part of the fiery old tyrant who used to walk up and down the aisle and denounce the railroad in smoking words? Who plowed her fields alone, with one hand?

On the wall is a sheet of paper with circles and perforations. "That's a target my father made at ten paces," says Frank's son. "He always fancied himself as a marksman."

We pass into the log bedroom. "Uncle Jesse slept on that bed three nights before he was killed," Bob remarks. I look at the decrepit, swaybacked old torture-rack and think of many things; and so must anyone who gazes at it.

On the wall is the crinkled mirror that Frank and Jesse used to shave by.

We go into the yard. Under this window Jesse lay when the Pinkertons were upon him. In that corner of the yard Zee crouched.

The stump of the old coffee-bean tree is there . . . and near it in the ground is a depression—yes! the very grave.

I gaze moon-eyed.

At first the house where Jesse had been killed was shunned; children would creep up, peep through the windows, then scurry away as if they had seen a ghost. The owner could not sell it; no one wanted anything to do with it. It was so little in demand that it rented for $8 a month. Jesse had paid $14.

Finally the death house began to be shown to a few curious visitors at fifteen cents admission. The guide had a singsong lecture about its 'bein' the original house where Jesse James was kilt.' But that didn't pay, and the house was sold for taxes. Now the city owned it. The city wanted to get rid of it. After what was considered a bit of luck the city sold it, for $1250.

In 1938 the wind changed. New York was having a World's Fair and somebody offered to buy the death house; he was going to take it to the Fair and exhibit it. St. Joseph's citizens suddenly found their pride. "No," they said feelingly. And the Chamber of Commerce began to put pictures of it in their bulletin, only a few pages back of the photographs of the Pony Express stables.

It was sold again. For $25,000.

The buyer jacked up the House on the Hill and moved it to Highway 71, to what is called 'The Belt.' He opened a filling station; if you filled 'er up you could go in free. Business began to boom; it boomed so much that people had to pay to see the house whether or not they filled up. In no time the owner said he would not take $100,000 for it.

He started a Jesse James Tourist Court and put up signs along the highway which said: 'Stop! This is the Jesse James House. See the Bullet Hole.'

Not far away is the bronze monument of a rider for the Pony Express, going like the wind. But nobody pays any attention to him. The Bullet Hole. That's what they want to see.

The place is now a tourist center, with a service station, hamburgers, beer, soft drinks, and a nearby dance hall. "We have just about everything," says the owner proudly. And what they don't have they're getting. The owner told me he was opening up the 'Jesse James Enterprises,' with a practice golf course, a bow-and-arrow target range, a pottery department, and a souvenir stand. It made me blink. The old house has come a long way.

There the death house stands today, with a wooden fence around it, much as it was when the shot was fired. On the front is the same printed notice that I gaped at as a young man, before it was moved from the hill: JESSIE JAMES HOME. The first thing you see when you step in is the work of tourists: names scribbled on every conceivable bit of wall space—scribbled, printed, smudged with lipstick. It makes one want to shoot from behind. And there in the wall, surrounded by a corona of scribbling, is the Bullet Hole. Once it was just that size, but tourists have pecked and chipped and carted away bits of plaster till today you can throw a potato through it. (The owner has worked a hardship on the tourists, for the Hole is now covered with a glass plate.)

On the wall, immediately above the Bullet Hole, is something to make one lift an eyebrow—the motto 'God Bless Our Home.'

On the floor you can see the spot where Jesse's lifeblood drained away.

There is practically nothing in the house that was in it that fateful night, mainly because of Zee James's auction. Some period pieces have been installed. There is a plush barber chair which was in a hotel barbershop; Jesse is supposed to have sat in the chair, but there is no proof.

As you stand there the scenes that took place so many years ago suddenly become real and vivid and moving. Why, this is the room where the family moved that Christmas Eve, the very room where Jesse played Santa Claus to his children! The room where he started to dust the picture and where the traitors moved between him and his holster. Bob Ford must have stood about *here!* And Jesse, hearing that faint click, must have turned his head about *there*. The room where Zee James supported in her lap his bleeding head and where the children sobbed at the dreadful thing that had happened to their father. Why, it was through this room that the public tramped, at the auction, buying the baby's high-chair for seventy-five cents. The room where Jesse's mother and his widow put the children to bed, their father's blood still on the floor! The room where Jesse's widow and mother sorted out his meager belongings, and where Mrs. Samuels kept crying over and over, "Oh! the traitors. Why did they do it?" What Americana is here, story and legend, here in this room with tourist names scribbled everywhere and the glass-covered Bullet Hole. You stand without speaking, then go out. A new batch of tourists is coming in, sharpening their pencils.

SOURCES

including a

NECROLOGY OF THE BANDITS

and a note on

THE JAMES FAMILY TODAY

SOURCES

INTRODUCTION

——The washday anecdote was refreshed in my mind by Alvin A. Clark, Maryville, Missouri. He was a neighbor to the Stafford family. The exact location of the Stafford farm is eight miles west and two north of Burlington Junction, Missouri, Colfax Township.

CHAPTER I

——The house where Frank was born no longer stands. It was given by Robert F. James, son of Frank, to Gerald Marsh, who lives at 408 North Water Street, Liberty, Missouri; there, in Mr. Marsh's basement, I saw part of the original lumber. Some of the door jambs had hound-tooth marks on them, for the Jameses were a hound-keeping family. Mr. Marsh makes fishing-line corks out of the lumber; these he gives to friends in memory of Frank James.

——Jesse Cole's life ended dramatically. He was a highly respected farmer in Kearney. One day he went into the back yard of his home, took off his coat and vest, rolled them up, and placed his watch on top of them. Then he lay down, opened his shirt, and with a revolver shot himself in the heart. He had been suffering from ill health.

——The information about Benjamin Simms, Mrs. James's second husband, was found in old records in the courthouse at Liberty, Missouri, by Mrs. Robert S. Withers, the historian of Clay County.

——Edgar Laffoon of Kearney, whose father was a schoolmate of the James brothers, furnished the name of the Pleasant Grove School. For a time it was called the Wilson School.

——I have seen the jail where Frank was confined. Only a part of the foundation remains. Some thirty years before Frank's visit it had held another notable prisoner, Joseph Smith, the founder of the Church of the Latter-Day Saints; and while I was there a group of Mormons arrived on a pilgrimage to the spot.

——From the *St. Joseph Herald* of April 6, 1882, comes the name of the officer who required Frank to take the oath of allegiance: Lieutenant Colonel William R. Penick. The oath itself (taken at Greenville, a village near the James farm which has ceased to exist except as a voting precinct) reads in full:

> I, Franklin James, of Greenville, County of Clay, State of Missouri, do solemnly swear that I will support, protect and defend the Constitution and the Government of the United States against all enemies, whether domestic or foreign, that I will bear the true faith, allegiance and loyalty to the same, any ordinance, resolution or law of any State, or legislature to the contrary notwithstanding; and, fur-

ther, that I will faithfully perform all the duties which may be required of me by the laws of the United States. And I take this oath freely and voluntarily, without any mental reservation or evasion whatever, with a full and clear understanding that death, or other punishment by the judgment of a military commission, will be the penalty for the violation of this, my solemn oath and parole of honor.

Franklin James

April 26, 1862

Chapter II

——The story about Bloody Bill Anderson and the steamboat was contained in a news dispatch in the *Kansas City Times* for April 10, 1882. The correspondent (whom I have been unable to identify) signed himself merely 'H.C.,' and said he had been with Jesse during the guerrilla days.

——The town of Rulo got its unusual name from a Frenchman named Charles Rouleau, born in Detroit, who married an Indian girl and founded the village on land which she brought him. The name eventually shook down to Rulo, and the town shook down still more—it hasn't even a mayor today, only catfish: that's the biggest and most exciting thing about the place, its catfish dinners. In summer they greet you halfway across the state.

——Additional information about Harlem has been supplied by Samuel A. Pence of 201 East Kansas Street, Liberty, Missouri. He says it was a small settlement at the north end of the

Hannibal & St. Joseph Railroad, across from Kansas City. (Later this railroad became part of the Burlington System.) For years, at this place, there was a ferry.

——The story about Jesse and the Leavell boy was told me by Robert S. Withers of Liberty, who heard it from Judge Leavell himself.

——The men regarded at the time as having been in the Liberty robbery were Arch Clements (usually considered the leader), Frank James, Cole Younger, Bill Chiles, J. F. Edmundson, Jim White, Oliver Shepherd, 'Red' Monkers, and Bud Pence. One of the curiosities of this raid was that Arch Clements had not yet surrendered to the Union forces at Lexington, Missouri. So far as he was concerned, the Civil War was still on. Nine months later he decided to surrender as a Confederate soldier, but on the streets of Lexington he got into an argument over which side was right—the North or the South—and was killed before he could get to the surrender office. (From accounts in the *Kansas City Journal* for April 6, 1882, the *Kansas City Evening Star* for April 6 & 7, 1882, and from dispatches in the *St. Louis Globe-Democrat* for April 1882.)

——According to the *Liberty Tribune* of February 16, 1939, Greenup Bird, who was cashier of the Clay County Savings Association, left a handwritten memorandum of the loot scooped up from the Liberty bank, as follows:

$40,000.00	in U.S. 3-70 bonds
8,668.18	in greenbacks and national currency
3,096.00	in Union military bonds
300.00	in Farmer Bank notes
5,008.46	in currency belonging to depositors
$57,072.64	

In addition there were three bags of gold, exact value unknown but believed to bring the total up to $62,000. I wrote the Treasury Department outlining the robbery and asking if those government bonds represented spending money to the bandits. The reply (from Robert A. Dillon of the Information Service) was:

"According to the records of the Treasury Department, United States Government Bonds in 1866 were outstanding in both registered and coupon form. The bonds could be sold to another directly, or through a bank, or dealer. The thieves would doubtless have been able to dispose of the stolen bonds. This disposal simply means by sale to an individual, or to an institution."

A local legend, passed along by Ed Brining, whose father was the clerk in the bank, tells that Mrs. Samuels had borrowed money from the county funds, and when the time came for repayment she showed up at the bank with revenue stamps which had been stolen from it. They were not accepted, so she paid in hard money. Since the burden of proof rested on the bank, nothing was ever done about it.

——I went to the Liberty bank. The outside, they tell me, looks much as it did at the time of the robbery. Only now it is 'The Tog'ry Shop,' run by Miss Nannie Chrisman. She told me I could go into the vault where the money was kept. I did—and it was full of dresses. What a comedown! They hung everywhere, like bats in a cave. I succeeded in knocking two to the floor. When I came out, Miss Chrisman had on her face an unmistakable look of relief.

As I was standing out in front trying to reconstruct the event, I saw a filling station with the name Wymore on it. When I inquired, the owner said he was a relative of the boy who had given up his life. It served to bring back a touch of the personal.

CHAPTER III

——Savannah, Missouri, is today famous for its cancer clinic. People from all over the Middle West go there for treatment. The banker who stopped the bullet on the day of the robbery eventually recovered, but forever after walked around with one shoulder higher than the other. I used to gaze on him with awe. To have been shot by Jesse James! That seemed about as high up in life as a person could get.
——The story of Jesse and the stolen mare is from the *Excelsior Springs Standard* for April 8, 1939.
——Eight warrants were issued after the Richmond affair. They were for Payne Jones, John White, Jim White, Isaac Flannery, Richard Burns, Andrew McGuire, Thomas Little, and Allen H. Parmer (the latter, about three years later, married Jesse's sister Susie). Also suspected was Cole Younger, but no warrant was sworn out. Jesse and Frank were suspected, but that was as far as it got. The law—after all this pother about warrants—accomplished not one thing. But angry mobs did. They grabbed three of the men and hanged them: Richard Burns, Andrew McGuire, and Thomas Little. (From the *Kansas City Evening Journal* for April 6, 1882, and Robertus Love.)
——Clay Seminary stood at the corner of Kansas and South Leonard Streets in Liberty. Most of it burned down in 1879, but one building survived and is today a Christian Science church.
——The scene of Jesse calling on his cousin is based on material in *The Commercial* of Weston, Missouri, for April 8, 1882; and from conversations with members of his family.

Chapter IV

——The anecdote of Jesse and Joe Miller comes from an interview with General Jo Shelby which appeared in the *Kansas City Journal* and was quoted by Governor T. T. Crittenden in his book, *The Crittenden Memoirs.*

——The tale of the Union soldier and his mother comes from the April 10, 1882, issue of the *Kansas City Times,* in a feature article again signed by the unidentifiable 'H. C.' The names of the two guerrillas who accompanied Jesse are given as John Hubbard and John Van Meter.

——Cole Younger's preliminary visit to Russellville as a cattle buyer hard up for small change, as well as the robbery itself, is recounted in a number of sources, mainly the *Kansas City Journal for* April 6, 1882; Edwin Finch's book, *Kentucky All Over;* 'Reminiscences,' by Charles H. Neal, which appeared in the *Kentucky Standard* of Bardstown for December 16, 1948; and from material supplied me by John W. Muir of Bardstown.

——Information concerning the Paso Robles trip has been most kindly furnished, and in great detail, by Mrs. C. S. Smith of 1225 Park Street, Paso Robles. She went to school with Drury Woodson James's four younger children (he had seven). Another source is the *History of San Luis Obispo County and Environs,* by Annie L. Morrison, published in 1917.

Unfortunately there is nothing, anywhere, about Jesse's voyage west, a great loss, especially as regards his passing through New York. Jesse James on Broadway . . . sets the imagination going. . . .

——The Baptist Church in Kearney, where Jesse was baptized, has been replaced by another building, and no souvenir or record of Jesse remains.

——Authority for the Gallatin bank account is Robertus Love, with some additional material that has come to light since he published his first-rate *The Rise and Fall of Jesse James* in 1926.

——A letter from Judge Thomas R. Shouse, now in the files of Elmer L. Pigg at Jefferson City, contains the story of the shooting of Sheriff Thomason's horse, and also of the later incident when Jesse paid off Oscar Thomason for the target practice obtained.

Chapter V

——The tale of Jesse and friend in the old swimming hole will be found on page 83 of *Jesse James, My Father*, by Jesse Edwards James, 'published and distributed' in Kansas City by the author, in 1889. Although this book contains material found no other place, some things in it are inaccurate. Perhaps this story is. But I couldn't resist it.

——Much information on the Corydon affair comes from an address entitled 'Train Robbers, Train Robberies and the Holdup Men,' delivered by William A. Pinkerton before the International Association of Chiefs of Police at Jamestown, Virginia, in 1907. The address is available in pamphlet form in the New York archives of the agency.

——*The Palimpsest*, the magazine published by the State Historical Society of Iowa in Iowa City, in its February 1936 issue identifies the Corydon riders as Jesse and Frank James, Cole and Jim Younger, Clell Miller, Jim White, and Jim Koughman. Two months later Clell Miller was arrested, taken back to Corydon, and tried. Nothing could be proved, and he was turned loose. The hand of the law did not descend on any of the other six.

——As a footnote to the humorous turn Jesse displayed at Corydon, I want to pass along a story told by Ernest U. Guenzel, III, which further illustrates Jesse's prankishness, even under considerable stress. Mr. Guenzel is vice-president of the First National Bank of Lincoln, Nebraska, and his grandfather (same name, less a Third) was aboard a train held up by the James-Younger gang. Toward the end of the business to hand, one of the bandits discovered a consignment of ladies' hats in the baggage car, whereupon the whole gang, led by Jesse, decorated themselves with the millinery, hopped on their horses, and rode gaily away.

——G. Schroeder of Wellman, Iowa, is the source of the anecdote about Jesse and the Reverend George Bayer. The latter died in Marengo, Iowa, and was known personally to Mr. Schroeder.

——The name of the cashier killed in the Columbia robbery was R. A. C. Martin. His picture hangs today on the wall of the Bank of Columbia as a memorial of the event.

——The Kansas City fairground robbery account is based on a fairly detailed article in the *Kansas City Journal* for April 6, 1882. The three men, according to this paper, were Jesse and Frank James and Bob Younger. Jesse was the one who grabbed the cashbox.

One man still lives who saw the robbery; he is John W. Wagner, conductor of the Wagner Funeral Home, Linwood and Wyandotte Streets, Kansas City. He says: "I was a boy of eleven. There were two gates. I was near the Twelfth Street gate when I heard shooting and, boylike, ran to see what the excitement was about. Three men were riding around and around, shooting. This was to distract the attention of the people from the actual robbery. These men rode down Campbell Street to the entrance on Fifteenth Street. I ran, too, thinking they were having a race. I did not actually see the man who got the money. I have only my memory to go on, but I'll never forget what I saw that exciting day."

——The *St. Joseph Herald* for April 4, 1882, gives the main details of the Ste. Genevieve affair. The name of the bank involved was the Ste. Genevieve Associations Banking House. Harry J. Petrequin, an attorney in Ste. Genevieve, has written me: "We still have the safe in our museum. It is a lock-and-key affair. The safe has iron straps around it for reinforcement."

Chapter VI

——The information about the first train robbery was obtained from Alvin F. Harlow's excellent book *Old Waybills*, published by D. Appleton-Century Company in 1934; the book that John Reno wrote about his own exploits, *The Life of John Reno, World's First Train Robber*, published by the Whitsett Print Shop, 204 South Chestnut Street, Seymour, Indiana, in 1879; and from fragments in the Coe Collection at Yale.

John Reno and the man who performed the *second* train robbery were both suitors for the hands of a local girl named Mollie. The second man needed money, so he held up a train, just as John Reno had done, and walked off with $7000, as

noted. But John Reno, who seems to have been watching his rival like a hawk, waylaid him when he was trying to elope with Mollie and took the money away from him. It shows pretty conclusively the kind of people who come from Indiana.
——Source of the Adair train robbery story is *The Palimpsest;* the pertinent article appeared in the February, 1936, issue, and was written by Philip D. Jordan. The name of the engineer who was killed was John Rafferty. The fireman was one Dennis Foley, William A. Smith the conductor, and John Burgess the guard. The time?—half-past eight at night. The *St. Joseph Herald* for April 4, 1882, also receives an assist for this section.
——Gad's Hill and Hot Springs transactions recorded in the *Kansas City Evening Star* for April 20, 1882.
——An illustration of the fear in which Jesse James's name was held (and which consequently kept potential informers potential) is given in a story told me by Raymond H. McCaw, night editor of the *New York Times.* His father was living in Pawnee City, Nebraska, when word got around that Jesse was due to rob the local bank. Mr. McCaw, Sr., rushed down, drew out his money ($480), hurried home, and buried it in a tin can in the back yard. There was some truth to the rumor, for the James gang did inspect another bank in that section. When the scare was over, Mr. McCaw dug up his money and again took a chance on the bank.

Chapter VII

——Details concerning the complicated courtship of Jesse James are to be found in the *Kansas City Evening Star* for April 20, 1882; and additional material has come from Mrs.

Stella McGown James. An account of the marriage was given in an interview with the Reverend William James, published in the *Kansas City Journal* for April 13, 1882. Jesse James, Junior, adds his confirmation.

——Robertus Love states that it was John Younger who killed Captain J. W. Allen, and Jim Younger who killed Daniels. The latter was buried in his home town of Osceola, and Allen, being a Chicago man, was shipped back there—express direct to the Pinkerton office, no doubt.

——The *History of Clay County*, published in 1920, gives information on Detective Witcher, and states that he left for the Great Beyond on March 10, 1874.

——An account of the San Antonio stagecoach robbery appears in the *St. Joseph Herald* for April 4, 1882.

——The following were in the Muncie robbery: Jesse and Frank James, Cole and Bob Younger, Clell Miller, and Bud McDaniels. The only man taken was Bud McDaniels. He got drunk, talked too much, and was arrested. He tried to escape from the officers and was shot for his pains. And that was all that ever happened to any of the Muncie men.

Chapter VIII

——According to numerous accounts, at the time of the explosion Jesse and Frank, Clell Miller, and Bill and Dora Fox were upstairs playing cards. This story presumably got started on its way by a bit of gossip printed in the *Kansas City Journal* for April 13, 1882, which was later picked up by Governor Crittenden and included in his *Memoirs*, and ever since has been fodder for many exciting Sunday newspaper and magazine articles. The story does not bear close inspection. But it must have fed many a writer's family.

——The authority identifying Ladd as the detective killed after the bombing is a letter by Jesse James, Junior, which appeared in the *Kansas City Star* for September 6, 1925. (*Note:* The main outline of Ladd's operations is contained in the *History of Clay County*, and in Judge Shouse's papers on file with Elmer Pigg. I paid a call on the New York office of Pinkerton's National Detective Agency, Inc., to find out more about Ladd, especially to try and find out what his real name was. Bad luck. The records for that section were kept in the Chicago office of the agency, and the Chicago Fire took care of them permanently. So, for the time being, Jack Ladd continues in history under an alias. Perhaps it's just as well.)

——Footnote to the Pinkerton version of the bombing: I examined the remains of the 'bomb,' which are to be seen today in the James home. On approximately half the original case, which is all that is left, there are no indications that any heavy iron straps ever formed a part of it. Furthermore, no such straps, or parts of such straps, were ever found after the explosion, or mentioned in accounts. Out there, the object is always referred to as a 'black-powder bomb.'

Chapter IX

——The story of the widow and the skinflint is one of the oldest and best-known of the Jesse James stories. I have heard, by word of mouth, many versions, yet all are substantially the same. One version, told in our section, was that the riders waited at a covered bridge, and there pounced on the man.

Another point in favor of its acceptance is that Frank James once or twice told the story; and no one who knew Frank James would ever accuse him telling something that was not true. He was the most close-lipped of all the members of the gang, and the least apt to brag. What he said could be depended on.

There is, in the library of the *Kansas City Star,* a worn and ancient clipping quoting a man named Wright (initials missing) who asserts he knew the facts; he says the incident happened near Jamesport, Missouri.

As for myself, I am inclined to accept the general idea of the story. It is the kind of humor that Jesse James would have indulged in.

Chapter X

——A booklet entitled *Robber and Hero,* written and published in 1895 in Northfield by Professor George Huntington of Carleton College, is the chief source of information about the robbery and the subsequent ride of the bandits. Further material is contained in another booklet, *The Northfield Bank Raid,* published by the Northfield News in 1933; and the whole picture has been filled in by that nonpareil Northfield historian, William F. Schilling.

——A note on the St. Paul hotels: The Merchants Hotel was at Third and Jackson, the European Hotel at 107 East Third Street (thanks to Lois M. Fawcett of the St. Paul Public Library).

——The information about the baseball game comes from George Edmond of the *St. Paul Dispatch-Pioneer Press.* He says that Frank Salvus of St. Paul, the author of *One Hundred Years of Baseball* and generally considered a top authority on the subject, believes that the league the *Red Caps* and the *Clippers* played in—the Northwestern—was not officially organized until 1877, but that the teams had played each other independently the previous season.

——Names of the men in the bank: Joseph Lee Heywood, A. E. Bunker, Frank J. Wilcox. The cashier, G. M. Phillips, was at the Philadelphia Centennial, for which he should have been thankful. The stone throwers: H. S. French, Justice Streater, and Elias Hobbs. The medical student: H. M. Wheeler. The hardware men: J. S. Allen, A. R. Manning. Other men who fired from the street: Ross C. Phillips, J. B. Hyde, James Gregg. And a note comes from Bill Schilling: "Why don't you add this about Lon Bunker? His initials were 'A. E.' but everybody called him 'Lon.' He left the banking business and became head of the St. Paul division of the Northwestern Newspaper Union, which supplied 'patent insides' to country newspapers." Glad to.

——Herman Roe, editor of the *Northfield News* for forty years and familiar with the story all his life, supplies me with a sidelight on Joseph Lee Heywood, the faithful but dead substitute cashier. He became Northfield's greatest hero. Banks in the United States and Canada raised $12,000 for his family. The Grand Army post of Northfield was named in his honor, and as long as the post existed a portrait of Heywood hung on the wall. He was an officer of Carleton College, and the college still has a Heywood Library Fund. In the First Congregational Church of Northfield there is today a memorial window to Heywood which bears the inscription '*Fidelitas*': that he was, but was he wise?

——In September, 1948, I went to Northfield to attend 'Jesse

James Day.' The robbery was to be reenacted. But it very nearly wasn't. They couldn't get the riders! Yes, the world had changed that much since the real robbery. Every man and boy, then, could have ridden, but now it took no end of scurrying about to find eight young men who could stay on as the horses galloped down the streets with blank cartridges hot upon them. It turned out there was a rodeo near, with professional riders, and the day was saved. It would have made Jesse James turn over in his grave.

Before the 'reenactment' there was a street parade, with a dozen bands from surrounding towns. The bands were led by highstepping, hipswinging 'majorettes.' That'd have made Jesse climb out.

CHAPTER XI

——I talked with three Northfield men who were living at the time of the raid: W. W. Pye, Charles Nichols, and Ed Doran. Mr. Pye said that his father was having a house built at the time. The stone mason was up high, working on the chimney. He heard the shots and could see the confusion in the street, and called down to young Will Pye, who ran next door to the old house and told his mother the news. In a few minutes the robbers dashed past and young Will was able to see them in their flight.

——An article in the *Sioux City Journal* for June 6, 1948, adds another piece of information to the Northfield record. It develops that the farmer Frank and Jesse borrowed the blind team from was named Andrew Nelson, and lived near a place called Valley Springs, Minnesota. The two horses were eventually picked up at Shindler, south of Sioux Falls, in what is now South Dakota.

——This same issue of the *Sioux City Journal* also sets down the names of the men who captured the Youngers and killed Charlie Pitts near Madelia: W. W. Murphy, Benjamin Rice, Charles A. Pomeroy, Sheriff James Glispin, George Bradford, James Stevenson, and Thomas L. Vought. They were called the 'Northfield Immortals.'

Chapter XII

——The surprise call of Frank and Jesse upon Farmer Rolph of Luverne would have remained denied to history without the assistance of the *Sioux City Journal*, issue of June 6, 1948.

——And for the story of the telegraph office inquiry I am indebted to the Historian of Minnehaha County, South Dakota: Mr. Charles A. Smith, 605 South Duluth Avenue, Sioux Falls.

——Having assured my unpopularity with the Garretson, South Dakota, Chamber of Commerce and other interested parties by doubting the legend of the Devil's Gulch, I now clinch it with a statement on the supposed 'Jesse James Cave' near Garretson. The Boys never hid in any cave at any time.

——The sad end of Charlie Pitts is told by Dr. Henry F. Hoyt himself, in his book *A Frontier Doctor*, published by Houghton Mifflin Company in 1929. And I should like to add a word of thanks to Paul Light of the *St. Paul Pioneer Press* for getting his readers to dig into their attics and hope chests for old papers shedding further light on Charlie's bleaching bones.

——The case history of Clell Miller's skeleton came to me via Herman Roe of Northfield, who got it straight from Dr.

Wheeler himself during a trip to Grand Forks to address the annual convention of the North Dakota Press Association.

Chapter XIII

——There are two sources for the information about the flight of the James families to Tennessee. One is conversations with Robert F. James. The other is no less than *Jim Cummins' Book* By Himself, issued by the Reed Publishing Company of Denver, Colorado, in 1903. The reader is referred to pages 173 and 174.

——Stanley F. Horn, the Nashville historian, gave me the piece about Frank James having made cedar buckets.

——A few years ago Mary James Barr visited the Smith family in Nashville and saw the room where she had been born. Emerson Smith and his wife read me a letter from her; it was warm and glowing and filled with appreciation for the kindnesses the Smiths had shown her.

——The name of the sheriff in Nashville whom Frank James made friends with was Timothy Johnson. It is said that Sheriff Johnson was a bit dazed, later, when he found that he had been fraternizing with $10,000, dead or alive. (Information from an interview with Frank which appeared in the *Nashville Daily American* for October 9, 1882.)

——The story of the belligerent Dude Young was told me by Stanley Horn. It also appears in an interview with Frank James in the *Nashville Daily American* for October 9, 1882.

——The story about Jim Cummins and the detective comes also from the *American*.

——Frank's official listing can be found under 'B. J. Woodson' in the Nashville directory for 1881, if you happen to have a copy handy.

Chapter XIV

——The arrival in Nashville was not the first visit for either Zee Mimms James or her four-year-old son. An article in the *Nashville Banner* for June 22, 1930, by M. B. Morton states that Jesse Edwards James (the middle name honoring John N. Edwards of Sedalia, Missouri, who had written a spirited defense of the James brothers under the title *Noted Guerrillas*) was born at 606 Boscobel Street in Nashville on August 31, 1875. Mr. Morton got his information from Gus A. Maddux, a Nashville real-estate man and owner of the house. The statement has been verified by Jesse Junior himself, in a letter to the author. Zee had presumably been sent down to Nashville to have the baby in comparative calm and safety; the time was shortly after the Pinkerton bombing, when Jesse was very much on the run. The name of the attending doctor was W. M. Vertrees.

I visited the house at 606 Boscobel Street and found evidence that Jesse too had stayed there around the time of his son's birth. (It must have been in fits and starts, but we can guess he was present at the great event, for he was not in the band that robbed the Huntington bank on September 1, 1875, and it would have to have been a pretty important thing that could keep Jesse away from his robbing.) The house, at the time of my visit, was owned and occupied by Mr. and Mrs. Angelo Calvo. I asked Mrs. Calvo if there were any souvenirs of the days when Jesse had lived there and she said yes, the remains of a stable in the rear where he had kept a horse bridled and saddled, and, in the basement, a 'hanging shelf.' And there it was, just like the one at the Felix Smith house where Frank lived. In the walls of the cellar was a secret recess disguised by a movable stone. Mrs. Calvo said her grandfather had told her that Jesse had kept his money in the wall. Her grandfather, she added, was an outlaw named Alex Scott, and she believed he had ridden with Jesse.

——The intelligence that Jesse joined the Methodist church in Nashville was part of an interview with Frank James published in the *Nashville Daily American* for October 9, 1882.

——The story of the meeting of Jesse James and Billy the Kid comes from two sources: M. A. Otero's *My Life on the Frontier*, and the previously mentioned *A Frontier Doctor* by Dr. Henry F. Hoyt.

To be as accurate as possible in what I was setting down, I sent the incident to Maurice G. Fulton, who is in charge of the Lincoln County Museum, Lincoln, New Mexico, and who is generally considered the greatest living authority on Billy the Kid. (Walter Noble Burns died in 1942.) His letter:

"Of the two who have written on the subject, I consider Hoyt the more reliable. For years I have considered his vignettes of the Kid as among the more precious of such testimonies.

"There may well have been a meeting of the two redoubtables at Las Vegas in the late summer, or fall, of 1879, at Scott Moore's hotel. At that time Billy the Kid was beginning his eighteen months retirement from the Lincoln County section. Governor Lew Wallace, and everybody else, were giving attention to the Indian outbreaks and Billy the Kid—after fulfilling his agreement with Wallace to turn state's evidence regarding the killing of Lawyer Chapman—had discovered that

Wallace could not carry out his part of the program because of the opposition of Rynerson, the district attorney. Accordingly the Kid had taken French leave of Lincoln and gone to Fort Sumner; hence it would have been easy for him to turn up at Las Vegas.

"That the Kid knew Scott Moore is attested by a letter of 1881, just after his conviction at Las Cruces, in which he is concerned about the selling of his mare which, as the spoils of capture, had fallen to Frank Stewart and from him to Scott Moore.

"I think your account is reasonably true, especially if considered from the viewpoint on Jesse James. If it were from the viewpoint of William H. Bonney, some things might be put differently. The Kid was a young rascal, with a mind alert to what was going on, and, I daresay, knew more about Jesse James than the latter did about him."

——The information about the Glendale robbery is based, chiefly, on material in the *Western Cultivator* for September 17, 1881 (ten days after the robbery). The paper was a Kansas City weekly. It gives this tidbit which I have never seen anywhere else: "There was on board a party of tourists from Penn Yann, New York, in charge of the land agent for the Fort Scott railroad. Suddenly the outlaws burst among them, discharging their guns and demanding that the passengers throw their money and valuables into a grain sack one of the bandits was carrying. The eastern tourists became extremely nervous."

The item about Jesse James and the engineer comes from the same paper, the same date.

Love says the following men took part in the Glendale robbery: Jesse James, Jesse's cousin Wood Hite, Ed Miller, Bill Ryan, Dick Liddil, and Tucker Bassham. Ed Miller was the brother of Clell Miller who departed this life at Northfield,

Minnesota. Frank James, it will be noted, is not included in the list.

——Three sources for the account of the Mammoth Cave stagecoach holdup: *Commonwealth of Kentucky vs. T. J. Hunt*, in the records of Barren Circuit for the March term, 1882; *Stage-coach Days in the Bluegrass*, by J. Winston Coleman, Jr.; and an article by Edwin Finch in the *Louisville Courier-Journal* for June 15, 1947.

The names of the passengers who contributed so generously to Jesse's charity drive were:

J. E. Craig, Jr., Lawrenceville, Ga.	$670.
Judge R. H. Rowntree (and his watch)	55.
S. H. Frohlechstein, Mobile, Ala.	23.
S. W. Shelton, Calhoun, Tenn.	50.
George M. Paisley, Pittsburgh, Pa.	5.
Miss Lizzie Rowntree (her watch, and a generous supply of jewelry).	

Phil Rowntree, a relative of the Judge, slipped his watch and wallet under the seat, and so contributed nothing to the roadside needy. He was lucky, indeed, for usually Jesse and his fellow-workers cuffed such a person over the head with their pistol butts; sometimes they shot him dead. It was best to contribute and try to forget it.

——Material about the Muscle Shoals affair comes again from the omniscient Stanley F. Horn, whose *The Army of Tennessee* is required American history. Apparently it was originally *Mussel* Shoals, after what was to be found in the river at the shoals, but as time went on various people (strong perhaps on muscle, but weak on spelling) began to write it *Muscle* Shoals; and at the time of the building of the first dam the government stepped right up and announced officially that it *was* Muscle Shoals. Mr. Horn tells me that some of the oldtimers still write it Mussel Shoals, government or no government.

——Mr. Horn also provides the information about Frank James and the sick friend.

——The name of the former detective who clapped hands on Bill Ryan was William L. Earthman. He was, at the time of the oyster episode, a collector of back taxes. Everybody hated him.

Chapter XV

——The source of the 'Respectfully, Joe' letter is Dick Liddil's confessions.

——John W. Muir sends me the information that the warm bed discovered by Detective Hunter was located in a hotel in Bardstown, Kentucky, now known as the Hotel Stephen Foster. Mr. Muir, a resident of Bardstown, is cashier of Wilson & Muir, bankers; he got the story, in turn, from his father.

——The *Louisville Courier-Journal* for May 16, 1937, carried a piece by Joe Hart which is the source of the anecdote concerning Jesse, D. T. Bligh, and the postcard. Mr. Hart quoted from an early scrapbook which is at present in the Louisville City Hall.

——With the appearance of the Fords a few vital statistics can be given: Charles Wilson Ford, born July 9, 1857; Robert Newton Ford, born January 31, 1862—as copied from the Ford family Bible, now in possession of Bob's nephew, Tom Jacobs of Jefferson City.

——The story of George Shepherd killing Jesse James came from a later news story in the *Kansas City Journal* for April 6,

1882, and from an interview with Frank James in the *St. Louis Republican* for October, 1882. A source of satisfaction to Frank, in this Shepherd matter, was that George Shepherd was the only member of the gang that Detective Bligh ever caught; and, as Frank said, "Shepherd was blind in one eye, and Bligh was lucky enough to come up on that side."

——The pane of glass on which Jesse scratched his name was removed from the window, but it still exists, and is at present owned by Felix Bean, who has it in his home at 1306 Morton Avenue, Louisville, Kentucky. Thanks again to John Muir for having put me in touch with former Congressman Ben Johnson for this story.

Chapter XVI

——Thomas M. Mimms, Zee's brother, according to an article in the *Kansas City Journal* for April 6, 1882, stated that Jesse and his family stayed at the following places in Kansas City: (1) A house on Woodland Avenue, between Thirteenth and Fourteenth Streets, where Jesse was known as J. T. Jackson; (2) Moved to a house on East Ninth Street, 'in the first block east of Woodland Avenue,' which was owned by one George Rick; (3) Then moved to 1017 Troost Avenue, where they remained a month.

——*Personal Note:* It was in St. Joseph that the author, a fugitive from the farm, did his first newspaper work, on the *St. Joseph Gazette.* He covered, mainly, the Y.M.C.A. and the undertakers. He used to pass the 'death house,' but it wasn't so highly regarded in those days. He saw that old ledger (of which more later) in Sidenfaden's mortuary establishment. But never did he dream he would one day be trying to write the story of the man who became St. Joe's most famous resident. Didn't appreciate it at the time, I guess.

——The story of Jesse playing Santa Claus is based on material in the *Western Cultivator* of Kansas City for September 17, 1882, plus conversations with the family.

——Harold M. Slater, of the *St. Joseph News-Press*, supplies me with the information that the city directory listing 'Thomas Howard' was compiled by the Hoyes City Directory Company, and printed by the St. Joseph Steam Printing Company.

Chapter XVII

——The story of Uriah Bond and Jesse James was supplied me by Uriah Bond's son, Martin Bond, a former neighbor of ours. As I write, Martin Bond is ninety-two-years old and lives at 1275 Westchester Place, Los Angeles 6, California. His full name is Uriah Martin Bond, but he has always been called just Martin. In his letter Mr. Bond gave me a glimpse of the days he had lived through in Clay County: "I was just a boy during the Border Warfare days, but I was old enough to know they were hell on earth."

——The Troy, Kansas, incident was told to me by Bartlett Boder, son of Louis Boder. He is president of the Missouri Valley Trust Company in St. Joseph.

——The anecdote of the police commissioner's underclothes comes from, among other sources, the *Kansas City Evening Star* for April 18, 1882.

——The same edition of the *Star* carried Jesse's butcherknife plan, as described by Charlie Ford to police.

——Jesse James, Junior, tells me the featherduster is now in the possession of Mary James Barr's son, in Kansas City.

——The material leading up to the murder and the murder itself has come, chiefly, from the newspaper accounts published the day after the event and on succeeding days. The first paper out with the sensational news was the *Kansas City Evening Star*, published April 3rd, the day of the shooting. Its headline is: 'STARTLING RUMOR.' The flash itself says: "A telegram from St. Joseph, Mo., says that Jesse James was shot this morning." The flash was signed 'John H. Leonard, *St Joseph Gazette*.' It would thus seem that Mr. Leonard was the first person to get the news to the outside world.

My old paper came out with an extra dated April 5th, with a headline that has become famous in American journalism: 'JESSE, BY JEHOVAH.' Others, with their dates:

The *Kansas City Evening Star*, April 4, 1882.
The *St. Joseph Herald*, April 4.
The *Evening Star*, April 5.
The *St. Joseph Herald*, April 5.
The *Chicago Weekly Tribune*, April 5.
The *Kansas City Weekly Journal*, April 6.
The *Kansas City Weekly Times*, April 6 (this has the best account of all).
The *Landmark*, Platte City, Mo., April 7, 1882.
Western Cultivator, Kansas City, Mo., September 17, 1882.
The *Kansas City Evening Star*, April 18, 1882.

All these were local papers, with the exception of the Chicago paper. But practically every paper in the United States carried the sensational news.

One of the curious sidelights was that the hometown paper of the James brothers did not mention the affair, which shows how intense the feeling was.

The reporter who most actively covered the story was Frederick Franklin Schrader of the *St. Joseph Gazette*. Most of the stories filed were based on his information. The Ford boys were inimical to him, so when he interviewed them in jail he told them he represented the *Chicago Times*. Later Mr. Schrader went to New York and became press agent for David Belasco. (He was the one who suggested the name for the Friars Club in New York.)

It is revealing to see how the newspapers handled the headlines; the 'heads' were brief, flippant, some in exceedingly bad taste:

BUSTED BANDIT (*Kansas City Evening Star*).
JUDGMENT FOR JESSE (*St. Joseph Evening News*).
GOOD BYE, JESSE! (*Kansas City Weekly Journal*).
JESSE JAMES BITES THE DUST (*The Landmark*).
JESSE'S JUDAS (*Denver News*).

CHAPTER XVIII

——The original spelling of the undertaker's name was Seidenfaden; later the first 'e' was dropped.

——James W. Graham himself told the story of how he photographed the dead Jesse, in an interview with Mrs. Ethylene Ballard Thruston which appeared in the *Kansas City Times* for November 12, 1948, one month before his death at the age of ninety-two. When he died he still had the original glass plates.

——Further to Judge Rowntree: It was discovered that at the time of the killing Jesse was wearing the watch he had taken from the Judge during the Mammoth Cave stagecoach robbery, and that Zee had on Miss Lizzie's diamond ring. The Judge's watch went back to him, and was passed on to his grandson, R. Harry Ray of Owensboro, Kentucky, from whom I have the following note:

"I have the watch you ask about. It was left me by my grandfather at his death, as I was his namesake and only grandson. The watch keeps excellent time. It is typical of the fine watches worn by men of that period, being a key-winder, very heavy eighteen-karat gold, with a closed face. My aunt, Miss Lizzie Rowntree, never recovered her diamond ring; I do not know what became of it after its discovery in the James house."

It has been printed endless times that the watch found on Jesse's body had been taken from a former governor of Arizona with the initials 'J. A. B.' This was based on the inquest testimony of Dick Liddil. It happens not to be true. Arizona has never had a governor with those initials. The watch had been presented to Judge Rowntree by a former governor of Kentucky, J. Proctor Knott. Dick Liddil either didn't look close enough or the court stenographer misquoted him.

——Two items in Zee James's testimony seem to be erroneous in view of other evidence: That she had arrived in St. Joseph on November 9, 1881 (it was actually November 8th); and that she was thirty-five years of age (she was thirty-seven).

——The coroner's jury was out fifteen minutes and came back with this verdict: "Upon our oaths do say that the body of the deceased is that of Jesse James and that he came to his death by a wound in the back of his head, caused by a pistol shot fired intentionally by the hand of Robert Ford." Then

the names of the coroner and jury: James W. Heddens (coroner), S. H. Sommers (foreman), W. H. Chouning, J. W. Moore, Thomas Norris, William Turner, W. H. George.
——The incident of 'Cousin Charlie' and his blue spectacles was reported in the *St. Joseph Gazette* for April 5, 1882, by an eyewitness.
——The World's Hotel, where Zee and Mrs. Samuels stayed, was at that time the biggest and fanciest hotel west of the Mississippi. The building stands today: a shirt factory.

Chapter XIX

——The name of the Kearney pastor was the Reverend J. M. P. Martin; the out-of-town minister was the Reverend D. H. Jones, from Lathrop, Missouri.
——The information about the sliding box is from an interview in the *Kansas City Star* for July 27, 1937, with Gale C. Henson.
——The lumber yard where George Shepherd worked was Baker & Cothesworth's, corner of Hickory and West Fifteenth Street, Kansas City (from the *Kansas City Journal*, April 6, 1882).
——The *Richmond* [Mo.] *Conservator* for May 24, 1882, gives the story of Zee James's lecturing plans.
——The note about Zee's book is from the *Kansas City Evening Star* for May 1, 1882. The name of the lawyer she hired was R. J. Haire.

Chapter XX

——Much of the material, in both this chapter and the entire book, which relates to Frank James was obtained from the famous interview which Frank R. O'Neil had with the bandit directly after he gave himself up. It was published in the *St. Louis Republican* (later the *St. Louis Republic*) and widely reprinted during October of 1882.

——The name of the friend with whom Frank stayed at Lee's Summit was Sim Whitsett.

——The hotel in Jefferson City where Frank stayed was the McCarty House. It stands at 120 East McCarty Street and is today used as a rooming house. An addition has been built on, so that it now extends out to the sidewalk. A bit of irony: John N. Edwards died there seven years later, while covering the state legislature.

——Although he didn't know it, the trial of Frank James was the beginning of a downhill run for William H. Wallace. He had gotten himself elected on a platform of 'Break Up the James Gang'; some of his efforts had led to Jesse's undoing. Reaction set in. Wallace, as the years marched on, became an ardent prohibitionist. In 1901 he ran for United States Senator; Missouri turned him down. In 1906 he ran for Congress; the district turned him down. In 1908 he ran for governor; the state said no. He died on October 21, 1937.

——The name of the preacher who identified Frank and gave the damaging testimony about Shakespeare was the Reverend Benjamin Matchett.

——One of the signers of the bond for Frank James that was

posted in Boonville was Wall C. Bronaugh, who wrote *The Flight for Freedom*, in which he recounted how he had been instrumental in getting the Youngers out of prison.

CHAPTER XXI

——The material on Frank James's later life was gathered from many newspapers of the period, and especially from conversations with Robert Franklin James, his son.

CHAPTER XXII

——Ann Ralston's croquet game appeared in the *Louisville Courier Journal* for May 14, 1937, quoted from an earlier newspaper.

——The main events of Ann's life with Frank James were related to me by Bob James.

CHAPTER XXIII

——A note from the *St. Joseph Western News* for May 19, 1882, concerning Ford's stage career: "Robert Ford, the slayer of Jesse James, is the biggest man in Kansas City. He is appearing on the stage three nights a week, for which he is paid $100 a night. The morbid curiosity of the people of Kansas City is beyond human comprehension."

At the time Ford was appearing in Kansas City, Nat Goodwin, the famous stage star, was also there. One day he went to a Turkish bath, and was astonished to come upon a man in the steam room, without a stitch of clothes on, who was holding an evil-looking pistol in his hand. The situation was so unusual that Goodwin engaged him in conversation. The man turned out to be Bob Ford. Ford, noticing Goodwin eyeing the pistol, explained that his life would not be safe if he did not have a weapon to protect himself. Ford boasted of his achievement, saying, "If Jesse James hadn't taken a fancy to me, I guess I wouldn't have had my chance." (From *Nat Goodwin's Book*, by Nat C. Goodwin.) It shows how his unpopularity was growing.

——The information about Bob and Dick Liddil setting themselves up as saloon keepers is from M. A. Otero's *My Life on the Frontier*.

——J. W. Graham, who took the death picture of Jesse, also took a photograph of the Ford boys (the negative has since been lost) in the cell where they were held directly after the shooting of Jesse James. In the interview published in the *Kansas City Times* for November 12, 1948, Mr. Graham said (and it goes to show the interest in Bob Ford that existed at the time): "Of course, we sold thousands of pictures of the Ford boys."

——Material on the killing of Bob Ford comes from several places. Newspaper sources: the *Creede Candle* for June 3, June 24, July 15, and September 2, 1892; the *Colorado Sun* for June 9, June 10, and June 14, 1892; Damon Runyon's syndicated column for August 14, 1940; and the *Colorado Magazine* for November 1944. Miss Dorothea F. Hyle, librarian of the Cass County Library at Harrisonville, Missouri, deserves my thanks for checking the statements in this chapter. And, finally, I was lucky enough to run upon a man who actually saw the shooting: Harry P. Taber, of 1203 Delaware Avenue, Wilmington 19, Delaware. Mr. Taber was, for a time, editor of a weekly, *The Amethyst*, which later became the *Creede Chronicle.*

——When arrested at Creede, Kelly gave his name as Ed O. Kelly, which gave rise to the error in the newspapers that his name was O'Kelly.

——The deputy sheriff who arrested Kelly was Dick Plunkett, the two doctors who examined Ford's body were named Norman and Anderson, and the lawyer who defended Kelly was B. F. McDaniel of Pueblo.

Chapter XXIV

——The story of the fight between Burdett and Kelly is told in detail in the *Daily Oklahoman* for January 14, 1904, and the *Kingfisher Free Press* for January 21, 1904. The author's thanks in particular for help on this chapter go to Mrs. Rella Looney, archivist in the Indian Archives Division of the Oklahoma Historical Society in Oklahoma City. She informs me that West Reno Avenue is still 'rugged.'

Chapter XXV

——The material contained in this chapter derives from many contemporary newspaper sources, and from conversations with Bob James.

Chapter XXVI

——The last years of Zerelda Cole James Simms Samuels were mainly described to me by her grandson, Bob.

Chapter XXVII

——The story about the blind ballad-singer and Bob Ford's sister is quoted by Vance Randolph in *Ozark Folk Songs;* he in turn got it from the *Springfield* [Mo.] *Leader* of October 18, 1933.

——Information on the cinematic history of Jesse James comes from the *Motion Picture Herald*, from material at the *Motion Picture Association*, and from the unfortunate movies themselves.

A brief and sorrowful listing of Jesse James pictures:

1. *Jesse James* (Paramount; October, 1927)
2. *Jesse James* (20th Century-Fox; January, 1939)
3. *Days of Jesse James* (Republic; December, 1939)
4. *Return of Frank James* (20th Century-Fox; August, 1940)
5. *Jesse James At Bay* (Republic; 1941)
6. *I Shot Jesse James* (Screen Guild, 1949)

Another sad thing is that the James family has never made a penny out of Jesse's movie lives. The best Jesse James, Junior, ever did was collect a salary for appearing in a picture called *Under The Black Flag*, made in 1920. But that had nothing to do with his father.

The Tyrone Power-Henry Fonda production was the biggest of all. In this one they had it that a railroad wanted to run tracks through the James farm and the James family protested, so a feud ensued and the railroad blew off the mother's arm. That was shifting history about in fine style. The James Boys were involved with railroads, all right, but the only one that ever came near their farm stayed three miles from it and never dreamed of ploughing through the house. When they made the movie they picked out Pineville, Missouri, as typical of the towns in Jesse's day, and then got to work to make it more typical. They altered the front of the courthouse, changed the stores, hauled in dirt and dumped same on the cement streets. Henry Fonda shot himself in the leg. Nancy Kelly tumbled off her horse into a barbed-wire fence. Lon Chaney, Jr., had his horse fall on him. Generally speaking, it was a tough day for the James Boys.

——As a footnote to the growth of the James legend, the mural by Thomas Hart Benton in the State Capitol at Jefferson City should be mentioned. Part of it (see the jacket illustration for this book) shows the Boys holding up a train. Benton used Daniel L. James, a third cousin, as one of his models.

Chapter XXVIII

——The fabulous banditry of Al Jennings (identifier of the most recent Jesse) lasted from August 18, 1897, to December 5th of that year. There were five in Al's gang; Deputy Sheriff

Bud Ledbetter took them all without firing a shot. Later Al Jennings ran for the nomination for governor of Oklahoma. He had about the same success.

——The name of the ex-slave who had been Jesse's 'camp cook' was John Trammell, a resident of Guthrie, Oklahoma.

——Among the curiosities of the Returned Jesses is a complete book proving that J. Frank Dalton was Jesse James. It was published in 1948 by LaHoma Publishing Company, Lawton, Oklahoma. It bears the names of Frank O. Hall and Lindsey H. Whitten.

CHAPTER XXIX

——All sources evident in the text.

NECROLOGY OF THE BANDITS

FROM the time he started until he was no more, Jesse James had twenty-eight men in his gang. This is the way they went:

Bud McDaniels tried to escape from jail in Lawrence, Kansas, but was shot hiding in the timber and was carried back to jail, where he died.

Thompson McDaniels (brother of Bud) was shot by farmers after the Huntington robbery.

Ed Miller was killed by Jesse himself.

Clell Miller (his brother) got it at Northfield, Minnesota.

Charlie Pitts was killed after Northfield. Ended up as a skeleton in a doctor's office, like Clell.

Bob Younger got life, compliments of the sovereign State of Minnesota. He died in prison on September 16, 1889.

Wood Hite was killed by Bob Ford.

Jack Keene went off to prison for fourteen years.

Arch Clements killed at Lexington, Missouri.

Andy McGuire was arrested and placed in jail in Richmond, Missouri. A mob broke in. That was the end of Andy.

Dick Burns's head was split open by a pal.

Payne Jones was killed while trying to steal a horse.

Cole Younger, after twenty-five years in prison, was pardoned and came back to his old home in Missouri, where he died with seventeen bullets still reposing in him.

Jim Younger served twenty-five years in the Minnesota guest house, was freed, then, a few days later, shot himself to death over a love affair, showing that love has its perils, too.

Tucker Bassham of Missouri was sent to jail, but was pardoned. Killed in Kansas. No great loss to either state.

The none-too-bright *Hobbs Kerry* went off to prison for seven years.

Clarence Hite was sentenced to twenty-five years in prison; contracted tuberculosis. Pardoned, died.

Bill Ryan was sentenced to twenty-five years as a guest of the State of Missouri. One day he was riding horseback in the timber. His horse became frightened and bolted. Bill Ryan's head struck a tree limb and that was the end of the best man Jesse James ever had.

John Younger (the youngest of the Youngers) was killed by a Pinkerton detective . . . the Pinkertons' only score, save Mrs. Samuels and Archie.

Jim Read killed in Texas by a deputy sheriff.

Bill Chadwell dropped dead on the streets of Northfield. A sudden seizure.

Jack Bishop tried to hide in Colorado. Didn't.

Dick Liddil turned state's evidence and died soon afterward, as was fitting.

Jim Cummins died in the Confederate Home at Higginsville, Missouri. His most brilliant work was in the field of horse thievery.

Frank James lived until 1915.

Oliver Shepherd died of deputy sheriff trouble. Considered catching.

Bob Ford. Never really a member of the gang, for he never attended a single robbery, but is usually considered a member. Died in Creede, Colorado, and none too soon.

Charlie Ford grew more and more morose. His end is told by Tom Jacobs, his nephew, who is still living. "One morning Charlie Ford and I started to the timber to hunt squirrels. I was about ten years old. As we were going across the barn lot, Charlie made an excuse to go back to the house. He was gone a few minutes, then I heard a shot. I ran back to the house and up the stairs. There he was on the floor, dead. He had shot himself through the heart. Some men, who were working on the road, came in, picked Uncle Charlie up and put him on the bed in the room. One of the men was the father of Forrest Smith, the present governor of Missouri. Charlie Ford did not shoot himself to death in a weed patch, as has been told so many times. What I have narrated is the true story of the death of Charlie Ford."

Other men rode with Jesse, but for the most part they were ex-guerrillas and did not for long pursue the exacting profession of banditry. Their names: Allen H. Parmer (married Jesse's sister Susie), Jim White, John White, Tom Little, Ike Flannery, Bill Hulse, Jack Hines, John Jarette, Bradley Collins, and Jim Anderson. They never made good.

For great help and comfort in the compilation of the above *Necrology*, I extend thanks to Charles E. Bell of 2511 Elliott Avenue, Louisville, Kentucky, a long time student of the James story, and to Herb Rice of Springfield, Missouri, a friend of the James family and a familiar of the life and times of Jesse James.

THE JAMES FAMILY TODAY

THE James family, in Missouri, is honored and respected. There are, as I write, two sons—Robert F. James (son of Frank), and Jesse James, Junior. (There are endless cousins and in-laws in Missouri, too—most of them highly thought of.)

The first time I met Robert F. James was on a golf course. I saw before me a short, dumpy, round-faced, rolypoly-looking man, staggering along under a golf bag. One end of a towel was stuffed into his trousers, the other dangled outside. Snatching up the towel, he gave his face a dab, then put the towel back.

"Oh," he said when we were introduced, "I'm just a second-growth celebrity."

I've thought of it many times. It is a key to him.

He knows he is a famous figure, but also he knows he inherited it.

He is a golf enthusiast in the most advanced stage. When he was 'farming' the old James place, he built a nine-hole golf course. This was before the days of the tractor, so he plowed with a team of horses on a walking cultivator—the hardest work, God knows, that has come down to man. One side of the golf course was near the house. Tourists came through the famous gate to see the historic house. He would watch them like a hawk. His wife would show them through the house; about the time they would come out, he would manage to be there and would call across and ask any visible male if he played golf. If the man did, Bob James would say, "Have you got your clubs with you?"

Sometimes the man would have them.

Then Bob James would tie his team to the fence, and in a few minutes he and the tourist would be banging away.

He is popular and full of pranks and jokes, a clubhouse favorite. One day he was playing at the Excelsior Springs course when his ball struck a meadowlark in such a way as to kill it. Instantly Bob's mind was at work. Without a word to anyone, he darted forward, picked it up, and dropped it in his golf bag.

When he came in, the regular session at the clubhouse began. "How did you get along, Bob?"

He beamed with satisfaction. "Fine. I got a birdie."

There was, it appears, a silence, for he seems not to be in that class at all.

"Well, I did," he said indignantly.

One of the others took it up and in no time a bet was placed.

"I'll prove it myself," said the injured man, bounding away to the locker room and coming back, in a moment, with the proof.

He got the money, too, I'm told by people who would never, never indulge in a golf-course fabrication.

He has many calls to lead parades at state fairs, appear at rodeos, and to head 'drives' of one sort or another. His health, as I write, is not good, but he responds to as many calls as he can.

In summer he lives in the old James house; in winter he lives in a furnished apartment in Excelsior Springs. He makes a living showing the farm (which is also rented for pasturage, but not 'farmed' in any other sense of the word). He drives out from Excelsior Springs, on clement days, and is there to show the never-ending tourists around. At certain seasons, the hotels in Excelsior Springs run excursions. Bob paces them and puts on his lecture. Recently Mrs. James was doing more of the lecturing.

Jesse's daughter Mary (who was in the kitchen at the time her father was shot, and ran in to see his body) went to school in Kansas City, and later married a prosperous farmer named Henry L. Barr. They lived on a farm near Kearney. Mary James Barr died on October 11, 1935, and was buried near her father. Her three sons live today in or near Kansas City.

As for Jesse Edwards James, the only other child of the bandit who lived, he turned his back on Missouri and went to California, where, as I write, he lives in Los Angeles. I have never met him; I know him only by correspondence. His health is not good. Once he had to go to a hospital. This was published in the newspapers, and for the first time the public learned he was living in that part of California. So great was the interest that people came and stood in the hospital yard and stared up at the window where he was supposed to be.

I asked Mrs. Jesse James, Junior, to bring me up to date on her family. "We have," she writes, "four daughters. Jo Frances James Ross has lived with Jesse and me for the past twenty-one years. She has been with the Bank of America, in Los Angeles, for eighteen years; she is an escrow officer. She was not happy in her marriage and brought her baby and came to live with us.

Her baby is now attending U. C. L. A., taking law. He is one of the finest.

"Lucille, our first-born, has a son twelve years old. In Kansas City I was a member of the Independence Avenue Christian Church. Lucille received a medal for having attended Sunday School for ten years without missing a single Sunday.

"Ethelrose, our youngest, was with the Federal Reserve Bank for eight years; then was married. No children.

"Estelle has twins. Both wonderful.

"Jesse was an attorney in Kansas City for more than twenty-five years—until he suffered a nervous breakdown. We came to California where he regained his health; here he practiced law until his health broke again.

"One more item of possible interest: My husband calls out to ask me to add a word about his baseball-playing, as he is proud of that. He played on the same team with Joe Tinker and with Johnny Kling. Both were good friends of his. Can you add that, too?"

I certainly can, Mrs. James, and glad to.

INDEX